T0344703

from the mists of the shoreless ocean
to the shining interior of the Heart cave
infinitely eager, perennially patient

THE NEW DYNAMIC OF PORTFOLIO MANAGEMENT

Innovative Methods and Tools
for Rapid Results

MURALI KULATHUMANI, MBA, CSM

Copyright © 2021 by J. Ross Publishing

ISBN-13: 978-1-60427-177-5

Printed and bound in the U.S.A. Printed on acid-free paper.

10 9 8 7 6 5 4 3 2 1

Library of Congress Cataloging-in-Publication Data
Names: Kulathumani, Murali, 1974– author.
Title: The new dynamic of portfolio management : innovative methods and
  tools for rapid results / Murali Kulathumani.
Description: Plantation, FL : J. Ross Publishing, 2021. | Includes
  bibliographical references and index. |
Identifiers: LCCN 2021003863 (print) | LCCN 2021003864 (ebook) | ISBN
  9781604271775 (paperback ; alk. paper) | ISBN 9781604278279 (epub)
Subjects: LCSH: Project management. | Information technology—Management.
Classification: LCC HD69.P75 K853 2021 (print) | LCC HD69.P75 (ebook) |
  DDC 658.4/04--dc23
LC record available at https://lccn.loc.gov/2021003863
LC ebook record available at https://lccn.loc.gov/2021003864

This publication contains information obtained from authentic and highly regarded sources. Re-printed material is used with permission, and sources are indicated. Reasonable effort has been made to publish reliable data and information, but the author and the publisher cannot assume responsibility for the validity of all materials or for the consequences of their use.

All rights reserved. Neither this publication nor any part thereof may be reproduced, stored in a retrieval system, or transmitted in any form or by any means, electronic, mechanical, photocopying, recording or otherwise, without the prior written permission of the publisher.

The copyright owner's consent does not extend to copying for general distribution for promotion, for creating new works, or for resale. Specific permission must be obtained from J. Ross Publishing for such purposes.

Direct all inquiries to J. Ross Publishing, Inc., 151 N. Nob Hill Rd., Suite 476, Plantation, FL 33324.

Phone: (954) 727-9333
Fax: (561) 892-0700
Web: www.jrosspub.com

CONTENTS

FOREWORD

It gives me great pleasure to write the Foreword for Murali Kulathumani's new book, *The New Dynamic of Portfolio Management*. Throughout my career in information technology, and presently as Chief Product Officer of a rapidly growing work execution company, I have always found the discipline of portfolio management to be valuable in choosing and monitoring investment choices that ultimately deliver the most value to the customer. I've found that portfolio management can make the difference between mere project activity and meaningful achievement of strategic outcomes.

Part of the challenge for leaders like me has been to visualize a roadmap of capabilities for the discipline of portfolio management so that we can take our organizations to the next level of maturity. In my opinion, while there are many good volumes about portfolio management in the market today, this new book is one of the first to propose a system to measure the capability of different portfolio functions.

Another aspect of portfolio management where the industry could use more exploration has been the gap between portfolio theory and the realities or constraints encountered in real life. While the theory of portfolio management is well established, there remains a considerable gap in applying this theory to the varied situations that are encountered in organizations today. Every organization is in a different place in terms of process maturity and I believe there is always a need to address the gap between theory and practice. This is where this book plays a valuable role in making the reader aware of how to navigate the space between the "ideal" and the "real" while delivering on the promise of portfolio management.

A third aspect of this very readable book that appealed to me was its emphasis on rapid implementation using tools that are readily available. Once again, the popular impression of portfolio management is that it takes too long to deliver any tangible value to the organization. This book successfully anticipates and counters that perception by focusing on rapid implementation from the get-go.

Finally, the approach taken in the book of starting with a *basic* portfolio before graduating to an *advanced* portfolio is a welcome approach for the simple reason that most organizations are early in their development of portfolio capabilities. For such organizations, it is a relatively easy path to attaining a basic portfolio which will provide considerable capabilities to manage and deliver projects. This, in turn, builds the credibility of portfolio management which can then be leveraged to build the advanced portfolio with all its attendant benefits. I also found the chapter on strategic transformation to be valuable and thought-provoking in explaining the strong link between strategy and the portfolio.

From a C-suite perspective, perhaps the most compelling feature of this book is the detailed exploration of how the portfolio office and the C-Level are connected in the delivery of value to the organization. Several aspects of this topic gave me pause for thought and are worth exploring for any C-level executive seeking to optimize the output of their organization.

Although dealing with technical topics and detailed methodologies, the book has been written in an easy-to-follow manner with handy illustrations aiding the reader in comprehension of the ideas and techniques. In conclusion, I believe this book stands apart from similar works in the field and is a must read for anyone interested in portfolio management as well as decision makers looking to achieve strategic transformation through portfolio management.

Gene Farrell
Chief Product Officer, Smartsheet

PREFACE AND ACKNOWLEDGMENTS

"The main thing is to keep the main thing the main thing."
—Stephen Covey

This quote sums up portfolio management in a nutshell and was the driving philosophy behind this book, which is my second on portfolio management. As we enter the third decade of the century, we are witnessing the Third Wave of Project Management—the exponential mushrooming of projects across all industries and no longer just under the domain of IT. Given this massive increase in projects, what does success look like? This book is a detailed, definitive answer to that question.

Part of the driving force behind this book was the feedback I received after writing my first book, *Breakthrough Project Portfolio Management* (J. Ross Publishing, 2018). Several respected peers and practitioners liked the book and suggested that I write a second offering that would be geared more to organizations that were starting from scratch. I too noticed from personal observations that the right tool would significantly accelerate successful portfolio management in organizations. I also noticed through actual implementations at several organizations that certain portfolio management capabilities were easier to attain than others. With these factors in mind, I had four main goals in writing *The New Dynamic of Portfolio Management*, which are covered in the first three sections:

- Outline the foundational aspects of portfolio management that organizations need to understand to start seeing immediate results.
- Establish the credibility of the portfolio office.
- Provide a pathway to allow organizations to build and then move past the initial building blocks of portfolio management in order to obtain an advanced portfolio and all the attendant benefits.
- Introduce a versatile, flexible tool that allows organizations to accelerate portfolio management delivery and demonstrate in sufficient detail how to utilize that tool.

An effective portfolio always works in partnership with other functions such as Finance, the office of the CIO, and certainly the business. And it usually takes more than one person to implement an effective portfolio—it takes a whole team, hence, the chapter on the portfolio office. Also, there is something to be said about the perennial and inescapable role of politics in portfolio management and how governance is key to success. These topics found a natural home in the fourth section of the book.

Most books, and certainly this one, do not take shape in a vacuum. A whole host of people were instrumental in the creation of this text. Foremost among them are mentioned below, but many more were involved in the interactions that enabled the narratives in the book. Perhaps the foremost person is Stephen Buda from J. Ross Publishing. His encouraging receptivity to the book's idea and his ample patience in waiting for me to deliver the promised manuscript is much appreciated.

Next, the whole team at Smartsheet needs to be lauded for their phenomenal support in curating the book idea and making valuable resources available to me at vital times during the formation of the book. First, Anna Griffin, the CMO of Smartsheet, who got the ball rolling and introduced me to the amazing team at Smartsheet that formed my working group over many months of effort. Second, Patricia Rollins, who was the driving force of the effort and kept the momentum going through thick and thin. Thanks are due to Andy Simpson, who provided very valuable suggestions through his deep knowledge of the platform and was a great source of ideas. I also appreciated the conversation and useful inputs from Robin Sherwood, a senior leader at Smartsheet and a thought leader in the portfolio management industry. Kara Lumley was also a great collaborator and needs to be recognized for her unflagging enthusiasm in this project. Last, but not least, thanks to Tim Sweeney for making the vital introductions to the Smartsheet team.

On a personal note, I would like to convey my gratitude to my family for their unstinting support through the long months spent on this endeavor. Specifically, thanks are due to my son, Appavu, for taking the time to proofread several versions of the manuscript to get them print ready. Finally, I would like to acknowledge the editing and production staff at J. Ross Publishing, specifically Donna Oliver. Their patient and meticulous edits turned my sometimes-telegraphic prose into meaningful and readable content.

Ultimately, portfolio management is the art of the possible—to win by keeping *the main thing the main thing*. In the face of change, adverse developments, unforeseen risks, and organizational inertia, the portfolio manager is still expected to navigate the portfolio to the safe harbor of impactful strategic results. If this book assists in that endeavor, I will consider my efforts to be successful.

—Murali Kulathumani

INTRODUCTION

HOW TO USE THIS BOOK

The goal of this book is to enable you to transform your current portfolio into a world-class portfolio. Whether you already have a portfolio, or are starting to build one from scratch, the contents of this book will inform you about the capabilities of a high-performing portfolio *and* help you get there. The objective is to provide the reader with a complete understanding of all the building blocks of a portfolio and then detail the nuances involved in implementation. The chapters, which sequentially cover the essential and advanced capabilities of a portfolio, are structured in a simple, intuitive way and also cross-reference each other to provide the reader with a logical construct of how the different capability areas interact.

PREREQUISITES

The book assumes very little in terms of prerequisites on the part of the reader. A basic knowledge of projects, coupled with passing understanding of finance terms and modern organizations, are all that it takes for a user to understand and start implementing the concepts explored in this book.

OVERVIEW OF THE BOOK STRUCTURE

The book is divided into four sections. Section I is brief but covers all the basics needed to make portfolio management work. Chapter 1 describes the evolving project portfolio landscape and the massive growth in the number of projects. Chapter 2 deals with the basics of project management since that is the bedrock of any portfolio. Chapter 3 explains the basics of Smartsheet, laying the groundwork for a tool that is used throughout the book.

Section II covers a central theme of the book, namely, the implementation of a basic portfolio. For many organizations, the basic portfolio is the easiest path to build a structure that immediately starts delivering value. In this section, Chapter 4 starts off with an introduction of the foundational capability of portfolio intake and assessment, while Chapter 5 walks through the actual implementation of portfolio intake using Smartsheet. Chapter 6 then introduces the concept of portfolio reporting and performance monitoring, while Chapter 7 shows how to implement those capabilities using Smartsheet. Chapter 8 then approaches the human element of portfolio management with an extensive treatment of portfolio resource management and how to implement it using Smartsheet. Chapter 9 forays into an area that determines success or failure for most portfolios—annual planning. Chapter 10 builds upon that introduction with an extensive treatment on how to orchestrate annual planning using Smartsheet. This marks the end of Section II, a hugely impactful collection of capabilities that make up the basic portfolio.

Some organizations have mastered the basics and are ready to advance to the next level. Section III details implementation strategies for the advanced portfolio with the introduction of budgets, benefits, and strategic planning. Chapter 11 directly addresses issues around allocating budgets to projects in the portfolio and includes a section on implementation using Smartsheet. Chapter 12 revisits the concept of portfolio performance monitoring in the backdrop of the advanced portfolio. Chapter 13 then deals with the sophisticated techniques surrounding balancing the advanced portfolio. Chapter 14 delves into the much needed, but often ignored, topic of benefits realization. Finally, Chapter 15 explores the intricate relationship between strategic transformation and portfolio management, while enumerating the benefits of having the two work in tandem. Section III describes the advanced capabilities that mark the best-of-breed portfolios and includes a detailed look at portfolio governance and how to ensure that it successfully provides direction for the portfolio.

No successful portfolio operates in a vacuum. Section IV explores in depth the support systems that play a huge role in making the portfolio successful. Chapter 16 begins by addressing the dominant factor that can make or break portfolio performance—the politics at work in organizations and how to successfully navigate them. Chapter 17 underscores the importance of a team in making big portfolios work, with the concept of a portfolio office. Chapter 18 continues with the concept of portfolio governance and shows how governance is the key to preventing portfolios from going off the rails. Chapter 19 explores the important relationship between the CIO and the portfolio office, while Chapter 20 follows up on the relationship between Finance and the portfolio office. Chapter 21 highlights the critical role played by the change management function in preparing the organization for changes rolled out by the portfolio office in the course of implementing portfolio management. Finally, Chapter 22 concludes Section IV with an exploration of the solutions to the most common problems faced by portfolio managers as they try to roll out capability enhancements in their organizations.

Throughout the book are Key Concept boxes that provide the reader invaluable material that summarizes important lessons to learn or things to know. Please do not skip over these call-outs.

CHAPTER STRUCTURE

Every chapter begins with an introduction to the central topic of that chapter. As part of the introduction, a summary listing of the chapter's contents is provided to enable the reader to get a bearing of how the chapter will unfold. This is typically followed by another section that elaborates on the introduction with a closer, more detailed discussion, including why this area of portfolio management needs to be covered. Several chapters employ the technique of progressive elaboration of the topic at hand, using tables and diagrams as appropriate. For most chapters, there typically follows an explanatory section that deals with how to set up the building blocks of a certain capability using our tool of choice, Smartsheet. Some chapters include a section that describes the levels of portfolio capability maturity for that topic and the attendant characteristics of each level. Finally, a chapter summary provides a synopsis of most chapters.

COMPARISON WITH FINANCIAL PORTFOLIO MANAGEMENT

A singular difference between this book and most other volumes on portfolio management is the use of financial portfolio management to introduce some topics in project portfolio management. I believe that most people are familiar with financial portfolios for the simple reason that they are likely to have a personal investment portfolio. It is therefore reasonable to expect people to grasp project portfolio concepts when they are introduced as a variant of the already-familiar financial portfolio concepts. However, this comparison is applied judiciously and, where appropriate, the difference between the financial and project portfolio concepts are highlighted.

THE PORTFOLIO OFFICE AND THE PORTFOLIO MANAGER

Although the portfolio office consists of more than just the portfolio manager, it needs to be remembered that many organizations only have one person—namely the portfolio manager—managing the portfolio. This is especially true for organizations that are just starting on their portfolio journey. Where there is a larger portfolio office, the portfolio manager is understood to be the prime driver within the portfolio office and that the other members of the portfolio office function under his/her direction. Therefore, the terms *portfolio office* and *portfolio manager* are used interchangeably, unless expressly indicated otherwise.

THE CONTINUOUS JOURNEY OF PORTFOLIO MANAGEMENT

Every portfolio is at a different level in terms of capability because of many factors, including the context of the larger organization. Consequently, it's natural that every portfolio manager will approach the book a little differently based on their current place in the journey. To aid in this approach, references have been inserted that enables the reader to look up other chapters where a topic may have been introduced or explored in greater depth.

FOCUS ON IMPLEMENTATION

This book was written with an emphasis on impactful implementation in the real world. Accordingly, every concept that is discussed is then followed up with a detailed introduction on how to implement that capability using Smartsheet. Although the basic or simplest Smartsheet approach is provided, it is understood that the platform is versatile enough to allow multiple different solutions to achieve the same portfolio capability. The reader is encouraged to explore and experiment using the Smartsheet platform, which is constantly being improved to deliver additional ease of use. Finally, the tables and figures used in the various chapters have been made available in their original form as a resource to jump start the reader's implementation journey.

CONCLUSION

Portfolio management can be a challenging endeavor. It can also be a rewarding journey, especially as the organization begins to become aware of its potential. *The New Dynamic of Portfolio Management* tries to enable both the reader and their organization to become successful on that journey, both by describing the different components that make a portfolio and offering the subtle nuances which have been proven effective by observation and experience. It is my fervent hope that the reader can deploy the content of this book to create a high performing portfolio in their own organization.

—**Murali Kulathumani**

ABOUT THE AUTHOR

Murali Kulathumani, PMP, has over 22 years of IT management experience. He has successfully managed large project portfolios at leading Silicon Valley firms such as Facebook, Cisco, Symantec, and Kaiser Permanente. Murali has extensive knowledge of the full spectrum of portfolio capabilities and pioneered a simplified form of earned value management, called *mEVM*, which has been well received by industry practitioners and several organizations. In fact, it has become the standard at a billion-dollar business unit of a leading health care provider in the United States.

Mr. Kulathumani has a technical degree in Electrical Engineering from Bangalore University and an MBA from Purdue University. Murali earned the Project Management Professional (PMP)® designation from the Project Management Institute and is a Certified Scrum Master. He is the author of *Breakthrough Project Portfolio Management* (J. Ross Publishing, 2018) and is a consultant, trainer, and professional speaker. Murali has also taught courses as an adjunct professor at Purdue University.

SECTION I

The Foundational Basics

1

UNDERSTANDING THE NEW PROJECT AND PORTFOLIO LANDSCAPE

INTRODUCTION

Almost everything is a project these days and every kind of organization now does projects—not just IT. It is commonplace to see significant numbers of projects in most companies. To manage these projects, everyone now must wear the project manager hat. In this chapter, we'll look at a few basic things:

- What is a project?
- What can go wrong in a project?
- What is the role of a project portfolio?
- What does a good portfolio look like?
- The need for a portfolio manager.

WHAT IS A PROJECT?

Although the term *project* is extremely commonplace, everyone has a slightly different take on what it means. The official definition of a project is as follows:

> KEY CONCEPT: A project is a temporary endeavor undertaken to create a unique product, service, or result.[1]

And the official definition of project management is provided below:

> KEY CONCEPT: Project management is the application of skills, tools, and techniques to project activities to meet project requirements.[2]

A project is simply a series of tasks that needs to be performed to get to a specific goal. There has been an explosion in the number of projects in practically every type of industry. Chapter 2 will feature an extensive tutorial on project management.

WHAT CAN GO WRONG IN A PROJECT?

The short answer: anything and everything. It is an accepted fact that most projects will run into trouble at some point. The fundamental reason for that lies in the nature of project management: every project is an experimental endeavor to "create a new product, service, or capability with finite resources and budget within a finite time while meeting concrete performance criteria."[3]

With all these constraints and unknowns in effect, it should come as little surprise that projects get into trouble. Here is a partial list of what can go wrong in a project:

1. Incomplete capturing of scope: "We didn't realize we had to do all that!"
2. Optimistic timeline: "No idea it would take so long!"
3. Budget constraints: "It cost way more than we thought, and still isn't complete."
4. PM (in)ability: "Jim's a good guy, but he's never seen these kinds of difficulties in a project before."
5. Inadequate design: "IT never said it had to work with both internal and external systems."
6. Organizational partner problems: "Finance never finalized the design and now they want to rethink the project!"
7. External problems: "The vendor said they could it in 3 months and now they're 6 months late!"

> KEY CONCEPT: There are many factors that can (and do) cause a project to fail.

We can all relate to some version of the above issues that land our projects in deep trouble. However, there is one common factor above all that determines whether a project succeeds or fails—*visibility*.

Visibility makes all the difference. Think about an important project that executive management is betting their jobs on. If key project indicators started showing the project going sideways—not meeting scope, schedule, and quality milestones—do you think the executive team would let that continue? Of course not, you can bet they would start taking strong action. Whatever the reason (internal politics, project manager problems, wrong timeline, etc.), the issue would get fixed in a hurry and the project would stand a higher chance of getting back on track.

So why doesn't this happen on every project? Why do approximately 50% of projects underperform and/or fail? The answer is a lack of visibility.[4] There simply aren't enough hours in the day for management to do a deep dive on every project. And with the explosion in the number of projects, the available time for management to examine each project only decreases. Because of this lack of visibility, most projects are left alone until they begin to fail in a visible, public way. By that point, it may already be too late to save it (or the project manager's job, in many cases).

> KEY CONCEPT: Without visibility, there is a high chance that a project could fail.

WHAT IS THE ROLE OF A PROJECT PORTFOLIO

In common usage, the word portfolio is simply a generic term used for a grouping of things, and the term in project management refers to a grouping of projects. The purpose of a portfolio is to establish centralized management and oversight for many projects and/or programs. A portfolio also helps establish standardized governance across the organization. The purpose of creating and managing a portfolio is to ensure the business is taking on the right projects that align with the company's values, strategies, and goals.[5] But the main reason a portfolio exists is to provide visibility and control over the projects running in the organization.

> KEY CONCEPT: A portfolio provides visibility and control over a group of projects.

There are many other advantages to having a portfolio:

- **Single window:** Quite simply, the biggest advantage of a portfolio is that it's a single window that shows all the projects. As organizations get bigger, there are so many active projects that seeing them in one place is a huge achievement.
- **Standardization:** Managing projects as a portfolio ensures that all projects follow similar standards. This could be as simple as always publishing the project manager's name in a standard place next to the project's title.
- **Intervention:** When projects are reported as part of a portfolio, it becomes easier to spot projects that are not doing well and intervene early.
- **Risk management:** By managing risk across a set of projects, management can adjust and control risk much better.
- **Strategy alignment:** Portfolios are ideal vehicles to identify which projects are aligned to a company's strategy and which are not. Effective project portfolio management requires a keen understanding of the relationships between strategy development and strategy implementation.
- **Forward looking:** A good portfolio can actually show where the company will be in its strategic journey ahead of time. If you can't see the future of your organization by looking at your portfolio, you have no chance of getting there.
- **Success rate enhancement:** According to the Project Management Institute, organizations with mature project portfolio management practices complete 35 percent more of their programs successfully.[6] They fail less often and waste less money.

> KEY CONCEPT: Portfolios are very useful structures for managing large numbers of projects.

> KEY CONCEPT: Projects are likely to fail without being managed in a portfolio.

WHAT DOES A GOOD PORTFOLIO LOOK LIKE?

A well-structured portfolio does not have to be a complex and costly setup. However, there are a few basic characteristics that a good portfolio needs to have:

- **Comprehensive:** Stakeholders can rely on this portfolio to have "The official list of all projects" with nothing missing.
- **Updated:** The basic portfolio is expected to have up-to-date information. Even if the information is not updated every day, it sticks to a service level agreement of keeping things current (e.g., all projects in the portfolio are updated at least once a week).

- **Well described:** Each project in the portfolio has a basic set of attributes that are populated with meaningful data. This enables decision makers to make decisions based on correct, substantial data. Each project should at least convey the name of the project, the project description, and the project owner.
- **Well reported:** It should be quick and easy for various stakeholders to see their projects in the portfolio. For example, the head of the finance department should easily be able to access a list of finance projects in the overall portfolio. All organizational leaders should be able to see the subset of their projects in the portfolio without having to ask someone to create that list.
- **Regulated (controlled):** A good portfolio has some kind of gate control; projects don't just get entered into the portfolio without at least the portfolio manager becoming aware of it and approving the entry. This ensures the portfolio manager can confidently vouch for the portfolio and its projects.
- **Scalable:** As mentioned previously, there are more and more projects around us. Therefore, any good portfolio should be scalable to accommodate the increase in the volume of projects.
- **Flexible:** If there is one constant in organizations, it's change. Department names can change. Processes can change. A capable portfolio should be flexible enough to evolve with the changes without causing excessive change management burdens on portfolio users.

These characteristics together describe a robust portfolio, one that would make most executives and organizations happy.

> KEY CONCEPT: Portfolios don't have to be complex or costly, but need to have some basic capabilities.

THE NEED FOR A PORTFOLIO MANAGER

In the previous section, we saw how portfolio management can help increase overall project success rates. However, portfolios don't just come into existence or manage themselves. The following are some common reasons why organizations find it challenging to start a portfolio and get it running:

- People can't follow instructions: It may sound like a cliché, but people simply cannot follow the most basic instructions. The management of a portfolio that solely relies on people to follow instructions usually fails.
- Conventional project portfolio management (PPM) tools can be too hard to configure: These tools are invariably hard to use and difficult to configure. Project managers and project team members avoid these wherever possible and try to work around them, defeating the concept of *one portfolio containing everything*.
- Unconventional PPM tools can be too basic: On the other end of the spectrum, many organizations try to operate a portfolio using Excel spreadsheets. Excel is easy to start with but hard to maintain because the end user can change columns, headers, or almost anything. Soon, the spreadsheets fall out of sync with different people creating new columns and attributes which don't match the rest of the team.
- Hard to scale: Some teams do start with Excel and manage to maintain a working portfolio. However, they run into trouble when the portfolio grows. For example, it may be possible to publish a portfolio report containing 50 projects with a weekly effort of 2 hours. When this

portfolio grows to 100+ projects, the effort involved will grow dramatically and prove to be unmanageable.

In short, it can be a challenging task to manage a portfolio which actually provides major benefits. That, in turn, creates a natural need for a portfolio manager to manage it. In the hands of a capable portfolio manager, a basic portfolio can be built that is neither complex nor costly. It is for those people that this book is written. If you are a project or program manager aspiring to move up the value chain, this book will teach you how to become a successful portfolio manager using one of the most versatile portfolio management platforms in the marketplace—Smartsheet. If you are already a portfolio manager, this book, with the help of advanced Smartsheet tools, will show you how to dramatically increase the capability of your portfolio.

REFERENCES

1. Project Management Institute (PMI). *Project Management Body of Knowledge (PMBOK® Guide)—Sixth Edition*. PMI, 2017.
2. Ibid.
3. Kulathumani, Murali. *Breakthrough Project Portfolio Management*. J. Ross Publishing, 2018.
4. IT project success rates finally improving—CIO.com (https://www.cio.com/article/3174516/it-project-success-rates-finally-improving.html).
5. Definition of portfolio management from: https://www.wrike.com/project-management-guide/faq/what-is-portfolio-in-project-management.
6. Delivering on Strategy—The Power of Portfolio Management (https://www.pmi.org/-/media/pmi/documents/public/pdf/learning/thought-leadership/deliver-strategy-portfolio-management.pdf).

2

A SIMPLE GUIDE TO PROJECT MANAGEMENT BASICS

INTRODUCTION

Everyone manages projects, whether as a certified project manager handling a portfolio or as a team player managing work processes as needed. In our world of doing more with less, finding methods and best practices to enhance your efficiency is essential.

That's why this project management guide is so valuable. It will help you learn the basics, discover useful strategies that you can implement today, get started on your next project with a range of pre-built templates, and gain the resources needed to manage all the work you do.

You don't have to use every one of these strategies in your project plans, but it's useful to have this toolset to choose from when planning a project.

PROJECT INITIATION

How to Manage a Project

Starting a new project is exciting, but you must do your due diligence ahead of time to ensure you start off on the right foot. What follows are the key details of the *initiation* phase, including how to create a project charter, define scope, identify objectives, and set expectations.

What Is the Project Initiation Phase?

The initiation phase encompasses all the steps you must take before a project is approved and any planning begins. The goal is to define your project at a high level and tie it into the business case you wish to solve.

> KEY CONCEPT: Project initiation is the first activity before a project is approved and any planning begins.

You should be able to answer two questions: why are you doing this project and what is the business value you expect to deliver? Consider the feasibility of your project and all the stakeholders that may be affected or require involvement.

Create a Project Charter

Once the initiation phase is underway and you've been given the green light, you need to create your project charter, or project initiation document (PID). The project charter outlines the purpose and requirements of the project.

It includes details, like business needs, key participants and stakeholders, scope, objectives, and overall goals. The project charter provides a foundation for defining project decisions and ensuring they are in line with company goals.

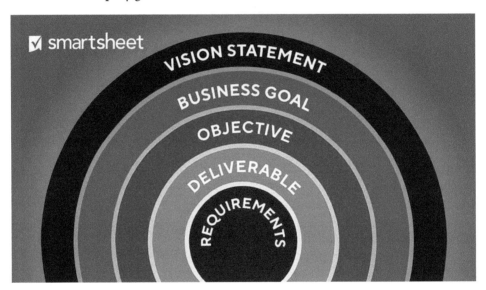

Although typically around one to two pages in length, your charter can be longer depending on the size, type, and complexity of the project. Here are some items you should be sure to include in your project charter:

- Title
- Brief description
- Background
- Goals/Deliverables
- Scope
- Impact on other business systems and units
- Stakeholders
- Roles and responsibilities
- Milestones
- Budget
- Constraints, assumptions, dependencies, and risks
- Success measurements/ROI (return on investment)
- Project approval

Define Scope

Project scope is the identification of the project's goals, deliverables, budget, and schedule. While scope can change over time, it's essential that you define it early on to set expectations with all stakeholders.

Because a successful project is measured by its ability to complete the stated requirements on time and on budget, it's important for the requirements to be clearly defined at the onset. Completing this step early on not only sets expectations but also provides a framework for you to fill in the details in order to deliver your project on time.

Defining project scope means you identify the project's purpose and deliverables along with the resources you'll need to execute your plan. Some of the items you should determine are:

- Project objectives
- Deliverables
- Constraints
- Assumptions
- Exclusions
- Schedule
- Budget

Additionally, the Project Management Institute (PMI) outlines the following six phases of defining scope:

1. **Plan Scope:** Decide how scope will be defined, monitored, and controlled.
2. **Control Scope:** An ongoing phase where you manage stakeholder expectations.
3. **Collect Requirements:** In this phase, you define project requirements needed to carry out your project.
4. **Define Scope:** Once you have requirements you can finally define scope including what is out of scope.
5. **Create Work Breakdown Structures (WBS):** This common project management tool breaks the broad project scope into a hierarchy of tasks.
6. **Validate Scope:** In this phase, internal and external stakeholders formally sign off on the proposed project scope and deliverables.

Identify Project Objectives

Like the scope, having set goals and objectives for your project can help you avoid risks and steer a course to project success. Having clear objectives will help your team stay on track because they know precisely what they're working toward.

An *objective* is specific and measurable and must meet time, budget, and quality constraints. A project may have one objective, many parallel objectives, or several objectives that must be achieved sequentially. Although it can be difficult to write clear objectives, consider the targeted key performance indicators (KPIs) that are specific to the business case you are trying to solve. One way to create clear, concise objectives is using the SMART method:

- **Specific:** Define objectives clearly and in detail, leaving no room for interpretation.
- **Measurable:** Identify the KPI you'll use to determine if you met your objectives.
- **Attainable:** Pick objectives that are reasonable for the team to successfully complete.
- **Realistic:** Set objectives that the project team believes can be achieved.
- **Time-bound:** Set a date or specific period that you plan to accomplish the objectives.

Invite the Right Stakeholders

Successful project managers ensure that they have the right stakeholders involved early on in the initiative. Many project managers often overlook less obvious—yet critical—stakeholders, so it's important to consider everyone that may be impacted by or have interest in the project plan, deliverables, and outcome.

The other thing to remember is that stakeholders can be internal *and* external. To maintain transparency throughout the project, guarantee that you have the right tools and processes in place to communicate effectively with all stakeholders. To determine the level of involvement and communication that each stakeholder may need, consider the following five important factors:

1. Who are the stakeholders who have the most influence on your project?
2. Which stakeholders will be most affected by your project?
3. How should you handle important people who aren't considered stakeholders?
4. Who controls the resources?
5. What are the top motivations and interests of your stakeholders?

You may even consider mapping the various stakeholders on a stakeholder map, based on level of influence and interest, to determine who needs what and when.

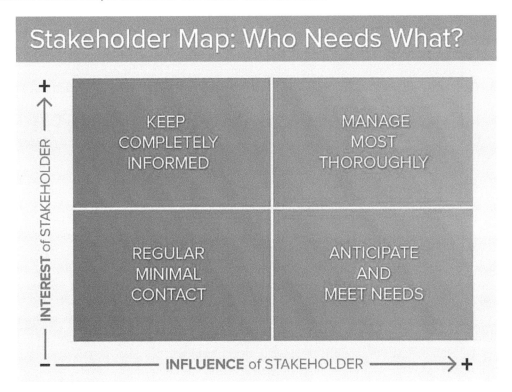

Set Expectations

Setting clear expectations of project objectives and goals, deliverables, timelines, resources required, and budgets is key to the success of your project. Of course, it's virtually impossible to anticipate every issue that may occur and throw project timelines for a loop. However, putting the effort in up front to consider and communicate all of the potential issues, and then being transparent as things change, will make a world of difference in keeping all parties on the same page. Here are some key factors to consider when setting expectations:

- Ensure the project charter is complete and well thought-out.
- Plan for risks and potential hiccups.
- Estimate realistic timelines and budgets but allow for some padding.
- Share project plans with all internal and external stakeholders.
- Set milestones throughout the project timeline to show incremental progress.
- Provide regular updates and real-time status reports.
- Be honest if things go wrong.

THE PROJECT PLANNING PHASE

The project planning phase is key to setting the roadmap for your team to follow to reach your intended project outcome. Nail this phase and your likelihood of delivering a successful project increases exponentially. This section will detail how to create your project plan broken out into phases and milestones to help estimate specific project costs, assess required and available resources, and determine potential risks and ways to mitigate them.

> KEY CONCEPT: Project planning is the act of creating the roadmap of activities needed to successfully execute the project.

Create a Project Task List Organized by Phases

With all the factors involved in a project, it's easy to overlook a detail that could potentially lead to missed deadlines or budget overruns. Any project or plan can be made more manageable by breaking it down into individual tasks. One way to do this is by creating a WBS (discussed later in this chapter), which is a visual representation that shows the scope of a project broken into manageable sections.

From there, your task list can be displayed in a variety of ways. Whether on a whiteboard or in an online task management tool, finding what works for you and your team and the project at hand is key to ensuring nothing is missed. Some project managers and teams find it helpful to use a task list template to quickly get started with their lists. Once you have your task list created, start grouping tasks together into phases and then set milestones for each phase. This will help you determine which tasks must happen when and which tasks are dependent on others.

Create Your Timeline

Now that you have your task list set, you're ready to create your timeline. A timeline is helpful to provide a visual representation of all the tasks within your project and how they are connected or dependent on each other. At this point, you will estimate and set start and end dates for each of the tasks within your list. Determining duration of individual tasks will help give you an idea of the finish date of your project. Be sure when estimating dates that you provide a small buffer to account for any issues that may arise.

Although there are many ways to create a project timeline, one that successful project managers often use is a Gantt chart (discussed later in this chapter). Gantt charts are visual timelines that display tasks as bars and enable you to track progress, map your critical path, show dependencies, and make updates by changing task duration.

Consider Available Resources

With your timeline ready to go, you need to consider which resources are available to keep your project on time and on budget. Making the best use of the resources you have is what will help get your project to the finish line. Resource management is designed to allocate human and tangible assets—finances, materials, and equipment—efficiently and effectively. Yet, it is one of the most difficult processes to control, maintain, and achieve success.

It is also important to assign roles and responsibilities to your team members at this time. This sets expectations up front, ensuring that each team member knows what they are responsible for. Within your project plan, define who is going to do what, by when, and then stick to it.

Estimate Project Costs

No matter what type of project you are managing, successful projects require accurate cost estimates. Cost estimations forecast both the budget and the resources needed to execute your project. In turn, project objectives are achieved within the approved timeline and budget. A *cost estimate* is the sum of all costs required to successfully complete a project through its duration. Although there are many ways to categorize the types of cost items, the most simple way is in two categories: direct costs and indirect costs.

- **Direct costs:** Expenses billed to a single project, such as project team wages and costs to produce physical products.
- **Indirect costs:** Expenses that are not associated with a single project, but rather are used by multiple projects simultaneously.

Beyond direct and indirect costs, project expenses can also fall into any of the following categories:

- Labor
- Materials
- Equipment
- Services
- Software
- Hardware
- Facilities
- Contingency costs

Assess Potential Risks

Risks are an inevitable part of any project. That's why it's critical to consider and assess potential risk before jumping into the execution phase. First, it's helpful to think through and list if/then scenarios. For example, "If we go over budget in this first phase, then X will happen or need to happen." In this case, "X" could be an adjustment made to scope, budget, timeline, etc. Next, create a risk assessment matrix, which is used to help evaluate and prioritize risks based on the severity of their impact and their likelihood to occur. A risk assessment matrix (see below) is a chart that shows the severity of an event occurring on one axis against the probability of it occurring on the other.

RISK ASSESSMENT MATRIX

RISK RATING KEY	LOW	MEDIUM	HIGH	EXTREME
	0—ACCEPTABLE	1—ALARP (as low as reasonably practicable)	2—GENERALLY UNACCEPTABLE	3—INTOLERABLE
	OK TO PROCEED	TAKE MITIGATION EFFORTS	SEEK SUPPORT	PLACE EVENT ON HOLD

		SEVERITY		
	ACCEPTABLE	TOLERABLE	UNDESIRABLE	INTOLERABLE
	LITTLE TO NO EFFECT ON EVENT	EFFECTS ARE FELT, BUT NOT CRITICAL TO OUTCOME	SERIOUS IMPACT TO THE COURSE OF ACTION AND OUTCOME	COULD RESULT IN DISASTER
IMPROBABLE RISK IS UNLIKELY TO OCCUR	LOW – 1 –	MEDIUM – 4 –	MEDIUM – 6 –	HIGH – 10 –
POSSIBLE RISK WILL LIKELY OCCUR	LOW – 2 –	MEDIUM – 5 –	HIGH – 8 –	EXTREME – 11 –
PROBABLE RISK WILL OCCUR	MEDIUM – 3 –	HIGH – 7 –	HIGH – 9 –	EXTREME – 12 –

(LIKELIHOOD — vertical axis label)

By assessing existing and potential risks, you can estimate their impact, adjust your project timeline accordingly, and then plan for responding to the risks if they occur.

PROJECT EXECUTION

The project *execution* phase is where deliverables are developed and completed, and it often feels like the meat of the project since a lot is happening during this time. This is where all the work you've put into planning the project will be executed. This section will discuss how to direct and manage the execution of the project plan, communicate with stakeholders on progress, and orchestrate status meetings and reports.

> KEY CONCEPT: Project execution is the part of the project where the work happens and deliverables are completed.

Types of Project Meetings

It's more essential than ever to maintain open communication during the project execution phase to ensure that everything runs smoothly. Depending on your project, there are different types of meetings that may be helpful throughout the duration of your project.

Project kick-off meeting: The project execution phase generally starts with a project kick-off meeting. All stakeholders and team members should be invited to talk through the project plan and discuss any foreseeable issues or concerns.

Stand-up or Scrum meeting: Also known as a daily huddle, morning roll call, or daily stand-up, these meetings bring project team members together to talk about what they accomplished the previous day, what they plan to do that day, and what obstacles they face. The focus here is on collaboration and accountability between team members.

Status or progress meeting: The project status or progress meeting generally happens on a weekly or monthly cadence throughout the life of the project. This meeting brings together all stakeholders to discuss what's been accomplished, milestones achieved, what's coming down the line, and any issues that need to be addressed.

For both the project kick-off and status meetings, project managers should send out an agenda prior to the meeting and have someone in attendance to document meeting minutes. This will help attendees plan and prepare for the meeting, while also allowing team members to look back on the minutes as a system of record for items discussed.

Manage Stakeholder Communication Plan

Creating strong lines of communication with all stakeholders throughout a project is key to ensuring it runs smoothly and maintains stakeholder confidence. Earlier in the initiation phase section of this chapter, a list of factors to consider when creating your stakeholder management and communication plan was provided. Now, in the execution phase, it's time to implement your plan. Here are best practices for communicating with stakeholders throughout your project:

1. **Be prepared** and stay two steps ahead in planning on how and when to communicate to your important stakeholders.
2. **Anticipate the needs of stakeholders** and respond to them before they become an issue.
3. **Ensure that all stakeholders have access** to the whole project plan so they can check in on progress without needing to bug you.
4. **Create a roll-up view** of high-level progress and KPIs so that stakeholders can view specific indicators without having to get into the details of project tasks.

PROJECT MONITOR AND CONTROL

While the project is underway, the project manager must have a constant pulse on how progress is tracking and have a real-time way to capture, track, manage, and report on their project status. This includes knowing whether tasks and milestones are being completed on time, if the budget is in line with actual costs, and more.

> KEY CONCEPT: Project monitor and control is the activity of watching over the project's progress and shoring it up as needed.

Identify and Mitigate Risk Early

It's inevitable that projects face issues. These issues can include budget risks, timeline risks, incidents, emergencies, opportunities, and more. Project managers who complete their risk assessment early on will have a better chance of avoiding issues, but they still must have a real-time view into their work to identify and mitigate unforeseen risks before they impact the overall project timeline and budget.

Since no project is without risk, having the right risk management tools and processes in place can help you identify, monitor, and resolve risks far more efficiently than relying on your own ability to be in the right place at the right time. Some benefits of using a risk management software include:

1. **Greater transparency:** Project managers are able to tackle and prioritize project risks with the best risk/reward outcomes.
2. **Reduced compliance and legal costs:** Integrating corporate governance and risk management compliance processes means lower costs for all.
3. **Better internal controls:** Project managers that closely monitor and manage their risk show deeper ownership of their projects than those who don't monitor as closely.
4. **Strengthened project operations:** The more knowledge a project manager has, the better they can be at predicting risk for future projects.

5. **Increased stakeholder trust:** Showing that you have the right tools in place to stay ahead of risk puts stakeholders' minds at ease.

Track Key Performance Indicators

Project managers must use KPIs to determine whether the project is on track. Here are some of the top KPIs to measure project performance:

1. **Project objectives:** A project that is on schedule and on budget is a good indicator to determine if the project will meet its original objectives.
2. **Quality deliverables:** Measure whether task deliverables are being met and if they meet specific standards set within the project requirements.
3. **Effort and cost tracking:** Project managers must track effort and costs associated with resources to see if the budget is on track.
4. **Project performance:** This tracks changes that occur in the project including amount and type of issues that arise and how they are addressed.

TIP: Creating a real-time project-specific dashboard (like the one below) to track high-level KPIs and then sharing it with all stakeholders will help reduce the time spent answering status questions.

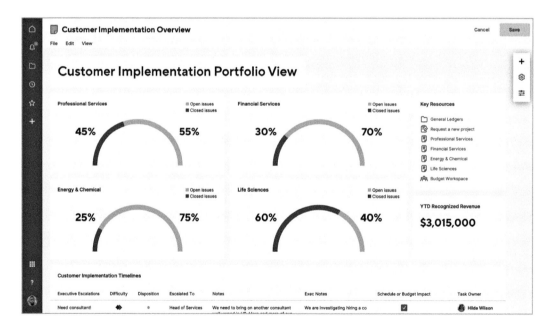

Manage Documentation

Documentation is an important part of any project. Whether you prefer waterfall over agile, kanban over Scrum, keeping records of what happened and changes that occurred throughout the project's life cycle will add to overall success. Especially when there are clients or external stakeholders involved, having organized documentation can be the deciding factor when disagreements or issues occur. Additionally, having a well-documented project provides historical insights that can be used on future projects.

The key here is organizing your documentation so that you aren't searching through folders, email, messenger apps, project management tools, etc., to find the documentation you need. Create a single location to manage all project documentation so that you can quickly access the information you need and keep details in context.

Know the Status of Your Project

Part of the project manager's role is to keep key stakeholders up-to-date on status throughout the duration of the project. Not knowing the status of your project when asked can send red flags that you aren't tracking your project closely and may reduce stakeholder trust in both you and the project. One way to guarantee that you know the status of your project at any moment is with a project status report. A project status report should capture all the business-critical activities, developments, and risks associated with a project. Essentially, a project status report is a snapshot of where a project stands and how various aspects of the project are doing. Additionally, status reports help to:

- Create and enable buy-in from stakeholders
- Provide transparency into progress toward milestones
- Identify issues and risks, so course correction can happen quickly
- Pinpoint work done by individuals, teams, or departments, so you can allocate resources as needed
- Provide a high-level gauge of project health
- Create a method to keep project managers and teams accountable
- Prevent scope creep

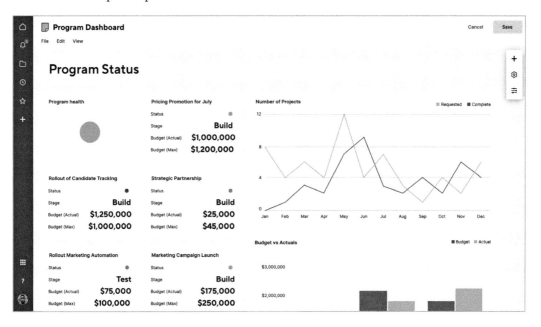

Control Scope Creep

Changes happen throughout a project and are to be expected. But, because the scope is defined at the very beginning of the project during the initiation phase, it's easy for stakeholders to try to add to that scope months down the road when the project is under way. It is essential that the project manager add requests to the requirements and prioritize based on value. If you say "yes" to every change request without evaluating the value and the impact on the timeline and budget, you will have a never-ending project that becomes a money pit.

PROJECT CLOSING

The project closeout phase represents the completed project. Final deliverables are handed over at this time, vendors who were hired for project-specific work are terminated, and valuable team members are recognized.

> KEY CONCEPT: Project closeout is the finishing phase of the project, where activities are brought to a controlled finish.

Project Closeout and Retrospective

Once the project is finished, the project manager still has a few tasks to complete. Many project managers hold a meeting—often called the postmortem or project retrospective—to evaluate what went well in a project and identify any project failures. Project managers need to create a project punch list, including tasks that didn't get accomplished during the project, and work with stakeholders to resolve them. Additionally, project managers need to complete a final project budget and project report and collect all project documents to store them in a single location for future reference.

Conducting a project retrospective is important to consider how well the project was initiated, planned, executed, and controlled. This is not necessarily to point out failures and successes, but rather to provide greater value through lessons learned. Documenting lessons learned allows an organization to record, maintain, and reuse insights on future projects.

> TIP: A cloud-based work execution platform makes it easy to collect, manage, and save all project closeout documentation in a single location throughout the project life cycle.

PROJECT MANAGEMENT TOOLS

As a project manager, you must find the right processes and tools to help you and your team deliver projects within the specified requirements. With the right tools in place, you can focus more on managing the project and delivering quality end products, and less on managing the process. The following section discusses some top project management tools and techniques that successful project managers use to plan, track, and manage their projects.

Program Evaluation and Review Technique (PERT)

With any project, time is important. But as complexity increases, sticking to timelines is even more critical. This makes it vital for project managers to be able to accurately estimate how long a task will take, and if there are any dependencies to completing each task. To accomplish this, PERT was developed.

PERT is often used with one-off projects where time is more important than cost. PERT work is represented in a chart or diagram that provides a visual into all scheduled tasks in a project sequence.

Project managers can then analyze how much time it will take to accomplish each task, and then forecast the overall project timeline.

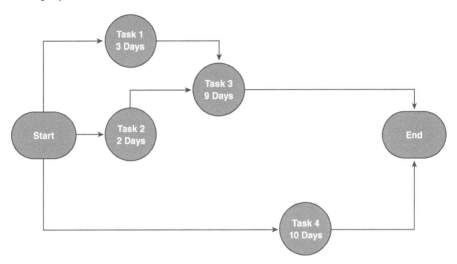

Here are some of the ways project managers use PERT:

- Estimate a completion date
- Gauge risk when there is a drop-dead date
- Find where you have flexibility in the schedule
- Improve scheduling of tasks

Kanban Board

A kanban board is most commonly used to visualize and track work being done (or needing to be done). It acts as the information hub for all task status and progress, since you can view all items on a single board. Tasks move across the board from left to right through the different stages of a workflow. This easy-to-set-up tool can also be overlaid with current processes and workflows. When setting up your kanban board, you will have (at the very least) the following three columns: *To-Do*, *Doing*, and *Done*. From there you can add any additional columns that align with stages of your project or workflow.

When deciding whether to use a physical board (post-it notes on a whiteboard) or an online kanban board, consider the following factors:

- Do you need real-time access to status?
- Will you have multiple team members working on the same project?
- Are your team members all located in the same physical space?
- Will you need to share your kanban board with external stakeholders?

Depending on your answers to the previous questions, you may want to consider an online kanban board that will enable you to share your board with all stakeholders no matter where they are located, and collaborate on project tasks in real time.

Gantt Chart

A Gantt chart (see next page) is a visual timeline that makes it easy to see how a project is progressing. Project tasks are organized on a horizontal bar chart that shows task durations, dependencies, and milestones. With a Gantt chart, you can plan out all of your tasks, making complex projects manageable.

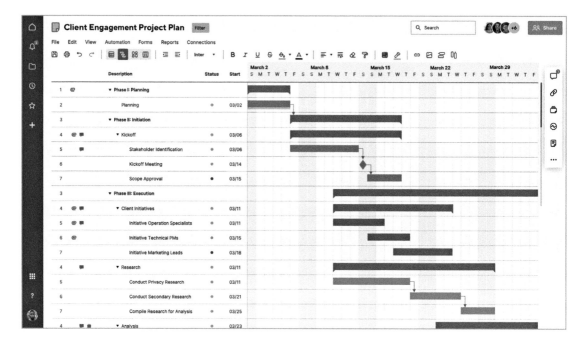

Use a Gantt chart to determine the overall project timeline and to assign roles and responsibilities to your team to ensure no task is missed. Some of the benefits of using a Gantt chart allows you to:

- Determine all necessary tasks.
- Know when tasks need to be completed.
- Discover the critical path (discussed next).
- Keep your team informed on progress.
- Simplify complex tasks.

Although there are many tools out there that can help you create a Gantt chart, make sure you consider the following factors before selecting one:

- Will it integrate with your daily workflow?
- Is it easy to create and update?
- Does it provide real-time updates when changes are made to the schedule?
- Is the Gantt view customizable?
- Can you view and update your chart on different devices (e.g., desktop versus mobile)?
- Is it easy to share your Gantt chart with your team?

The answers to the above questions will help determine the right platform to use for all of your Gantt chart and project needs.

Critical Path

Depending on the size and type of your project, it may require you to manage hundreds of tasks and dozens of dependencies, which can make it tricky to identify the most important tasks—the ones that, if missed, could send your project over schedule. That's why it's essential to have the right tools in place to identify the critical path for your project.

The critical path helps to identify the important tasks to keep on track throughout the duration of your project. Here are three benefits of utilizing a critical path:

1. **Identifies the most important tasks:** It clearly identifies the tasks that you will have to closely manage.
2. **Helps reduce timelines:** When the critical path is displayed on your project timeline, it provides a new level of visibility to determine where you can make adjustments.
3. **Compares planned with actual:** Using the baseline schedule developed from the initial critical path analysis can help track schedule progress.

Originally created as a hand-drawn diagram, you can now automatically identify the critical path within most online project management software. Be sure that your software allows you to overlay your critical path on your project timeline Gantt chart, and is easy to turn on or turn off.

Work Breakdown Structure

A WBS is a visual tool for defining and tracking a project deliverable and all the small components needed to create it. As defined by the PMI Project Management Body of Knowledge, a WBS is a "hierarchical decomposition of the total scope of work to be carried out by the project team to accomplish the project objectives and create the required deliverables."

To create your WBS, start with the desired outcome, which you then break down into the smaller deliverables or tasks. The deliverable can be a physical object, a service, or an activity. A visual representation of a WBS is below:

Project Name			
	Task 1		
		Subtask 1.1	
			Work Package 1.1.1
			Work Package 1.1.2
		Subtask 1.2	
			Work Package 1.2.1
			Work Package 1.2.2
	Task 2		
		Subtask 2.1	
			Work Package 2.1.1
			Work Package 2.1.2

Often an overlooked tool within project management, here are some of the benefits of creating a WBS:

- Provides a visual representation of all parts of the project.
- Offers an ongoing view for stakeholders into how the project is progressing.
- Defines specific and measurable outcomes.
- Breaks the work into manageable chunks.
- Provides a way to make successful experiences repeatable.
- Sets a foundation for estimating costs and allocating team members and other resources.

Project Roadmap

The project roadmap is a key visual tool (see below) to quickly convey the overall project purpose and plan. It is a high-level, easy-to-understand overview of the important pieces of your project. Share this helpful resource with stakeholders to provide a quick snapshot of what the project aims to accomplish, important milestones, key deliverables, dependencies, and possible risk. This key communication tool should include the following details:

- **High-level project overview:** Be succinct and concise when documenting your goals and objectives. Aim for a few sentences at most.
- **Schedule overview:** Provide a high-level view of the timeline. Don't worry about including too many details: simply link to the project plan from your roadmap.
- **Key milestones:** Highlight a few important dates. This quick view into milestones will help set expectations with less-involved stakeholders.
- **Dependencies:** Show important deliverables and how they contribute to project success.
- **Key contacts:** Identify the go-to people on your project team, what their focus is, and how to get a hold of them.

Project Name	Goals *Why is this work important?*	Objectives *What are you planning to accomplish?*	Key Deliverables What are the major outputs of this work?
	Schedule Overview + Dependencies *Show workstreams here, too.*		
Key Milestone 1 *IMPORTANT DATE!*	Key Milestone 2 *IMPORTANT DATE!*	Key Milestone 3 *IMPORTANT DATE!*	
Key Project Contacts			

Additionally, to be effective, your project roadmap should be updated frequently—ideally in real time. This ensures that stakeholders are looking at the most up-to-date information and will reduce the number of requests you receive for real-time updates.

3

A SIMPLE GUIDE TO SMARTSHEET BASICS

INTRODUCTION

In the previous two chapters we covered some broad ground about portfolio and project management and Smartsheet is a great platform to implement project and portfolio management quickly and easily. Therefore, in later chapters, we'll be walking through how to implement simple and effective designs in Smartsheet that deliver effective portfolio management results.

At the same time, we don't want to assume that the reader has any knowledge of Smartsheet. This chapter will walk the reader through basic Smartsheet operations that will be needed in later chapters. Smartsheet is remarkably easy to get started with and is also very flexible. The user-friendliness of the platform is partly because it draws on everyone's familiarity with spreadsheet features. It then proceeds to make simple and useful upgrades on top of those capabilities. In this chapter, you'll learn how to use Smartsheet to create and customize a basic sheet.

BASIC SMARTSHEET OPERATIONS

Creating a Sheet

A sheet is the foundation of your work in Smartsheet and where all of your data lives. The way you set up your sheet will determine how you can take advantage of Smartsheet's many capabilities.

The default sheet view is the familiar looking grid, which you can easily customize with multiple column types, hierarchies, attachments, collaborative communication, and more. The three other sheet views—Gantt, Card, and Calendar—are discussed later in this chapter.

Create or Rename a Sheet or Other Smartsheet Item

1. In the left side rail, click the **Solution Center** (plus) icon.

2. In the left panel, click **Create**, and select the desired tile for the item that you want to create. (More information on these below.)

> TIP: In the Solution Center panel, you can also search for a template using the search field and categories.

3. When prompted, enter a name for the item, and click **OK**.

> NOTE: The item name can contain up to 50 characters.

The screen will refresh to display your new item—it's ready for you to start working.

Rename an Item

You must be the owner of an item to rename it.

1. From the **Home** in the left panel, right-click on the name of the item and select **Rename**.
2. Type the new name for the item (limit of 50 characters) and click **OK**.

Overview of Smartsheet Items

1. *Grid*—Has no predefined columns—it's a clean slate. Use this when you want to start from scratch.
2. *Project*—Includes common columns needed to create a project and enable Gantt chart functionality.
3. *Cards*—Provides what you need to start a card-based Kanban-style project.
4. *Task List*—Includes several predefined columns, including Task Name, Due Date, Assigned To, Done, and Comments.
5. *Form*—Creates a basic three-column sheet with a form attached to it. Use this when you know you'll want to collect information from others with a form.
6. *Report*—Compiles data from multiple sheets and only shows items that meet specified criteria.
7. *Dashboard/Portal*—Allows you to create a visual summary of sheet data or an information hub.

Rows and Hierarchy

Smartsheet has smart rows that allow you to build hierarchy, and easily organize, track, and move data.

Hierarchy: Indent or Outdent Rows

You can create a hierarchy on your sheet by indenting rows. When you indent a row, it becomes a child of the row above it (the parent row).

> NOTE: Hierarchy is created from the child row. It is not created by designating a row as a parent.

Note that hierarchy creates relationships between rows, it doesn't control row formatting.

Indent a Row

Click on a cell in the first row you'd like to indent, and then click the **Indent** button on the toolbar. The row above it will become the parent row.

> NOTE: If the **Indent** button is unavailable, you may be trying to indent a blank row. In order to create hierarchy, data needs to exist in *both* the parent and child rows. Make sure neither row is blank before indenting.

> TIP: You can also use the keyboard shortcut Ctrl +] or Command +] on a Mac.

Indents are displayed only in a sheet's Primary Column; however, the relationship is applied to the entire row.

Remove Hierarchy

To remove the parent-child relationship, click on a cell in the child row and then click the **Outdent** button on the toolbar.

> TIP: You can also use the keyboard shortcut Ctrl + [or Command + [on a Mac.

Expand or Collapse Indented Rows

When you expand or collapse rows and then save the sheet, this changes the sheet structure for all collaborators shared to it. That is, everyone who uses the sheet will see the same rows collapsed and expanded that you do.

To show or hide the indented items beneath a parent row, click **expand/collapse** ▾ in the parent row's Primary Column.

▾ **Administration**
Complete TPS Report
Send TPS Report to Engineering
Correct Accounting Glitch
▾ **Software Engineers**
Update Bank/Credit Union Mainframe
Stabilize Load Balancers

To expand or collapse all sub-items on a sheet, right-click on the Primary Column header and select **Expand All** or **Collapse All**.

Hierarchy Best Practices

Keep the following in mind as you work with hierarchy:

- There is no fixed level of indenting. You can continue indenting rows on your sheet to create multiple levels of hierarchy.
- When you click and drag a row that has items indented below it, the child rows will move with the selected item.
- You can't delete a parent row without also deleting its indented child rows. (To delete the row without deleting the child rows, remove the parent-child relationship first.)
- When dependencies are enabled on a project sheet, parent rows reflect a roll-up summary of the start date, end date, duration, and % complete values entered for the indented child rows.

Smartsheet columns are like columns in a typical spreadsheet, but they also have special properties that make using your sheet easier and more powerful.

Column Type Reference

Column types help you get better control over what data is allowed in columns—use specific types to ensure more consistent data entry. In Smartsheet, you'll work with default columns and configurable columns:

- **Default columns**. These cannot be changed or removed.
- The **Primary** column. This column will always have a type of Text/Number. The Primary Column type cannot be changed.
- **Configurable columns**. You can choose from the following column types:
  - Text/Number
  - Contact List
  - Date
  - Dropdown List (Single Select)
  - Dropdown List (Multi Select)
  - Checkbox
  - Symbols
  - Auto-Number/System

Who Can Use This Capability

Licensed users with **Owner** or **Admin** permissions to the sheet can add to or edit a column.

Default Columns

Every sheet has a primary column. This column is mandatory and cannot be deleted from a sheet. The value in this column is frequently the main descriptor for the row: it will always have a type of Text/Number. The primary column type cannot be changed.

These column display icons alert you to certain row-specific content or activities:

- The **Attachments** column ⬭. The Attachments icon will appear on each row with an attachment. Click the icon to review the attachments.
- The **Comments** column ⬭. The Comments icon will appear on each row containing comments. Click the icon to review the comments.
- The **Row Action Indicators** column ⓘ. This column will display an icon for Pending Reminders ⬭, Update Requests ⬭, Locks ⬭, and Allocation Alerts ⬭ associated with the row.

> NOTE: If multiple row actions exist for the row, the column will display multiple icons.

Configurable Columns

Text/Number

This column type can include text, numeric values, or any combination of the two. Text/number is the best choice for comment columns that might have long entries or number-focused columns, such as the projected expense for a sheet tracking a budget.

You can apply formatting to a text/number column to display values in currency or percentage format by clicking the column header and then clicking the **Currency Format** or **Percentage Format** button in the toolbar.

> NOTE: If the first character of a number is zero followed by another digit or by a letter, Smartsheet will prepend the value with an apostrophe and store it as text. It does this so that the leading zero will be retained and displayed with the number. If you want the number to be stored as a number—so that you can perform calculations with it, for example—you'll need to double-click the cell and remove the apostrophe and any leading zeros.

Contact List

This is the best choice for columns such as Assigned To, Owner, Approved By, and so on. This column type enables you to assign rows to collaborators shared to a sheet or to contacts from your Smartsheet Contact List. You can also use the column to send reminders to shared collaborators and generate reports that show a list of tasks assigned to a specific team member.

When you use this column type, you have the option to specify preferred contact values in the **Values** box. Acceptable values for this list are a contact name and email address, a name only, or an email address only.

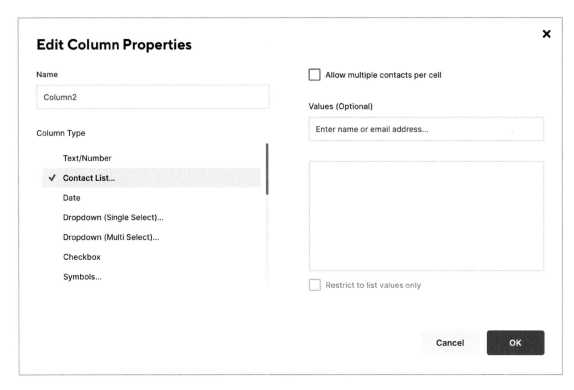

If you've set up preferred contacts in the contact column, you'll be able to quickly access them by clicking the dropdown arrow ▾ in a Contact list cell or corresponding Smartsheet form field. In the cell, you'll also see contacts and email addresses that have been assigned to other rows on the sheet.

> NOTE: A Smartsheet form field associated with a contact column will only include preferred contacts. If no preferred contacts have been set, anyone submitting through the form must type the contact's name or email address rather than selecting from a list.

You can add to the list by manually typing a new name or email address into a cell. As you type, the list will expand to display a relevant list of matching contacts from your Smartsheet Contacts List, as well as from the User Management screen (available with multi-user plans).

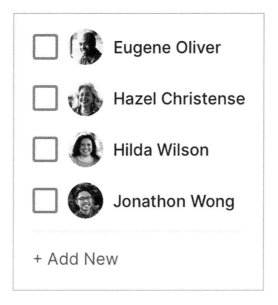

TIP: If you start typing a name or address and aren't seeing the list auto-resolve, this means you don't have any contacts matching what you've typed. Add the contact to your list to make sure that you can run reports and send reminders to them. Click the dropdown arrow ▾ in the cell, then select **Add New** to add the contact to your list and assign it to the row.

To remove names or email addresses from the auto-resolve dropdown list, remove them from the other cells in the column and from the Edit Column Properties form. People who are shared to the sheet will always appear as suggestions when you type in a Contact List column.

Date

The cells in this column will display a calendar icon that collaborators can click to choose a specific date. You can also manually type in dates or use keyboard shortcuts to populate the cells. Date columns must exist in the sheet to enable dependencies or to display items in the Calendar view.

The dates will appear in the format set up in the Personal Settings of your Smartsheet account.

Dropdown List (Single Select)

This column displays a list of values from which you can choose a single value.

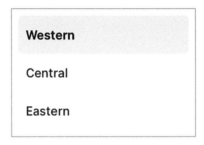

When you select this column type, you'll have the option to type the values that you want to appear in the list. Separate each list item onto a separate line by pressing Enter or Return on your keyboard.

To remove an item from the Dropdown List, select it and then press Backspace or Delete.

Dropdown List (Multi Select)

This column displays a list of values that you can choose one or more values from. When you select this column type, you'll have the option to type the values that you want to appear in the list. Separate each list item onto a separate line by pressing Enter or Return.

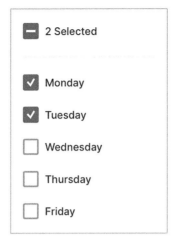

Checkbox

The column presents a checkbox that can be checked or unchecked. A checkbox will appear in the cell only if a value has been entered into another column in that row.

Symbols

A Symbols column will display a visual image. Use a Symbols column to describe the status of a row. You cannot add your own (custom) symbols to the column.

Auto-Number/System

This type of column will automatically generate values for every row in the sheet that contains data. Auto-numbering can be useful when you want to assign row IDs, part numbers, invoice numbers, or customer numbers without manually typing them in. System columns can show you who created each row, who last modified each row, the time each row was created, and the last time each row was modified.

When you set them up, System column cells are initially empty: the values will be generated as soon as you click **Save** to save the sheet.

Use the Best Column Type for Your Data

Column types help you get better control over what data is allowed in columns. Use specific types to ensure more consistent data entry. You can also add a column description to provide more information about your column.

For information about the different column types in Smartsheet, see Column Type Reference.

Who Can Use This Capability

Licensed users with **Owner** or **Admin** permissions to the sheet can add or edit a column.

Edit a Column to Change Its Type

To change an existing column type, use the **Column Properties** window: click the dropdown arrow ▼ under the column header and select **Edit Column Properties**.

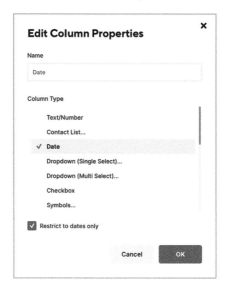

> NOTES:
> - Even when a column property is set, it's possible to type text freely into a cell (one exception is read-only System columns).
> - If you're the sheet Owner or are shared to the sheet with Admin-level permissions, you can prevent others from adding free text by checking the **Restrict to** checkbox when you edit column properties or create a new column.
> - If a column is enabled in the project settings of a sheet, its type will be displayed as **Date/Time**, **Duration**, or **Predecessors** and the column type won't be editable.

Include a Column Description

Explain important information about a column in a custom tooltip; people can access the information by hovering over an information icon below the column header. Use a column description, for example, to document how you want a particular column to be used and what type of data you expect the column to contain.

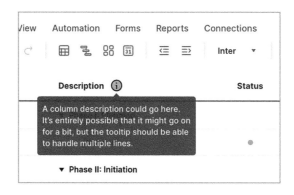

NOTES:
- You must be the sheet **Owner** or shared with **Admin**-level permissions to add or edit a column description.
- The column description has a limit of up to 250 characters (this limit may vary depending on the language or character type you use).
- Column descriptions are visible only in sheets—they cannot be viewed in reports or dashboards.

Create a Column Description

1. Right-click a column header and select **Add Column Description**. The Column Description window appears.

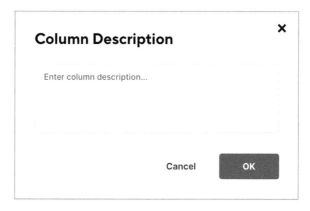

2. Type your column description in the form and click the **OK** button to set the description.

An Information icon appears below the column header.

That's it! Now anyone shared to the sheet can view the column description by hovering over the information icon.

Edit Column Description Information

1. Right-click the column header and select **Edit Column Description**.
2. In the Column Description window, make your desired changes and click **OK**.

Maintain Consistency in Data Collection with Dropdown Columns

You can use the **Single Select** and **Multi Select** dropdown column types to standardize the collection of key information:

- Allow collaborators to select one or more values that apply to them
- Easily track and report on the standardized values collected

Who Can Use This Capability

Licensed users with **Owner** or **Admin** permissions to the sheet can add or modify columns. Licensed users with **Editor-level** sharing permissions or higher can modify dropdown list values in cells within unlocked rows and columns.

Set Up a Dropdown Column in Your Sheet

To create a Dropdown List column:

1. Click the dropdown arrow below a columns header and select **Insert Column Right** or **Insert Column Left**, depending on where you want to place the additional dropdown column. The Insert Column window appears.

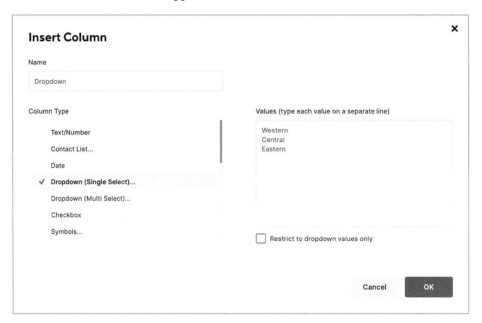

2. Type the name of the column in the **Name** box.
3. Select the **Dropdown (Single Select)** or **Dropdown (Multi Select)** column type.
4. Type the values that you want to appear in the list under **Values**. (You can separate each list value onto a new line by pressing Enter or Return.)
5. To restrict users from entering free text values, check **Restrict to dropdown** values only.
6. Click **OK**.

NOTES:
- Values in dropdown cells are ordered based on their order of appearance in the values list.
- Values may contain punctuation, letters, numbers, and emojis.
- If the text equivalent of a hyperlink is inserted under Values, it will appear as plain text in the values field, but is a clickable hyperlink when selected from the dropdown.
- Email addresses under Values will appear as plain text in the dropdown.

That's it! The Single Select or Multi Select dropdown column is inserted into your sheet. Now you can start collecting standardized values from collaborators.

Edit Dropdown Column Properties

If you want to add or remove values from the dropdown list, you can do so by editing the dropdown column properties.

To edit the column properties:

1. Click the dropdown arrow below a column's header and select **Edit Column Properties.** The Edit Column Properties window appears.

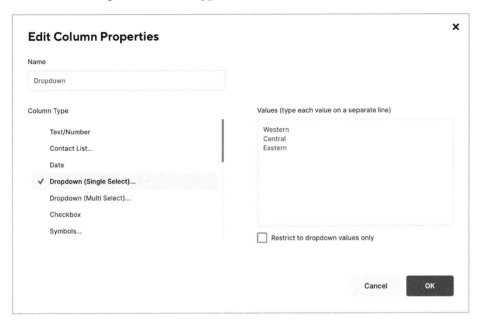

2. Modify the values listed under **Values.** To remove a value from the dropdown list, select it and then press Backspace or Delete.

> NOTE: Values in a Single Select or Multi Select dropdown field on a form will need to be modified in the **Edit Column Properties** window.

3. Click **Save.**

Note the following if you decide to switch between column types:

- When switching between Single Select and Multi Select dropdown column types, the values listed under **Values** in the column properties will remain the same. The only difference is that Single Select allows you to select a single value from the dropdown list, while Multi-Select allows you to select multiple values.
- When switching from a Single Select or Multi Select dropdown column type to a non-dropdown column type, any cells that contain a single dropdown value will be shown as text, and any cells that contain more than one dropdown value will be shown as line-delimited text.
- When switching from a non-dropdown column type to a Single Select or Multi Select column type, the entire content of each cell will be captured and added as one value in the **Values** section of the dropdown column properties.
- When switching from or to Single Select or Multi Select column types, reports containing those columns will need to be updated.

Choose the Right Dropdown Column Type

When you select values from dropdown columns on the sheet, the dropdown list will appear differently based on the dropdown column type selected.

The Single Select dropdown column will allow you to select a single value from the dropdown list:

The Multi Select dropdown column will allow you to select one or more values from the dropdown list by checking the checkbox next to each value. Each value selected from a Multi Select dropdown will be captured in the cell:

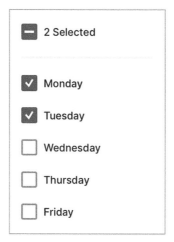

To remove captured values from cells, double-click the cell and click the **X** next to the captured value you want to remove, or uncheck the checkbox next to the value in the dropdown list.

Tips and Best Practices for Working with Dropdown Columns

Keep the following in mind when modifying cells in dropdown columns:

- If the dropdown column has not been restricted to list values only, you will be able to enter a free text value in the cell by double-clicking the cell and typing the value. These free text values will be added to the dropdown list in the cell it has been added to but will not be added to the **Values** section of the dropdown column properties.
- In Multi Select dropdown columns, free text values are saved alphabetically at the end of the cell they are added to.
- There's no limit to the number of values that can be selected in a Multi Select dropdown column (up to normal cell character limits).

Smartsheet allows you to attach and manage files directly in your sheet so you can access all of your work in one place. Files can be attached from your desktop and the most popular cloud storage providers.

Attach Files Stored on Your Computer to a Sheet

You can attach almost any type of file to a sheet, row, or comment. This is useful when you want to relate files to items that you're keeping track of in Smartsheet. You can attach files stored on your computer or files stored in supported third-party cloud storage services.

Attach Files to a Sheet or Row

How you attach files depends on where you'd like them to be connected. You can attach files on the sheet level or attach files directly to a specific row or comment.

To attach files at the sheet level:

1. Select the **Attachments** icon 📎 in the right panel.

The Attachments panel appears.
2. **Drag and drop** any files you'd like to attach onto the right panel.

You can also select the **Attach Files to Sheet** button at the bottom of the right panel to navigate through your directory more extensively and find the files you need.

To attach files to a specific row:

1. Select the row you'd like to attach the file to.

2. Select the **Attachments** icon  in the right panel.

The Attachments panel appears.

3. **Drag and Drop** the files you'd like to attach to the right panel.

TIP: You can also select the **Attach Files to Row** button at the bottom of the right panel to navigate through your directory more extensively and find the files you need.

Behaviors of Row-Level Attachments

- Rows that already contain attachments will display the **Attachments** icon to the left of the row number.
- You can only attach files to one row at a time.
- You can't associate any already attached file with a different row or area of the sheet.

Attach files as you comment:

1. Select the **Comments** icon in the right panel (sheet comments) or select the dropdown arrow at the start of a row and select **Comments** (row comments).

2. Select the **Attachments** icon (right side of the **Add comment** box) and select the files you want to attach.

3. Type your comment and select **Save**.

Supported File Types, File Sizes, and Other Requirements

The vast majority of file types are supported for uploading, including (*but not limited to*):

File type	Examples of extensions
Most image formats	.jpg, .png, .gif
Portable Document Format	.pdf
Microsoft Office Suite	.docx, .pptx, .xlsx

Supported browsers and upload quantities:

- You can upload *100 files at a time*. While there isn't a limit to the total number of attachments allowed on a row or sheet, you are bound by the amount of storage space included in the sheet owner's subscription.
- A browser that supports HTML 5 is required to upload files larger than 30 MB.

File Types that Are Not Supported

For security reasons, Smartsheet may restrict the file types that can be uploaded or downloaded; for example, you cannot upload an executable file type (.exe).

Maximum file sizes based on user and method of upload:

User or upload type	Maximum file size
Licensed user	250 MB
Free user	250 MB
Trial user	30 MB
Anyone uploading files from a Smartsheet form	30 MB

Conversations

Conversations allow Smartsheet to manage both work, as well as the critical team communication about the work, in one place.

Users can reply to @mentions directly from email, saving time by not having to switch apps. This makes conversations easier to use and reference and improves confidence that replies will be received and maintained.

Have Conversations in the Context of Your Work

With **Conversations** you can track work *and* have discussions about that work in one place. Conversations can apply to an entire sheet or to a specific row or card in a sheet. You'll work with comments in the Conversations panel.

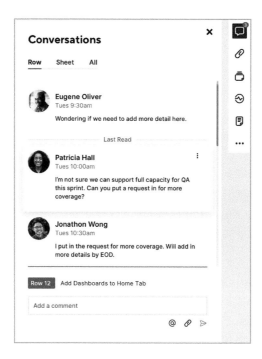

To direct a comment to a specific person, type @<email address> (for example, @sally.smart@ smartsheet.com) in the comment to tag that person.

Interact with Comments in a Sheet

For sheets, rows, and cards, you'll see all the available comments in the Conversations panel. To review conversations, click the **Conversations** icon in the right panel.

Comments are displayed in a conversation in chronological order based on the date they were created: the most recent comment will appear at the bottom of the Conversations panel.

Here are some tips for working with the displayed comments:

- Click **All** or **Sheet** at the top of the pane to view different collections of comments. Click **Sheet** to display only comments that apply to the entire sheet.
- To move to the row on which a row-level comment was made, click the row number next to the name of the person who wrote the comment.

Create a New Comment for a Row (Grid View) or a Card (Card View)

To create a comment for a specific row, click **Add a comment** in the Comment column of the row.

To create a comment for a specific card (Card View), right-click the card and click **Comments**.

NOTE: To add a line break to a comment, type Shift + Enter (Shift + Return on a Mac).

Create a New Comment that Applies to the Entire Sheet

Use sheet comments to have general conversations about the sheet that are not specific to a particular row.

1. Click the **Conversations** icon in the right panel to open the Conversations panel.
2. At the bottom of the panel, type in the **Add a comment** box.
3. Click **Post comment** (or press Enter or Return).

Reply to an Existing Comment

Click **Reply**, type your reply, and click **Post comment** (or press Enter or Return).

Edit, Email, Print, or Delete a Comment or Thread

Click the **More Options** icon ⋮ to the right of the comment to see the additional actions you can take with it.

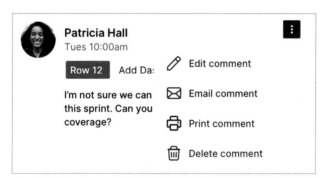

Select the desired command to edit, email, print, or delete a comment or comment thread (note that to edit or delete comments you'll need appropriate permissions).

Use file attachments to give context to comments. To provide more context to a comment, you can include an attachment with it. To do this, click the **Attachments** icon at the bottom of the **Add a comment** box.

To remove an attachment from a comment:

1. From the comment that includes the attachment, click the menu to the right of the comment and select **Edit** comment.
2. Hover the mouse over the attachment and click **Delete** to delete the file.
3. Click **Save** to save the change.

Type @<email address> to tag someone in a comment. They'll receive a notification that includes a link to the comment so they can quickly find it and respond.

Here are some things to keep in mind when you use @mention:

- The recipient tagged in the comment will have two options: reply in Smartsheet or reply directly via email.

- If the recipient has Viewer permissions, they will not have the option to add a comment. They will receive an invitation to view the sheet instead.
- If you @mention someone who isn't shared to the sheet—and you are the Owner, an Admin, or shared with Editor—Can Share permissions—you'll be prompted to share the sheet with them so that they can have access to the comment when selecting "Reply in Smartsheet."

Use Comments in a Workspace

If you're keeping sheets in a workspace, you may want to include comments relevant to all sheets in that workspace. To create a comment in a workspace, navigate to the workspace and click the Comments icon in the upper-right portion of the workspace.

Workspace comments appear in a separate window (there is no Conversations panel in a workspace). Here you'll see comments about the workspace only. To view comments for a specific sheet in the workspace, you'll need to first open the sheet. Conditional formatting allows you to create rules on your sheet, whereby the formatting of individual cells or entire rows will update when certain criteria are met.

Conditional Formatting

Conditional formatting rules apply formatting automatically to rows or cells based on the values they contain.

In the section below we'll see how to do the following:

- Create a Rule
- Modify, Clone, or Rearrange a Rule
- Delete or Disable a Rule

> NOTE: The conditional formatting feature won't change cell values. To change cell values based on criteria, you'll want to use a formula.

Create a Conditional Formatting Rule

1. Click **Conditional Formatting** 🖽 on the toolbar to display the Conditional Formatting window.
2. Click **Add New Rule** to create a new, blank conditional formatting rule.

Set the Conditions for the Rule

1. Click **<set condition>** to display the **Set Condition** window.

   The condition you set determines what will trigger the formatting. For example, if you'd like to apply a background color to all rows assigned to Jonathon, select the column named **Assigned To** in the left pane and the criteria **Jonathon** in the right pane.

NOTES:
- The available criteria will vary depending on the column type. For example, for a Checkbox column, you can apply formatting based on whether the box is checked. For a date column, you can apply formatting based on the date being "in the past" or "in the next [x] days" (among other options).
- Smartsheet looks at the numbers in a column formatted for percentage (for example, a % Complete column) as values between 0 and 1. Use decimal values (examples: .25 for 25%, .5 for 50%) to get the correct comparison.

2. To further customize your rule (for example, if you want to specify that a **Comments** column contains the value "urgent"), click **define custom criteria**.
3. To display formatting on rows that fall outside of the condition, select the checkbox to **Apply format when condition is NOT met**. In the example above, selecting the checkbox would apply formatting to rows NOT assigned to Jonathon.
4. When you're finished setting the condition, click **OK**.

Set the Format for the Rule

1. From the **Conditional Formatting** window, click **this format** to choose the formatting to apply if the condition is met. The formatting options will appear within the window.

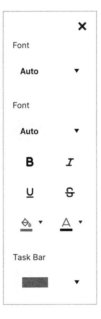

By default, the formatting is applied to the **entire row**. If needed, click **entire row** to limit the formatting such that it's only applied to certain selected columns in the row. When the rule is set up to apply formatting to *multiple* columns, you'll see an ellipsis (. . .) in the rule description.

If **Start Date is today** then apply **this format** to the **Task Name column**   abc

NOTE: If multiple rules have the same condition and formatting, they will be consolidated into a *single* rule.

2. Click **OK** to close the Conditional Formatting window.

Formatting Options

Use this option	To do this
Font and Font Size	Set the font type (Arial, Tahoma, Times, Verdana or Auto) and size
B, *I*, U̲, S̶	Apply **bold**, *italics*, underscore, and/or strike-through to the font
(Background Color)	Apply a background color to cells
(Font Color)	Apply a color to the font
Task Bar Color	For rows that meet the condition, apply a color to the card border in Card View or the Gantt and Calendar bars in Gantt View or Calendar View. A color will be applied to a card, Gantt bar, or Calendar bar only if you've applied the rule to the **entire row**.
	Note that if your aim is to alter the cell or row background color, click the **Background Color** button.

Add a Condition, Clone, or Rearrange a Rule

Add a Condition

1. Click **Conditional Formatting** in the toolbar to display the Conditional Formatting window.
2. Click the dropdown arrow ▼ to the left of the rule in the **Conditional Formatting** window to view additional options.

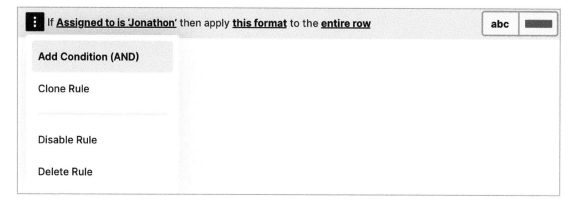

3. To add more conditions to a rule, select **Add Condition (AND)**.

   This creates an "and" operator in the rule, indicating that multiple conditions must be met for the format to be applied.

For example, you could use the above steps to create a rule with the following two conditions:

> If <u>Assigned to is 'Jonathon'</u> **and** <u>Status</u> is <u>In Progress</u> then apply <u>this format</u> to the <u>entire row</u>.

This rule formats all of Jonathon's tasks that are currently in progress. The boxes to the right of the rule display a preview of how the formatting will look. The left box shows that the text will be grey, italicized, and have a strike-through applied. The right box shows that the color blue will appear on Gantt and calendar bars of rows that meet the criteria.

Clone a Rule

Cloning is useful for replicating an existing complex rule for use in a similar new rule. To clone a rule, click the dropdown arrow ▾ to the left of the rule and select **Clone Rule**.

Rearrange Rules

To establish the order in which rules are executed, you can rearrange them. To rearrange a rule, click it and drag it up or down in the list.

Rules are applied in order from top to bottom. If rules conflict, the rule that is higher in the list takes priority. For example, if your first rule formats the row orange if <u>Start Date is today</u> and the second rule formats the row red when <u>Assigned to is 'Jonathon,'</u> any row that has both <u>Start Date is today</u> and <u>Assigned to is 'Jonathon'</u> will turn orange because the first rule takes priority. Note that rules are additive rather than exclusive, so if one rule turns the text red and another turns the cell background red, both rules will still be applied.

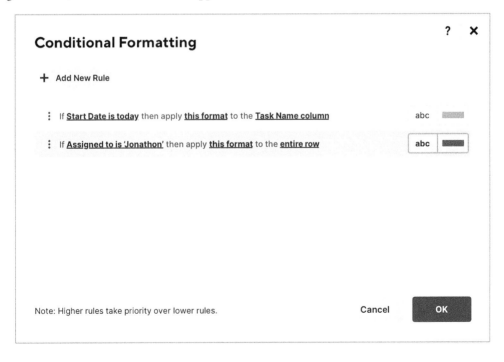

Delete or Disable a Conditional Formatting Rule

1. Click **Conditional Formatting** ▦ in the toolbar. The **Conditional Formatting** window appears listing all existing rules.

2. Choose one of the following:
    - **To temporarily turn off** a conditional formatting rule (for example, if you think you may want to use it later), disable it by clicking the dropdown arrow to the left of the rule and selecting **Disable Rule**. (Select **Enable Rule** to enable it later.)
    - **To delete the rule entirely**, click the dropdown arrow next to the rule and select **Delete Rule**.

WORKING WITH A PROJECT PLAN IN SMARTSHEET

In the previous section, we learned how to perform some of the most frequently used Smartsheet operations. Next, we'll look at one of the most common use cases in Smartsheet—making a project plan. This section will be referred to in future chapters as well since maximizing your project plan is one of the most powerful features of Smartsheet.

What Is a Project Plan?

A project plan is basically a list of tasks within a project. It's an essential part of any project manager's toolkit. A project plan is designed to deliver the intended scope of a project, facilitate communication among stakeholders, and track planning assumptions and decisions. It is a living document that can include a stakeholder list, a scope statement, a project schedule, schedule and cost baselines, baseline management plans, and a communication plan. It can (and, most likely, will) change over the course of a project. It is worth noting that a project plan is not just a project timeline, although that is an important component of the plan.

You should always create a project plan before starting a new project. Start with what you want to achieve from the project and break it down into the things you need to do in order to accomplish the goal. Then, once you have a high-level plan of all the things that need to be done, you can think about timing, budget, resources, and more.

At the very least, a project plan should answer the following questions about a project:

- Why?—Why are we starting this project? What is the problem that this project will address or solve?
- What?—What are we working on? What are the major deliverables and goals?
- Who?—Who will be involved in the project and what will be their responsibilities?
- When?—When should the project start and end? What are the milestones?

How to Build a Project Plan in Smartsheet

1. **Select a Project Template**

   1. Go to Smartsheet.com and log in to your account.
   2. From the **Home** tab, click **Create**, and choose **Browse All Solutions**.
   3. Type "*Project with Gantt Timeline*" in the **Search** box or select **Projects** from the category list.
   4. Click on the **Project with Gantt Timeline** tile, then click the blue **Use** button.
   5. Name your template, choose where to save it, and click the **Ok** button.

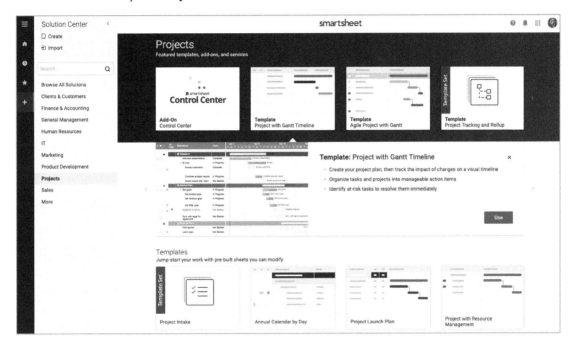

2. **List Your Project Information**

   A pre-made template will open with sample content filled in for reference and the sections, sub-tasks, and sub-sub-tasks already formatted. With Smartsheet, it's easy to add or delete columns depending on the scope of your project. Simply right-click on a column and select **Insert Column Left/Insert Column Right** to add a column or **Delete Column** to remove a column.

   1. Add your tasks under the **Task Name** column. You'll notice that the hierarchy is already formatted for you. So, be sure to enter the project phase name or group name to the Section 1, Section 2, and Section 3 fields (this is called the parent row).
   2. Enter your tasks and sub-tasks under the parent rows.
   3. On the left side of each row, you can attach files directly to a task (perfect for attaching stakeholder lists, budgets, and more) or start a discussion about a certain item.

			At Risk	Task Name	Status	Start Date	End Date	Assigned To	% Complete
			ℹ		ℹ			ℹ	ℹ
1			⚑	⊟ Section 1 - enter your own text here		03/16/25	03/25/25		40%
2	🔗 💬		⚐	Sub-task 1 - enter task and timing	Complete	03/16/25	03/21/25	(AW) Abby Wright	50%
3			⚐	Sub-task 2	Complete	03/21/25	03/24/25	(AH) Adam Hart	50%
4			⚐	Sub-task 3	In Progress	03/23/25	03/24/25	(AH) Adam Hart	0%
5			⚐	Milestone 1		03/25/25	03/25/25		
6			⚑	⊟ Section 2		03/26/25	03/31/25		
7			⚐	Sub-task 1	In Progress	03/26/25	03/27/25		
8			⚑	Sub-task 2	Not Started	03/27/25	03/31/25		
9			⚐	Sub-task 3	Not Started	03/27/25	03/31/25		
10			⚑	⊟ Section 3		03/29/25	04/08/25		
11			⚐	Sub-task 1		03/29/25	04/03/25		
12			⚐	Sub-task 2		04/03/25	04/07/25		
13			⚐	⊟ Sub-task 3 - set multiple levels		04/05/25	04/08/25		
14			⚐	Sub-task 1		04/05/25	04/07/25		
15			⚐	Sub-task 2		04/05/25	04/08/25		
16									

3. **Add Start and End Dates**

   1. Add start and end dates for each task. If you click and drag either end of the task bars in the Gantt chart, Smartsheet will automatically adjust the dates in your table.
   2. Click a cell in either date column.
   3. Click the calendar icon and choose a date. You can also manually enter a date in the cell.

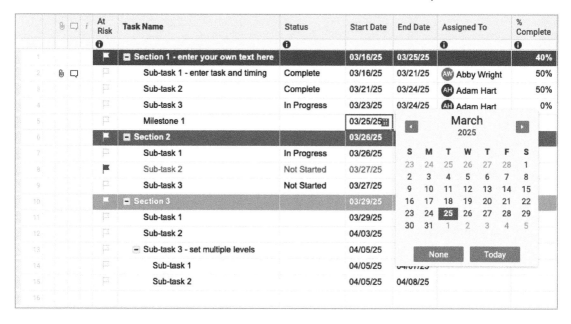

4. **Enter % Complete and Assigned To Information**
   The **% Complete** and **Assigned To** columns provide more information about your project and improve transparency by allowing team members to see who is doing what and the status of each task. On the Gantt chart, the thin bars inside the task bars represent the percentage of work complete for each task.

   1. In the **% Complete** column, enter the percentage of work complete for each task.
   2. In the **Assigned To** column, choose a name from your contact list (in the dropdown menu) or manually enter a name.

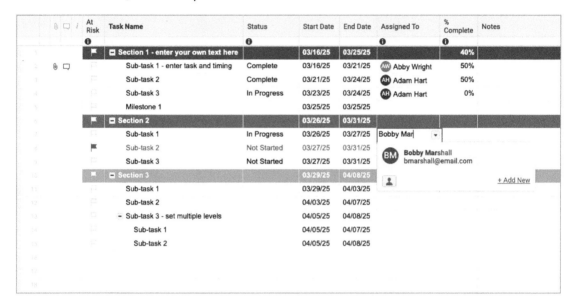

That's it! Your basic project plan is finished. You can add additional columns, but the best practice is to only add columns when absolutely necessary.

CHAPTER SUMMARY

This chapter reviews some of the most popular Smartsheet features and actions. While this is a useful reference for most users, this is not meant to be a comprehensive guide to Smartsheet. The user is encouraged to go to the Smartsheet website and access the latest features and help articles.

SECTION II

Implementing the
Basic Portfolio

SECTION II INTRODUCTION: THE BASIC PORTFOLIO

WHAT IS A BASIC PORTFOLIO?

Every organization needs to start somewhere in their portfolio journey. There are some aspects of portfolio discipline that are easy to attain and some that need an advanced level of capability. Up to this point in the book, we have discussed the need for a portfolio, and this section is aimed at organizations that understand this and have just started their portfolio journey.

In other words, this is where organizations should start if they are looking to build a basic portfolio and get to *Level 1*. Although the term *basic* creates an impression of *limited*, we need to remember that most organizations are currently way below *basic*, so a *basic portfolio* would be a major upgrade compared to where they are now. A basic portfolio will add many useful capabilities to organizations that have nothing in place currently.

What is a basic portfolio? It is a portfolio that primarily deals with four foundational capabilities that are key to gaining control of organizational projects:

1. Controlling the intake of projects into the portfolio
2. Reporting on the state of the projects in the portfolio
3. Understanding and managing how resources are deployed in the portfolio
4. Managing the activity of annual planning

In the next seven chapters, we examine what goes into the making of a basic portfolio. The chapters typically start with a discussion of each of the capabilities listed above and then go on to explain how to implement these capabilities using Smartsheet. After implementing a basic portfolio, the organization is capable of understanding and controlling what projects are being worked on and how to deliver optimal value to stakeholders.

4

PORTFOLIO INTAKE AND ASSESSMENT

INTRODUCTION

Portfolio intake is the process of regulating the work that enters the portfolio. It is vital to get this working correctly because the portfolio should be considering proposals aligned with the strategic direction of the portfolio (i.e., "meaningful stuff") and not wasting precious resources on misaligned proposals (i.e., "stuff no one really wants but we're doing anyway"). However, speed is also important here—we want a way to quickly decide if we want to work on a project or put it on the back burner. In this chapter, we will learn about the following aspects of portfolio intake management:

1. Describe portfolio intake
2. Explain the need to gather project details during portfolio intake
3. State the characteristics of a high-performing project intake process
4. Specify the two types of portfolios and detail how the portfolio intake will work for each
5. Explain some challenges and best practices that work in almost every situation

The goal is to have robust intake management while keeping the portfolio nimble and responsive.

> KEY CONCEPT: Portfolio intake is possibly the single most important starting point in setting up a portfolio that delivers value.

WHAT IS PORTFOLIO INTAKE?

If there's one constant in the workplace it's that there will always be more requests than there are resources to fulfill them. There's always a ton of projects that need to be done, but with our limited resources (people *and/or* money), we can't do them all. Therefore, we need to focus on which projects we will do and which we'll politely refuse. This process of managing the incoming requests and selecting what we work on is called portfolio intake (i.e., demand management). Portfolio intake controls what gets into the portfolio.

> KEY CONCEPT: Portfolio intake is the process of controlling which projects get into the portfolio.

Here are some broad factors to think about when creating and managing the intake process:

- **Strategic fit:** "Does this even belong in this portfolio?" Some project requests simply don't belong. It's best to screen them out at the intake stage.
- **Resources needed:** "What will it take to do this project?" Before we start on a project, we need to know what resources it will take. At a minimum, it needs to be tagged as small, medium, or large.
- **Customer:** "Who is the customer?" Capture which department or organization we're doing this for.
- **Estimated start date:** "When do we expect this project to start?" Know when we expect to work on this project.
- **Estimated finish date:** "When do we expect this project to finish?" Know when we expect to deliver value.
- **Goal alignment:** "Which goals will be moved forward by doing this project?" It is vital to know what capabilities this project will add to our strategic roadmap.
- **Benefits:** "What is the ROI?" Are the benefits soft (e.g., productivity savings) or hard (e.g., revenue growth, actual cost reduction, etc.)? Know exactly what value will be added to the enterprise by doing this project.

These are the minimum suggested set of fields to have. Based on your organization's needs, you can have more if required.

> KEY CONCEPT: The above listed fields are the minimum needed for an effective portfolio intake.

WHY GATHER ALL THESE DETAILS DURING PROJECT INTAKE?

You may encounter push back from your stakeholders for asking these questions before starting a project. That's fairly common, but there are some good reasons why these attributes are gathered during project intake:

1. We only want to take up viable project proposals. A viable project proposal should have thought through all the above attributes and be ready to provide the answers.
2. If you don't gather these data elements now, it's very hard to get them later. Once a project starts, the stakeholders are quite reluctant to provide all the missing info.
3. By asking project proposals to provide this information, the portfolio manager can decide what the priority of this new request should be. That helps to determine when and how to commit resources to this new request.

> KEY CONCEPT: Portfolio intake is the best time to collect basic details about each project.

CHARACTERISTICS OF A HIGH-PERFORMING PROJECT INTAKE PROCESS

No matter how you implement it, an ideal portfolio intake has the following characteristics:

- **Efficient and responsive:** Approval or non-approval should be expedited. A well-defined service level agreement (SLA) should be in place to make intake decisions. Don't leave the requesters in limbo.
- **Easy to use:** The stakeholders should find it easy to submit a complete proposal. There should be resources and training that enable a stakeholder to know what to do when submitting a proposal. At the same time, only complete proposals should be submitted to the intake.
- **Effective governance:** All intake proposals should be reviewed by appropriate governance and quick decisions whether to approve or reject should be made. If there is no such governance body, the portfolio manager should be able to approve/deny projects.
- **Fiscally responsible:** Prior to approving a project, a governance body (or portfolio manager) should have a clear idea of what this does to the available portfolio funds or resources. In other words, the portfolio manager should know the impact of this new project on existing projects.

> KEY CONCEPT: A good portfolio intake process strikes a balance across several different factors.

PORTFOLIO TYPE AND ITS IMPACT ON PORTFOLIO INTAKE

Although we outlined the characteristics of an ideal portfolio intake process earlier, in reality, the intake process will be heavily influenced by the kind of portfolio. Two broad portfolio types are defined below:

1. The tactical/functional/operational portfolio
2. The transformational or strategic portfolio

The Tactical Portfolio

A tactical portfolio is one that mostly does operational projects, and its characteristics include:

- Projects are shorter in duration
- Projects are typically not strategic
- The portfolio handles many projects

Examples of projects that are found in a tactical portfolio include:

1. Modifying the columns in a sales dashboard
2. Changing permissions on a software system
3. Making configuration changes to an ERP module
4. Updates to the company's website, etc.

All the above efforts are important but unlikely by themselves to bring about dramatic change in the organization's capabilities or result in strategic transformation. Strategic considerations are typically not mentioned.

KEY CONCEPT: A tactical portfolio is one that mostly includes operational projects.

Operation of a Tactical Portfolio's Intake

There are two modes of operation for a tactical portfolio.

Mode 1:

In a portfolio where the budget is tracked, the portfolio manager conducts the following actions in managing the intake of a tactical portfolio:

- All proposals are submitted using a common tool and/or standard format. See Chapter 5 for more details on actual implementation.
- The portfolio manager holds a periodic meeting (weekly or biweekly is recommended) to review proposals.
- A representative group of leaders or their representatives are invited to the meeting.
- Redundant and/or duplicate proposals are identified and possibly eliminated (e.g., two different stakeholders submitting duplicate requests that are named similarly).
- Cross-team impacts are identified. Questions that need to be answered include: Who would be impacted by this project? Which team(s) need to work on this project?
- All the teams impacted are expected to state their level of effort within an SLA (e.g., two weeks).
- The combined cost of these efforts is rolled into the final dollar estimate for the proposal and funding approval is secured from the governance body (or whoever executive management nominates; sometimes the finance department approves).
- A project manager is identified and the project is given to that person to run.

KEY CONCEPT: Mode 1 of a tactical portfolio intake involves budget management and is more detailed. See Chapter 11 for a discussion on budget management.

Mode 2:

In a portfolio where the budget is not tracked, the tactical portfolio intake process is rather simple:

- All proposals are submitted using a common tool and/or standard format.
- The portfolio manager does a scan of the proposal for correctness and missing info and duplicate proposals are resolved. Projects with missing info are sent back to submitters.
- Cross-team impacts are identified and notified.
- A project manager is identified, and the project is given to that person to run.

KEY CONCEPT: Mode 2 of a tactical portfolio intake is used where no budget management is involved and is simpler than Mode 1.

Things to Keep in Mind While Designing an Intake Process for a Tactical Portfolio

The following considerations are most important for a tactical portfolio:

- **High volume:** In a tactical portfolio, the volume is likely to be very high since each effort is quite small.
- **Need for speedy processing:** For the tactical portfolio to be effective, it needs to operate in a way that does not slow things down.
- **Alignment is not a major concern:** Unlike a strategic portfolio, there's no strategic fit to worry about. The screening process is more of answering yes/no to the following questions:
  - ◻ Does this effort belong in our portfolio?
  - ◻ If it belongs, do we have the resources to do it?

The Transformational or Strategic Portfolio

A transformational or strategic portfolio is one that seeks to transform the capabilities of the organization and is consistent with the strategic vision. Here are the characteristics of a transformational portfolio:

- It usually has longer duration projects or sets of projects in a program.
- The projects are directly aligned to the organization's strategy (projects must succeed for the strategy to succeed).
- The projects are fewer in number but cost more and may take longer to execute.

See Chapter 15 for an extensive discussion about the strategic considerations of a transformational portfolio.

> KEY CONCEPT: A transformational portfolio is one that mostly does large, strategic projects.

The Strategic Portfolio Intake Process

Given the framework just described, here's how the strategic portfolio intake process would work in a two-tiered arrangement.

Tier 1: Understanding the Proposal Completely

- When a proposal is received, the portfolio manager matches it with one or more strategic priorities. The proposal owner could also specify to which strategic priorities their proposal aligns.
- The link to the strategic priority must be validated by the priority advocate for that strategic priority. This validation by the priority advocate is necessary because sponsors are often not clear about what priority their project aligns to. This validation also guards against stakeholders trying to misalign their project with important strategic priorities in the hopes of securing approval and funding.
- There needs to be a clear specification of what this project is expected to contribute in terms of the strategic roadmap. This clear specification should preferably be accompanied by the strategic roadmap.

- Estimation/Calculation is done to show whether the portfolio can afford to do this project and where the financial reserves would stand if this project is approved. If there are a batch of projects being considered in this intake round, the projection should show what the combined cumulative financial impact would be (of approving all the projects). This can spur productive discussion about project prioritization, at least for the time being.

Tier 2: Review by Governance

Portfolio governance is a team of senior managers that provides oversight and decision making for a portfolio. They are the body that approves (or rejects) key decisions regarding projects in the portfolio. Portfolio governance participates in intake as it's important to screen new proposals seeking to be a part of the portfolio. Governance performs the following actions on intake:

- Reviews fully developed proposals, including estimates of effort and expense.
- Determines financial impact of approving one or more proposals.
- Makes final go/no-go decision on each proposal.
- Returns some proposals with requests for more information that are then reconsidered at subsequent sittings.

> KEY CONCEPT: A transformational portfolio has two-tier intake: Tier 1 qualifies the project and Tier 2 performs governance review/approval.

Intake Considerations of a Strategic Portfolio

The following considerations are most important for a strategic portfolio:

- **Modest volume:** Since these efforts are fairly large and transformational, the volume is likely to be modest compared to a tactical portfolio.
- **The need for a high degree of confidence in strategic alignment:** In a strategic portfolio, the emphasis is on only doing projects that are in alignment with the strategic mission of the portfolio. Therefore, before a proposal is cleared for funding and included in the portfolio, there needs to be a high degree of confidence in the alignment of the proposal to the strategic roadmap.
- **An expectation to spend effort in validating alignment:** It takes a good amount of time and effort to validate and ensure strategic alignment. A strategic portfolio's intake process is not necessarily fast moving.

CHALLENGES AND SUCCESS FACTORS FOR PORTFOLIO INTAKE

1. **Identify portfolio type and design intake accordingly**
   - The intake design process must match the type of portfolio.
   - A tactical portfolio will need a speedy intake or it will choke on the volume of proposals.
   - A strategic portfolio will need a carefully filtered intake or it will let through non-strategic proposals which undermine the portfolio's functioning.
   - Identifying the type of portfolio is the critical first step.

2. **Don't collect too many or too few pieces of information during intake**
   - Collecting too much information (having too many fields on the intake form) will result in stakeholders/sponsors trying to bypass the intake process.

- Stakeholders are also likely to complain about the intake process being slow/nonresponsive.
- On the other hand, having too few pieces of information means the portfolio manager must go after the stakeholders to collect additional information later.
- Generally, stakeholders are reluctant to provide this information and could also complain that the process is inefficient.
- The best practice is to collect only what is needed and design for speed/user-friendly performance.

3. **Establish an SLA for processing proposals and strive to meet it**
   - A portfolio can establish significant credibility by defining an SLA for processing a proposal and consistently meeting that SLA.
   - For example, a portfolio office can commit to providing a decision on a proposal within one week of receiving it.
   - For a strategic portfolio, this may take longer and therefore needs a longer SLA. It needs to be noted here that the SLA should be declared after a careful study of all the steps from receipt of the proposal to the disposition decision.
   - Once declared, every effort should be made to meet the SLA and demonstrate to the organization that the SLA is being met.

4. **Show the velocity of intake—visibility and transparency are key**
   - The portfolio manager needs to publish a regular report showing how many proposals came through the intake process for that period and how many were approved (or denied) within that time frame.
   - While this can be a little uncomfortable in the beginning (most intake processes take a little bit of time to find their stride and start processing proposals; during that time, the SLA may not be met in all instances), it offers a huge incentive to identify and remediate the instances when the SLA was not met.
   - It also serves a dual purpose of showing to the organization that portfolio intake is performing well and underscoring the point that all proposals need to start using the process.

5. **Expect to do plenty of hand-holding**
   - Stakeholders will need help filling out the project proposal template until the whole process gains traction.
   - The portfolio manager should be willing to help answer questions regarding the template and the entire intake process.
   - If the portfolio manager does not provide the needed support, stakeholders are likely to resist the process because they don't understand it.

6. **Maintain a web page to keep track of all proposals**
   - One widely noticed pattern in most portfolio intake systems is that there soon tends to be a mass of intake proposals which can become unmanageable.
   - This mass of proposals, most of them at different stages of processing, creates a logjam that is typically frustrating for stakeholders to navigate through.
   - To avoid this situation, the portfolio manager needs to implement a simple system of putting all the available information on a web page (or some similar place on the intranet) that people can look up on their own and understand where their proposal is in terms of processing.
   - Additionally, a weekly email with useful statistics, including the number of new project proposals, should be sent to all stakeholders.

7. **Start simple and over-communicate**
   - A fair amount of confusion can be expected when intake is first adopted.
   - It is recommended that the whole process be as simple as possible and that the portfolio office compensate for the newness of the process by over-communicating.
   - As the organization becomes familiar with how intake works, additional complexity can be slowly introduced.

8. **Take political cover**
   - In a world without politics, people would be generous with their patience and wait for all the glitches to be resolved.
   - In the real world, however, dissatisfied stakeholders may use a slow intake process as an opportunity to criticize the portfolio manager (or the portfolio function).
   - It is therefore recommended for the portfolio office to always *take cover* by communicating clearly and demonstrate in writing that all possible help was offered to stakeholders regarding the intake process.
   - Other defensive tactics include publishing an in-process list of proposals at every step and showing that stakeholders were regularly informed about the status of their proposals.

9. **Projects not approved: denied or sent to backlog?**
   - In some organizations it may be unacceptable to say that some projects are "denied approval."
   - In such cases it may be better to call the non-approved projects as "sent to backlog"—the understanding is that there is no current plan to start working on backlog projects.

> KEY CONCEPT: Several factors are involved in making sure portfolio intake works. The previous list will ensure that the portfolio intake process will perform optimally.

LEVELS OF PORTFOLIO CAPABILITY MATURITY

The following portfolio capability levels illustrate what you can expect at each level. This is useful to benchmark where you are now and how to get to the next level.

Level 1

- No defined intake process—there isn't a standard way to determine how projects are identified and started.
- No distinction between tactical and strategic proposals—proposals are handled as they are submitted, often slowing down the pace of processing.
- Due to a lack of an organized intake, the organization may be frustrated with the lack of speed in processing and the lack of predictable, standard steps.
- Little to no governance oversight over starting projects—as a result there isn't a regular pathway to initiate projects.
- There are no standard intake criteria to qualify a proposal—every project proposal is considered case-by-case for approval and funding.
- Since there is not a defined body that provides approval to start projects, some projects get started soon while others may stagnate.

- There isn't a clear idea of the impact to portfolio funds from approving a project. Consequently, too many or too few projects may be approved, causing a potential overspend/ underutilization situation at year end.
- There is little to no validation performed on projects that are purported to be strategic. There may not be a standard strategic plan to compare each project against to arrive at a decision.

Level 2

- A formal intake process exists and there is awareness that all projects must go through intake. However, the intake process may not be optimized.
- Although a conceptual distinction exists between tactical and strategic proposals, there may not be separate processing pathways for strategic and tactical projects.
- A lack of separate processing pathways for strategic and tactical projects results in some confusion about what steps apply to which type of proposal, causing proposals to take longer to process than expected.
- Although some governance exists before initiating new projects, there may not be enough governance in place before committing to strategic proposals.
- Although there are standard intake criteria to qualify a proposal, the criteria may not be comprehensive.
- The lack of comprehensive criteria may introduce some variability in assessing project proposals, leading to some projects getting approved quickly while others may take longer.
- As part of intake assessment, there is some analysis done about the impact to portfolio funds resulting from approving a project. Consequently, the portfolio avoids approving too many or too few projects.
- There is some validation performed on projects that are purported to be strategic. However, there may not be an officially approved strategic plan to compare each project against to arrive at a decision.

Level 3

- A formal, optimized intake process exists and there is awareness that all projects must go through intake.
- Separate pathways exist for tactical and strategic proposals—both are optimized for their respective type in terms of throughput and oversight.
- Having well-defined separate processing pathways for strategic and tactical projects allows proposals to be accelerated through intake without losing quality.
- Adequate governance exists for new projects, especially for strategic big bets.
- There are comprehensive intake criteria to qualify a proposal, ensuring that all proposals are assessed in a standard manner.
- As part of intake assessment, sufficient analysis is performed about the impact to portfolio funds resulting from approving a project. Consequently, the portfolio avoids approving too many or too few projects and optimizes the throughput of the portfolio.
- Comprehensive validation is performed on projects that are purported to be strategic. Strategic management is advanced and contains all the roles and artifacts, such as an officially approved strategic plan and priority advocates, which enable the validation of each proposal to ensure strategic fit.

CHAPTER SUMMARY

In this chapter we began by stating the importance of the portfolio intake process in ensuring that the portfolio is focused on meaningful projects. Portfolio intake is the process of regulating the work that enters the portfolio. The chapter then proceeded to explain the balance between regulation and the speed of processing proposals. We also explained the need to gather project details during portfolio intake and listed all the characteristics of a high-performing project intake process. We then specified the two types of portfolios—tactical and strategic—and how the portfolio intake will work for each. We finished this chapter with an explanation of some challenges and best practices that work in almost every portfolio intake situation and then described the levels of maturity in this portfolio capability.

5

IMPLEMENTING PORTFOLIO INTAKE USING SMARTSHEET

INTRODUCTION

In the previous chapter we saw how important it is to get portfolio intake working properly. In this chapter we describe how to actually implement portfolio intake using Smartsheet. We'll cover the following aspects:

1. The advantages and disadvantages of using Microsoft Excel as the portfolio intake tool
2. How Smartsheet is the ideal tool to implement portfolio intake
3. Outline a simple example of portfolio intake using Smartsheet
4. List some common challenges and outline best practices that work in almost every situation

The goal of this chapter is to enable you to start designing your own intake process using Smartsheet.

> KEY CONCEPT: Getting portfolio intake up and running is the key to starting a portfolio. Smartsheet makes this rapid and easy using its native features.

USING MICROSOFT EXCEL FOR PORTFOLIO INTAKE

Microsoft Excel is a common choice for most organizations starting out on the portfolio management journey. The advantages of using Excel are as follows:

- **Widely available:** Microsoft Excel is installed on most work machines and available pretty much everywhere.
- **Popular/Familiar:** Most people are familiar with Microsoft Excel and know how to operate it, making it easy to get started.
- **Simple to start:** One of the great advantages of Microsoft Excel is its simplicity. It only needs the names of the fields to start a portfolio intake sheet.
- **High user adoption:** Since nearly everyone has used it in the past, it's very easy to ask people to now use it for portfolio intake.
- **Flexible:** Microsoft Excel is extremely versatile because of its simplicity. It can accommodate nearly any need.

KEY CONCEPT: Microsoft Excel is a common starting choice for most organizations seeking to build their portfolio intake; however, there are hidden disadvantages.

As just listed, Microsoft Excel has many advantages, so why not just go with Excel for portfolio intake and possibly for the rest of portfolio management? As it turns out, there are some significant disadvantages that prevent Excel from being the go-to tool for portfolio management. Here are the prominent pitfalls of using Excel for portfolio intake:

- **Easy to start, hard to scale:** Excel is easy to use with only a handful of projects but becomes harder as the portfolio grows. Other complicating factors include multiple submitters and larger teams. As Excel fails, the credibility of the function also takes a hit.
- **Too flexible:** One of Excel's biggest advantages is also a big weakness. Anyone using an Excel sheet can change almost anything within the sheet. Safeguards exist but then begin to complicate the user experience.
- **Little support for validation:** Excel does have validation support (only allows certain choices in certain cells), but these can be easily defeated (for example, by copying and pasting).
- **Little routing support:** Once a sheet is filled, it is not easy to alert other stakeholders about it other than by manual methods (like sending an email that says, "I've submitted the form," or walking over to the person's desk!).
- **Limited access restrictions:** Anyone who can get to the Excel sheet can fill it out. There is no way to know who filled out which part of the form.
- **No change control:** One person could overwrite other peoples' responses on a form. There are no easy ways to find out which cell was changed and what was there previously.
- **Possible corruption:** It's been observed that when many people simultaneously use a file saved on say, SharePoint, unpredictable (and undesirable) consequences such as file corruption and loss of data could occur.

Many more drawbacks could be listed here. The bottom line is that Microsoft Excel is simply not a viable or scalable tool to implement portfolio intake or any other aspect of project portfolio management (PPM). We need another tool that has all of Microsoft Excel's strengths and none of its weaknesses.

KEY CONCEPT: There are significant disadvantages to using Microsoft Excel to build a portfolio intake process which make it necessary to consider other options.

IMPLEMENTING PORTFOLIO INTAKE WITH SMARTSHEET

We'll now implement portfolio intake using a sample set of project intake fields. These are just the absolute minimum set of fields to have. Organizations may have additional fields to track other attributes of interest. However, remember not to have too many fields—refer to the *Common Challenges and Best Practices* section later in this chapter to understand why.

Here are the steps to implement a Portfolio intake using Smartsheet:

Step 1: Create a new sheet.

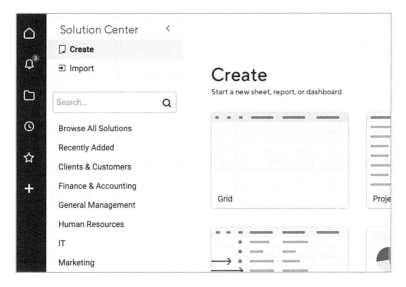

Step 2: Choose the "Grid" option.

Step 3: Name your sheet "Portfolio Intake Form."

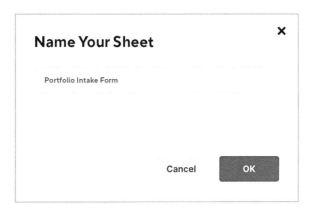

Step 4: Choose the fields of your intake form:

a) You should see the following view with one **Primary Column** and a few other fields titled **Column2, Column3**, etc.

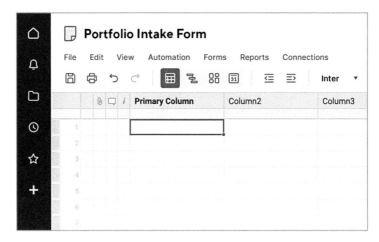

b) Let's start with the **Primary Column**—double-click on the **Column Header** (click on the words that say "Primary Column").

c) As shown below, you should get a screen that invites you to edit the **Primary Column**. Let's change the **Name** field to **Project Name**. Click **OK**.

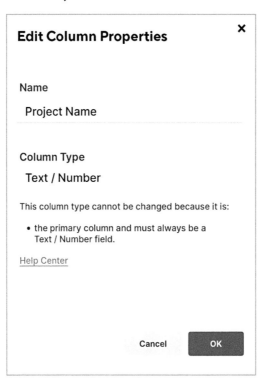

d) Like the previous step, rename the fields that say **Column2** through **Column6** to the following standard fields that are used in most portfolio intake forms:

    i. Column2—rename to **Project Description**

        ◻ Double-click on **Column2** and a dialog box will open

        ◻ Change **Name** field to **Project Description**

        ◻ Click **OK**.

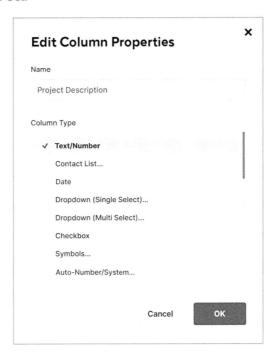

e) Do the same for these additional columns. Remember to choose the right kind of column type for each.

    i. Column3—rename to **Project Size**

        ◻ Double-click on **Column3** and a dialog box will open

        ◻ Change **Name** field to **Project Size**

        ◻ Choose Column Type **Dropdown (Single Select)** and populate the desired choices

            ○ Example for choices—"Small, Medium, Large"

        ◻ Remember to select **Restrict to list values only** for data integrity

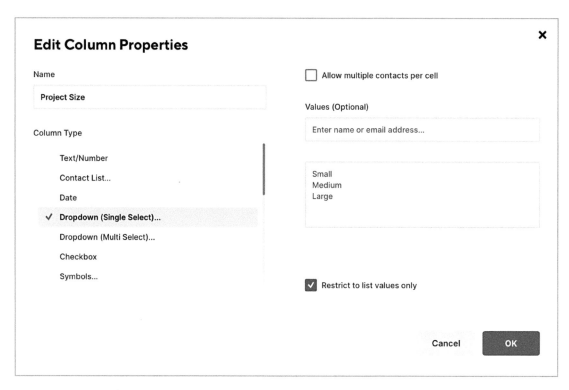

ii. Column4—rename to **Project Type**

 ▫ Choose Column type **Dropdown (Single Select)** and populate the desired choices

 ▫ Example for choices: "Marketing, Sales, R&D"

iii. Column5—rename to **Project Start Date**

 ▫ Choose Column type **Date**

iv. Column6—rename to **Project End Date**

 ▫ Choose Column type **Date**

Step 5: Now we create an intake form to populate the sheet we just made:

a) Within the Project Intake Sheet screen, go to **Forms** → **Create Form**. Click on **Create Form**.

b) You should see the Project Intake Sheet form shown here:

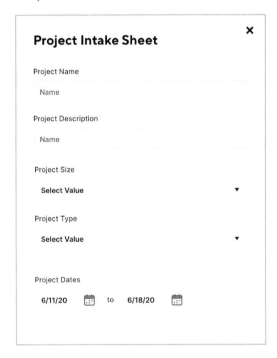

Step 6: Customize the portfolio intake form with specific details:

a) Proceed to edit the **Form Title** and **Description** according to your needs.

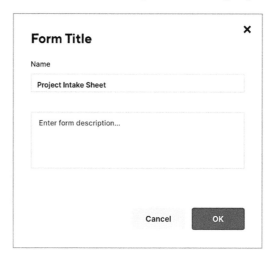

Here are some helpful hints for the **Form Title** and **Description** fields:

- Instead of a generic sounding title such as "Project Intake Sheet," it is a good idea to have a more descriptive title, such as *"Project Proposal Intake Sheet for the Marketing Support Portfolio."*
- In the description, consider adding more information such as:

    ▫ The purpose of this intake sheet

    ▫ What kind of projects are meant to be included in this portfolio

    ▫ What's the process after submitting the proposal through this intake form

    ▫ How long can the submitter expect to wait until they hear back

b) Edit the fields in the Intake Form:

    i. Refer to the figure below:

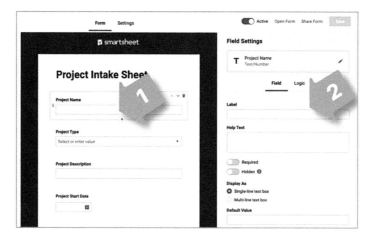

ii. Click on the **Project Name** column—the **Field Settings** pane on the right will appear.

iii. Edit the **Label** field if you want the display name of the field to be different from the Column Name. For example, the Column name could be "Project Name" while the Display name could be "Marketing Support Project Proposal Name."

iv. Add **Help Text** to help the user fill out this field correctly.

v. Check the **Required** flag if the user must fill out this field to submit the form.

c) Just like the above example, all the fields can be edited by clicking on them and adjusting the configuration in the pane on the right that pops up as soon as the field is clicked.

Step 7: Add additional fields to the portfolio intake form:

Organizations may choose to have additional fields beyond the bare minimum described above. Here's how to add these fields:

a) By clicking on **New Field** (look for the blue hyperlink at the bottom of the list of fields on the left), additional fields can be added to the intake form.

b) A **Create Column** pop-up appears in which the field name and other configurations such as column type must be provided.

c) A field (**Project Funding Source**, for example) is created (see #1 in the following screenshot) and must be dragged onto the desired position on the form (see #2):

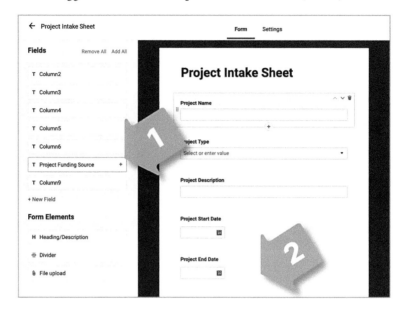

Step 8: Customize form elements

a) Heading/Descriptions let you add headings to sections of the form (useful if the form is long).

    i. Click on **Heading/Description** to make the Heading field appear (see #1 in the screenshot below).

    ii. Once the **Heading** field appears (see #2), click on the field settings to customize (see #3).

b) The **Divider** element lets you add a line between fields. It's a styling element and lets the user know that certain fields are grouped together.

c) The **File upload** element is a very useful feature. Imagine a project proposal is being reviewed and the reviewer wants just a bit of additional information beyond what is entered in the fields. What if there was an accompanying PDF, Word document, or email message from the CEO directing that this project be started ASAP? File upload makes that possible. One or more documents can be attached to the project proposal using this feature.

    i. Click on **File upload** (see #1 in the screenshot below) to make the **File upload** field appear on the form (see #2).

    ii. Observe the **Field Settings** on the right (see #3) to customize, as necessary.

    iii. Once the form is saved, this field can be used to browse and attach files which then accompany the project proposal form.

d) The complete **Portfolio Intake** form looks like this:

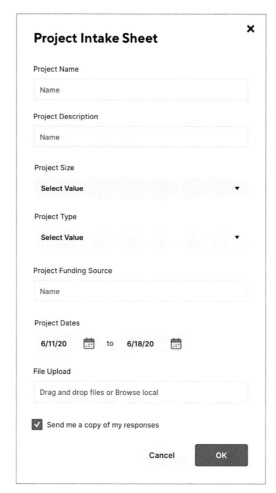

KEY CONCEPT: Smartsheet offers an intuitive and flexible interface to build a feature-laden project intake form that meets the needs of most organizations.

COMMON CHALLENGES AND BEST PRACTICES FOR THE PORTFOLIO INTAKE FORM

1. **Identify intake form fields with user input**
   - Consult users while designing the form fields for the intake form
   - This applies not only to the fields but also the choices in the dropdown of each field
   - By doing this, several fields that were not previously known may become apparent

2. **Don't collect too many or too few pieces of information on the intake form**
   - Collecting too much information (having too many fields on the intake form) will result in people trying to bypass the intake process
   - Stakeholders are also likely to complain about the intake process being slow/nonresponsive
   - On the other hand, having too few pieces of information means the portfolio manager must "fill in the blanks" later
   - The best practice is to collect only what is needed and design for speed/user-friendly performance

3. **Allow users to only submit complete forms**
   - On the Smartsheet form, there are options to make each field optional or mandatory
   - If allowed, users would rather leave one or more fields blank and hit submit
   - It then becomes the responsibility of the portfolio manager to acquire this information later (which is difficult) or decide on approving the project without this information (more difficult)
   - So, wherever possible, all or most of the fields need to be made mandatory (and filled in) before the form can be submitted

4. **Training users on how to complete the intake form is recommended**
   - It is always a good idea to train users prior to launching the Smartsheet intake form
   - This is a good opportunity to inform users about the process after filling/submitting the form
   - Also, it's a good time to share the URL of the form so users can bookmark it

5. **Ask users to select the option that says, "Send me a copy of my responses"**
   - At the bottom of the portfolio intake form is an option to send the submitter a copy of their responses
   - During training, users must be trained to click that box each time they submit a proposal
   - This ensures that they receive a copy of their submission, which they can then forward to other interested stakeholders
   - In practice, this has been observed to be very effective in keeping people in the loop about proposal submission.

6. **Use Smartsheet automation features as a follow-up to your portfolio intake submission**
   - There are two situations when it's useful to inform everyone about a new project proposal
   - One, it may be useful for a group of stakeholders to become aware that a project proposal has been submitted
   - Second, once a project proposal has been approved and is now a project in execution, it's again useful to automatically inform a group of stakeholders about progress
   - Both the scenarios above can be done easily with Smartsheet's standard features

KEY CONCEPT: Portfolio intake is the cornerstone of portfolio management and needs to be implemented carefully to ensure success. The best practices listed previously cover the range of situations that needs to be assessed and accounted for.

CHAPTER SUMMARY

In the previous chapter we saw how important it is to get portfolio intake working properly. In this chapter we detailed how to implement portfolio intake using Smartsheet. First, we covered the advantages and disadvantages of using Microsoft Excel as the portfolio intake tool (which is used widely as the go-to tool for portfolio management when starting out). We then explained how Smartsheet is the ideal tool to implement portfolio intake as it handles all the disadvantages of Excel. Then we outlined a simple example of portfolio intake using Smartsheet, covering form construction and the various fields in depth. We also listed some common challenges and outlined best practices that work in almost every portfolio intake situation.

6

PORTFOLIO REPORTING AND PERFORMANCE MONITORING

INTRODUCTION

What's the most important function of a portfolio? It's to report on how the projects in the portfolio are performing. The reason to monitor the performance of projects is to obtain an early warning if projects are failing so we can take corrective action. However, reporting on projects is more challenging than it seems at first. In this chapter we cover the following aspects of performance monitoring:

1. A discussion of why projects tend to go off-track and the need for reporting/performance monitoring
2. The difficulties involved in reporting on a portfolio of projects
3. An approach that works in reporting on a group of projects
4. A critical look at the popular red/yellow/green (R/Y/G) status system

KEY CONCEPT: A portfolio's most basic role is to report on the performance of the projects managed within it.

WHAT COULD GO WRONG ON A PROJECT?

The short answer: anything and everything. It is an accepted fact that most projects will run into trouble at some point. The fundamental reason for that lies in the nature of project management: every project is an experimental endeavor to create a new product, service, or capability with finite resources and budget within a finite time while meeting concrete performance criteria. With all these constraints and unknowns in effect, it's almost expected that some projects will get into trouble.

When several projects go off-course, the portfolio will start underperforming, too. That's why the prudent portfolio manager will spot and correct underperforming projects before they lead to an underperforming portfolio. Some projects simply can't be fixed—in that case, the function of the portfolio manager is to terminate them. For accomplishing all of the above, project reporting and performance monitoring is needed.

> KEY CONCEPT: Projects are likely to run into trouble. To detect and correct this, portfolio reporting is vital.

WHAT IS PROJECT REPORTING?

Project reporting is the activity of keeping track of the projects in a portfolio and displaying the information to all the stakeholders through reports. Project reporting typically provides the following:

- A list of projects in the portfolio
- The overall status of projects in the portfolio
- The milestone and risk status of each project in the portfolio
- A rollup of individual projects that gives senior management an executive view

WHY IS PROJECT REPORTING DIFFICULT?

Though it seems straightforward, project reporting is hard to do in most organizations. Here are the main reasons why:

- **Non-uniformity:** Left to themselves, everyone tracks their individual projects differently. One project manager may use an elaborate project plan. Another may not have a project plan at all. Others may be anywhere in between.
- **Different platforms:** Some project managers may use Microsoft Excel. Others may use Microsoft Project. Still others may use lesser-known tools. Bringing these different formats together is not easy.
- **Projects under the radar:** Some projects may have started without anyone on the larger team knowing about it. Without knowing about the existence of a project, it's impossible to include it for reporting.
- **Different attributes:** Imagine it was mandatory that everyone had to use Excel to track their projects and that every project had to have a project plan. Would reporting then be easy? Chances are that reporting would still be hard because the columns wouldn't match, the rollup would not work, and the whole point of reporting would be undermined.

> KEY CONCEPT: Several factors prevent portfolio reporting from happening easily. A careful effort is needed.

PROJECT REPORTING: AN APPROACH THAT WORKS

Without thinking of a specific tool or platform, the following design pointers will always work in building a reliable project reporting system:

1. **Start with intake:** The key to successful project reporting starts with project intake (see Chapters 4 and 5 for an extensive discussion on project intake). Here are the ways in which a well-designed intake process facilitates project reporting.

   a. **Eliminates "under-the-radar" projects:** By coming through a common (and standard) intake channel, projects are known and will be included in the reporting. This eliminates the chance of projects being excluded.

   b. **Enforces a standard metadata field set:** Another advantage of coming through a standard intake form is that all projects will have a standard set of metadata fields. For example, if the intake form makes all fields mandatory, a project cannot be submitted without a *start* and *end date*. Without this constraint, it is often possible to have projects that have missing attributes. With this arrangement, a project cannot start without all the above attributes.

2. **Decide on a common template:** All projects need to work off a common template. This includes having a common set of metadata fields as well as a similar project plan. This solves many issues in one clean sweep as explained below:

   a. **Projects can now be stacked:** Projects that follow a common template can be pooled or aggregated easily. What does that mean? For example, all projects that have a "start date" of January can be listed together under a category of "Projects starting in January."

   b. **Projects can be filtered and sorted:** Stakeholders usually want to see only the projects that are of interest to them. The benefit of a common set of metadata is that projects can now be combined and separated in useful ways. Consider these examples:
      • Projects can now be sorted according to budget, from the highest to the lowest.
      • All the projects managed by one project manager can now be shown in a separate list.
      • All the projects being done for a particular client (or department) can now be grouped together.

3. **Roll up to a common dashboard:** Showing all the projects in one easy-to-understand interface is important. First, it lets people see everything in one place—that's not a small feat to achieve. Many organizations struggle to do even that. But there are more advantages:

   a. **Seeing everything in one place lets people react:** People can act if they have visibility. Imagine there was one important project your VP thought should have started by now. If the VP doesn't see that project on the "all-projects dashboard" even after a few weeks, he/she can then ask, "Where's my project? What's the holdup?"

   b. **The dashboard is *official*:** If your project is on the dashboard, it's officially running. If it's not there, something's wrong and the stakeholders can go fix it.

   c. **The dashboard makes it easy to grasp the state of the portfolio:** Imagine a long list of projects, all being done by different project managers for different stakeholders. Such a list of projects and their details is hard for anyone to understand (see Figure 6.1). However, the visual dashboard in Figure 6.2 is easy to grasp and quickly offers stakeholders the information they need.

Project Name ▼	Project Description ▼	Sponsor ▼	Start Date ▼	End Date ▼
Project 1	Description 1	Sponsor 1	1/1/2021	1/31/2021
Project 2	Description 2	Sponsor 2	1/2/2021	2/1/2021
Project 3	Description 3	Sponsor 3	1/3/2021	2/2/2021
Project 4	Description 4	Sponsor 4	1/4/2021	2/3/2021
Project 5	Description 5	Sponsor 5	1/5/2021	2/4/2021
Project 6	Description 6	Sponsor 6	1/6/2021	2/5/2021
Project 7	Description 7	Sponsor 7	1/7/2021	2/6/2021
Project 8	Description 8	Sponsor 8	1/8/2021	2/7/2021
Project 9	Description 9	Sponsor 9	1/9/2021	2/8/2021
Project 10	Description 10	Sponsor 10	1/10/2021	2/9/2021
Project 11	Description 11	Sponsor 11	1/11/2021	2/10/2021
Project 12	Description 12	Sponsor 12	1/12/2021	2/11/2021
Project 13	Description 13	Sponsor 13	1/13/2021	2/12/2021
Project 14	Description 14	Sponsor 14	1/14/2021	2/13/2021
Project 15	Description 15	Sponsor 15	1/15/2021	2/14/2021
Project 16	Description 16	Sponsor 16	1/16/2021	2/15/2021
Project 17	Description 17	Sponsor 17	1/17/2021	2/16/2021
Project 18	Description 18	Sponsor 18	1/18/2021	2/17/2021
Project 19	Description 19	Sponsor 19	1/19/2021	2/18/2021
Project 20	Description 20	Sponsor 20	1/20/2021	2/19/2021
Project 21	Description 21	Sponsor 21	1/21/2021	2/20/2021
Project 22	Description 22	Sponsor 22	1/22/2021	2/21/2021
Project 23	Description 23	Sponsor 23	1/23/2021	2/22/2021
Project 24	Description 24	Sponsor 24	1/24/2021	2/23/2021
Project 25	Description 25	Sponsor 25	1/25/2021	2/24/2021
Project 26	Description 26	Sponsor 26	1/26/2021	2/25/2021
Project 27	Description 27	Sponsor 27	1/27/2021	2/26/2021
Project 28	Description 28	Sponsor 28	1/28/2021	2/27/2021
Project 29	Description 29	Sponsor 29	1/29/2021	2/28/2021
Project 30	Description 30	Sponsor 30	1/30/2021	2/29/2021
Project 31	Description 31	Sponsor 31	1/31/2021	3/1/2021
Project 32	Description 32	Sponsor 32	2/1/2021	3/2/2021
Project 33	Description 33	Sponsor 33	2/2/2021	3/3/2021
Project 34	Description 34	Sponsor 34	2/3/2021	3/4/2021
Project 35	Description 35	Sponsor 35	2/4/2021	3/5/2021

Figure 6.1   A confusing dashboard

In the next chapter we will look at exactly how to build a dashboard like the one shown in Figure 6.2.

> KEY CONCEPT: A regulated portfolio intake, a common project template, and a portfolio dashboard together form the foundation of robust portfolio reporting.

WHAT IS PROJECT PERFORMANCE MONITORING?

Project reporting, as we just saw, is the activity of keeping track of the projects in a portfolio and displaying the information to all the stakeholders through reports. Project performance monitoring is a subset of project reporting and it may be more correct to say that project performance monitoring is

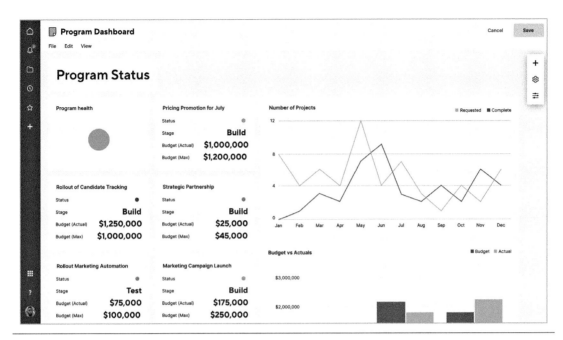

Figure 6.2   Much easier to understand

made possible by project reporting. It's the next step in the process. It describes how the projects are doing on the main areas of performance—scope, schedule, and budget:

- Is the project delivering on scope?
- Is the project on schedule?
- Is the project spending according to plan?

> KEY CONCEPT: Portfolio performance monitoring is the next step in robust portfolio reporting. It enables the identification of projects that are on track versus those that are not.

DRAWBACKS OF THE SUBJECTIVE R/Y/G METHOD OF PERFORMANCE MONITORING

One of the most popular (and least effective) methods of project performance is to mark projects red, yellow, or green on a subjective basis. Basically, the project manager can choose R/Y/G to show the status of the project. Although this method is easy (and hence popular), it is quite misleading and not an effective way to measure project performance. Here are some issues with this method:

- **No universal definition of R/Y/G:** The meaning of R/Y/G varies from project to project. There is no standard definition across projects. Therefore, a "red" for one project may not mean the same as a "red" for another project.
- **Everyone wants to avoid *red*:** The status of red is always underreported. That is, left to the subjective decision of project managers, most of them would find a reason to avoid reporting their project as red.

- **Sometimes yellow is the new green:** Some stakeholders tend to report their well-performing projects as yellow instead of green because yellow is seen as a *safe* color and as an insurance policy against future project problems.
- **Sometimes yellow means "we're trying hard":** Project managers may declare their status as yellow though their project is in deep trouble. The yellow is supposed to signify that they are making efforts to shore up the project.

From all the above reasons, the subjective use of R/Y/G status colors cannot be trusted to show what is really happening with the project.

> KEY CONCEPT: A subjective R/Y/G system is one where the project manager decides the status of the project. It does not work well at portfolio scale.

What's the Correct Way to Use R/Y/G?

A formula-based R/Y/G can be useful. A formula to decide if a project should be marked R/Y/G based on its milestone performance is the best approach. How does a formula-based R/Y/G work?

- Every project is broken out into tasks and milestones.
- Each task has a start date and end date.
- Each task also has a formula built in that automatically declares that task as R/Y/G based on whether that task is on time or delayed.
- All the reds, yellows, and greens are summed (again, with a formula) that determines whether the project overall is R/Y/G.

The advantages of this method are:

1. **Formula-based R/Y/G is objective:** There is no room for subjectivity in this system because two projects showing red are indeed comparable because the same formula measures their activity and finds them both in trouble.
2. **Formula-based R/Y/G is precisely defined:** Both at the task level as well as the project level, there is a precise formula that decides the color of the project. If there is a need to make the formula a little more (or less) exacting, it can be done.
3. **Formula-based R/Y/G is predictable:** A delayed task triggers a red for that row and many such delayed tasks predictably triggers a red for the whole project. This is similar for yellows and greens; if most tasks have a yellow (or green) status, the project goes to yellow (or green). This predictability helps project managers run their projects and eventually creates a more stable portfolio.

> KEY CONCEPT: A formula-based or objective R/Y/G system is one where an automated formula decides the status of the project based on milestone performance. It scales and is recommended for portfolio reporting.

CHAPTER SUMMARY

We started this chapter with a look at the need for portfolio reporting. The basic reason to report and monitor the performance of projects is to obtain an early warning if projects are failing so we can take corrective action. This naturally translates into a discussion of why projects tend to go off-track and the difficulties involved in reporting on a portfolio of projects. We then outlined a platform-neutral approach that works in reporting on a group of projects. We finally ended the chapter with a critical look at the popular R/Y/G status system and why a subjective R/Y/G doesn't work, but a formula-based R/Y/G can be successful.

7

PORTFOLIO REPORTING USING SMARTSHEET

INTRODUCTION

In the previous chapter we reviewed the importance of portfolio reporting. We also covered some design pointers to help make this happen. While it is possible to implement portfolio reporting using many platforms, including Microsoft Excel, it is a huge aid if it can be done "out of the box." One such solution is available using Smartsheet. A template set from Smartsheet (covered in detail in this chapter) does a great job of accomplishing all the reporting requirements outlined in the previous chapter.

In this chapter we cover the following aspects of performance reporting implementation:

1. The benefits of the portfolio reporting template set
2. Downloading the portfolio reporting template set from Smartsheet
3. Installing the portfolio reporting template set
4. An explanation of the components found in the portfolio reporting template set
5. Operating the portfolio reporting template set
6. Customizing the portfolio reporting template set

KEY CONCEPT: Portfolio reporting is a key component of portfolio management. Implementation of portfolio reporting is made easy through out-of-the-box features provided by the Smartsheet platform.

BENEFITS OF THE PORTFOLIO REPORTING TEMPLATE SET

The portfolio reporting template set is the quick and easy way to get a group of projects up and running, report on risks, and communicate milestones to stakeholders while having a view across all current projects. The benefits of this template are:

- Rapid implementation
- Quick value delivery
- Easy operation
- Easy to scale
- Built-in workflows to make the process work in an organization

Note that the portfolio reporting template set is also referred to as the *multiple project tracking and planning template set* and the *PMO template set*. We will refer to it as the portfolio reporting template throughout this chapter.

KEY CONCEPT: The Smartsheet portfolio reporting template set is the quick and easy way to jump-start portfolio reporting.

HOW TO DOWNLOAD THE PORTFOLIO REPORTING TEMPLATE SET FROM SMARTSHEET

1. Within Smartsheet, click on the + icon at the bottom of the Menu bar:

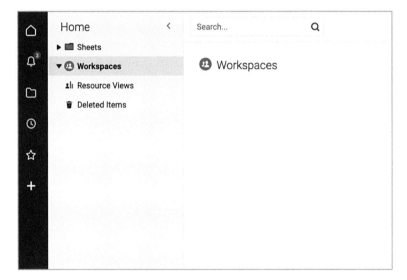

2. The Solution Center menu bar opens. In the search box, type "PMO Template Set" and click **Enter**:

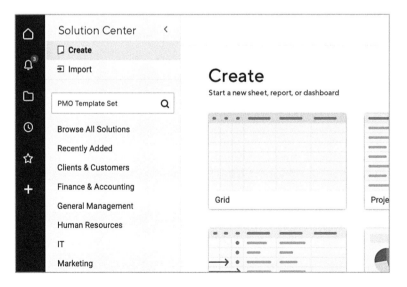

3. The **PMO Template Set** is returned as a search result. Click on it.

4. A pop-up appears with the tracking template and an introductory video. Click on the **Learn More** button on the right-most of this pop-up box:

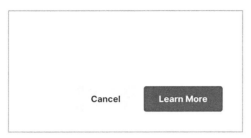

5. Finally, the download screen is visible. Click on **Get Template Set Now**:

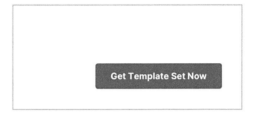

6. Verify that the template set has been downloaded into your Smartsheet account in the location shown below (under **Sheets**):

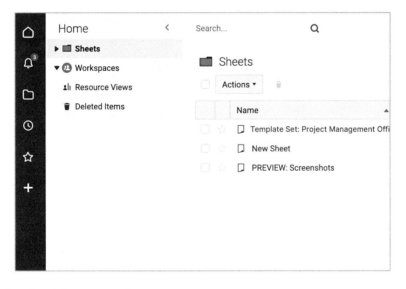

7. The download is now complete.

INSTALLING THE PORTFOLIO REPORTING TEMPLATE SET

1. First, create a new Workspace:
   a. Open the Smartsheet **Home** location.
   b. From the home menu, click the **Create** button in the upper right-hand corner.

    c. From the dropdown menu, select **Workspace**.

    d. Name the workspace. For our example, we'll call it "Portfolio Reporting and Tracker."

2. Drag the template set into the workspace:

    a. Select the template set folder (which we just downloaded) under your **Sheets** folder.

    b. Drag and drop the folder down to the **Portfolio Reporting and Tracker** workspace you just created.

3. Verify your workspace looks like this:

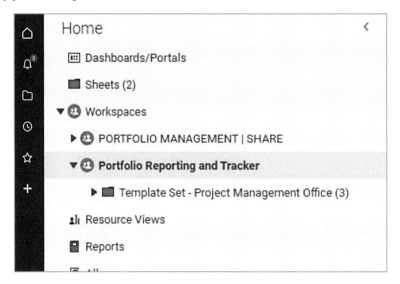

EXPLANATION OF THE COMPONENTS FOUND IN THE PORTFOLIO REPORTING TEMPLATE SET

The portfolio reporting template set is a self-contained unit, designed to do the following:

- Allow a group of project managers to submit projects for approval, and then plan, track, and report on multiple projects in one place
- Empower a portfolio manager to own and publish a portfolio level view of all projects and metrics in real time
- Automatically notify a group of specified people when new projects are submitted for approval

It does all the above using the following main components:

1. **Project intake sheet form:** This component allows project managers to submit project requests via the form for ease of intake and tracking
2. **Status and task reports:** Multiple dynamic reports to track project tasks and provide information rollup
3. **Project tracking sheet:** Project tracking sheet to provide a single point of truth
4. **Project and portfolio dashboard:** Roll-up dashboards at both the project and portfolio levels

HOW DO THE PORTFOLIO REPORTING COMPONENTS WORK TOGETHER?

The portfolio reporting components interact as shown here:

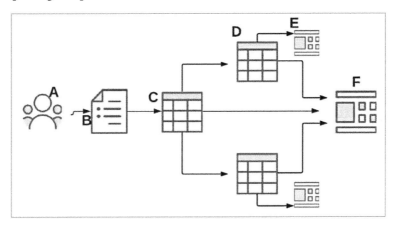

The process flow steps are explained below:

- **Step A.** Administrator or project manager decides to submit a new project
- **Step B.** Project intake form is filled out by the project manager
- **Step C.** The new project's details are added to the project intake sheet, which is the master list of all projects
- **Step D.** Project-level metadata sheets and other project related sheets are populated
- **Step E.** Project tracking and roll-up dashboards will be available for each new project
- **Step F.** The project overview dashboard is the roll-up information from all individual projects

Does all this seem a little overwhelming? No problem, each of the above steps are explained in detail below.

> KEY CONCEPT: The portfolio reporting template set is a self-contained unit with well-designed components that integrate to form a functioning portfolio.

OPERATING THE PORTFOLIO REPORTING TEMPLATE SET

First, we'll look at the project intake sheet form since that's where the whole process starts. The project intake sheet (Step B in the picture above) is where new projects are added to the portfolio. Projects can be added directly to this sheet (not recommended) or via the form on this sheet.

1. **How to access the project intake sheet:**
   - Refer to the following screenshot as a guide and perform the following steps:
     - ◻ Click on the home icon (see #1)
     - ◻ Go to the Portfolio Reporting and Tracker workspace we created earlier

> □ Click on the **Template Set—Project Management Office** folder (see #2)
> □ Click on the **Project Intake Sheet** (see #3)

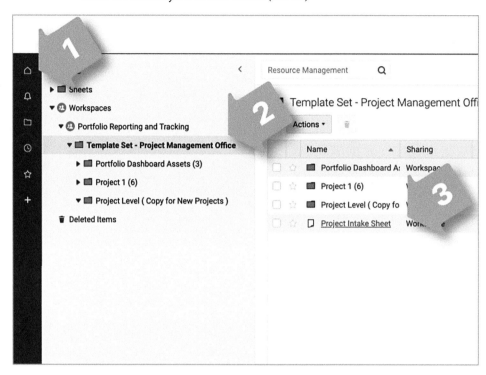

2. **Operating the project intake sheet and form:**
   • Once the Project Intake Sheet opens, click on the Forms menu option and then on **Manage Forms**.

- The form opens and looks like this:

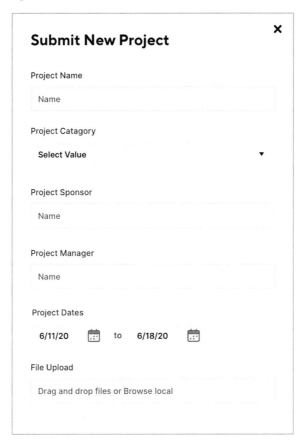

- There are 6 data points collected in this form to begin the project proposal intake flow:
  A. Project Name
  B. Project Category
  C. Project Sponsor
  D. Project Manager
  E. Target Start Date
  F. Target End Date

There is also an optional **File Upload** field.

- To open the form, click on **Open Form**:

- Fill out the fields with relevant information and click Submit. Remember to select the **Send me a copy of the responses** checkbox at the bottom:

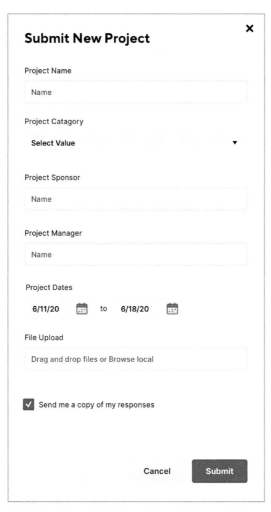

- Once you submit, go back to the project intake sheet and notice that the proposal you just submitted is now entered as a new row in the intake sheet.
- What if we need several others on the team to submit project proposal requests? To allow others to submit project requests, open the form and then click on **Share Form** as shown here:

- When the **Share Form** link is clicked, a dialog box opens to allow additional info to be added.
- Click **Share Sheet** after filling out the recipient's list and adding a brief message, as necessary.

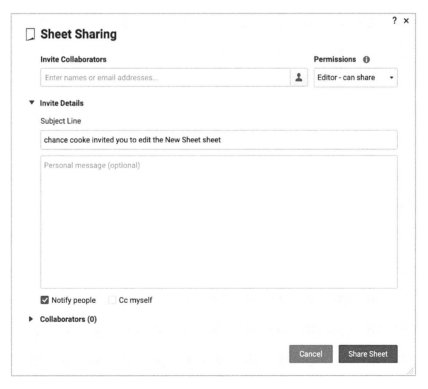

That's it! Your portfolio intake form is ready to accept project proposals.

COPYING THE PROJECT FOLDER

As soon as the project proposal submitted through intake is approved, a small action is needed to ensure that this new project (no longer just a proposal!) is included in the overall reporting of the portfolio. To do that, this new project must use the same template and other reporting arrangements that other projects are using. The simplest way to do that is to clone the project folder and rename it with the title of the newest project (which in this case is *Project 1*). Refer to the screenshot below for the sequence of actions described here:

1. Go to the workspace we defined for the portfolio reporting template (here shown as **Portfolio Reporting and Tracker**).
2. Within that workspace, right-click on the folder titled **Project Level (Copy for New Projects)**.
3. Click on **Save as New** in the pop-up that appears.

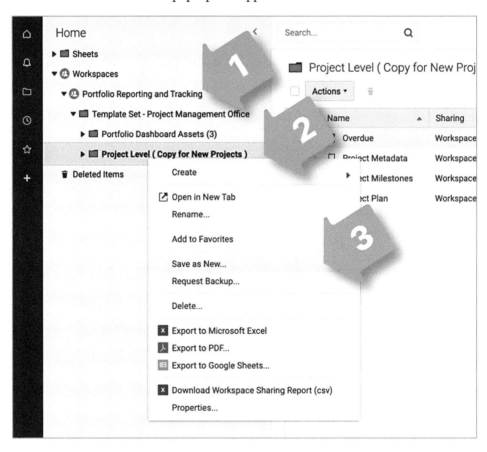

Next, the pop-up shown here appears:

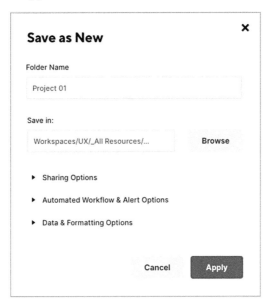

Proceed with the following steps:

1. Rename the folder "Project 1" (because that is the name of the new project proposal entered in the project intake form).
2. Hit **Apply**.

Notice that we now have a new folder for our new project (Project 1), as shown here:

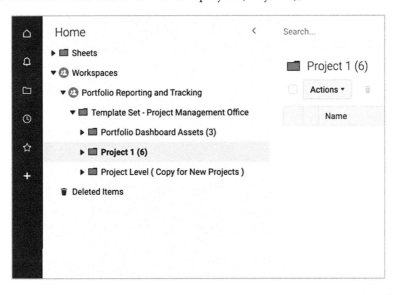

All the above steps will have to be done for each new project that is approved. Therefore, every new approved project will have its own folder in the workspace.

LINKING THE INTAKE AND PROJECT METADATA SHEETS—COPYING THE PROJECT ID

1. From the project intake sheet, copy the Project ID ("SM-005") for our new Project ("Project 1"):

2. In the new project folder that we just made for Project 1, open the **Project Metadata Sheet**.
3. Paste the Project ID "SM-005" over the placeholder Project ID "SM-001" as shown here:

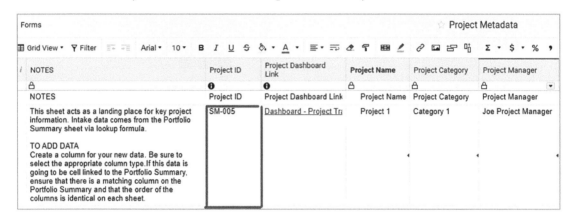

4. With the above action, notice that the information for Project 1 from the project intake sheet now populates the cells in that row in the project metadata sheet.

LINKING THE INTAKE AND PROJECT METADATA SHEETS—COPYING THE CELL LINKS

1. From Project 1's metadata sheet, copy the following cells: **Start Date**, **End Date**, **Schedule At Risk**, and **Project Status**:

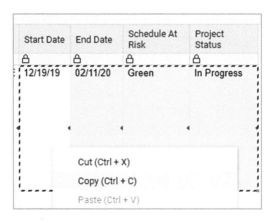

2. Go back to the project intake sheet.
3. Locate the row for Project 1 in the intake sheet. In that row, paste the copied cells into the identical columns.
4. Remember to Paste Special and select **Links to copied cells** as shown here:

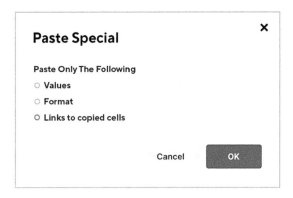

That's it! You've just created cell links across the whole template set.

CUSTOMIZING THE PORTFOLIO REPORTING SETUP

So far, we walked through the basic portfolio set-up model. However, most organizations will need to customize on top of that simple arrangement. Here are the basic customizations.

Customize Project Intake

Customizing Project Categories

Go to the project intake sheet:

1. Double click on the **Project Category** header—a pop-up appears:

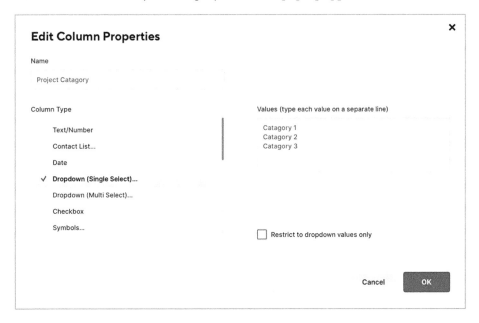

2. Edit the dropdown options for the categories to meet your requirements. Note that if you modify the categories, you will also need to modify Row 1 in the portfolio metric sheet. This sheet is found under the "Portfolio Dashboard Assets" folder under the "Template Set" folder.

Customizing the Project Intake Form

Go to the project intake sheet:

1. In the project intake sheet, click on **Forms** and then **Manage Forms**.
2. A pop-up will appear with all the form settings:

3. Edit the different text elements in the form to align with your requirements. Remember that this will change the portfolio intake form for everyone.
4. If needed, refer to Chapter 4 for detailed instructions on editing and customizing form fields.

> NOTE: It is not recommended to remove any of the six original fields as they are used at different levels of this template. However, additional fields can be added with no implications.

Customizing the New Project Approval Request

In many organizations a project proposal must be approved by the project sponsor before it can become a project in the portfolio. For this purpose, an automated approval request will be sent to the project sponsor (and possibly additional people or a mailing list) when a new project proposal is received. The following instructions explain how to customize this approval request to meet different needs.

1. First, go to the **Automation** menu and click on **Create a Workflow**:

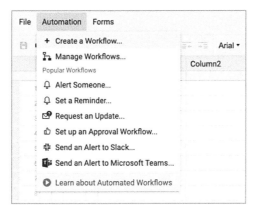

2. Customize the workflow by modifying the Triggers and Conditions as shown below:
   - Verify that the approval should go to the Project Sponsor (see #1).
   - Customize the subject and message at the request level—this will have to be done for both the "Approved" and "Declined" scenarios (see all the places marked #2).
   - Customize the alerts for both the "Approved" and "Declined" scenarios (see all the places marked #3).
   - Also select which columns' data should be included in each alert.

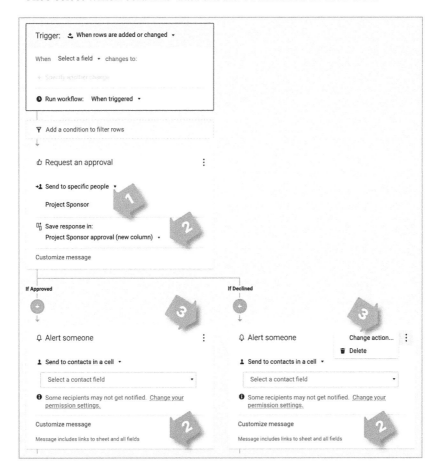

Smartsheet is versatile regarding the customizing of automation options to meet different needs. It is suggested that the user try different options with the intuitive interface to understand the possibilities.

CUSTOMIZE THE PROJECT PORTFOLIO DASHBOARD

The project portfolio dashboard is the information hub for all the projects you are tracking. Dashboards are made of different widgets that pull in real-time information from your sheets and reports. It is found under the **Template Set** main folder. The standard dashboard that comes with the Template Set is shown here:

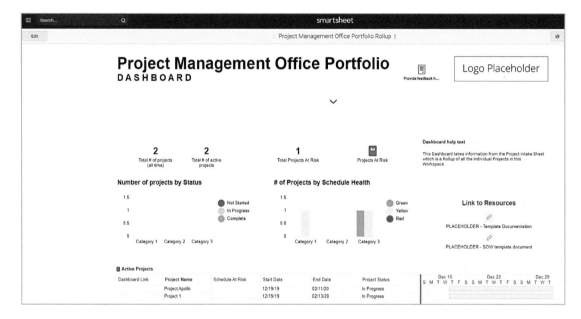

- Click **Edit** in the upper left corner of the dashboard to begin customizing. Hover your mouse over any widget and select the pencil icon to start modifying the widget and its contents.
- **Project Title** is a title widget. Double-click on it and edit if desired.
- The **Logo Placeholder** is an image widget and can be replaced with your company logo.
- **Active Projects** is a report widget, which displays the live reports in your dashboard.

In the lower part of the dashboard (not shown in the previous screenshot due to size), there is a Web Content widget placeholder:

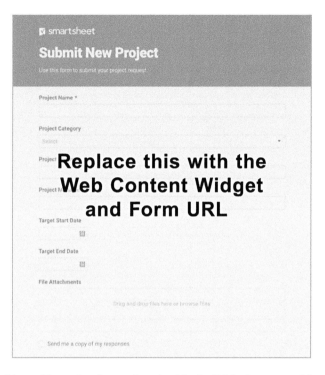

- This placeholder will need to be replaced with the Web Content widget as explained in the following steps:
  - Click on the **Edit** button in the top left-hand corner of the standard dashboard
  - Delete the placeholder by clicking on the recycle bin icon:

  - Remember, we're still in Edit mode. Click on the **Add Widget** button ⟨+ Add Widget⟩ in the top right-hand corner of the dashboard and select the **Web Content** tile in the dialog box that appears.

❏ In the **Edit Web Content** widget box that appears next, click on **Select URL**, and paste the URL on the portfolio intake form as described below:
  ○ Access the form management dialog box for the Project Intake Sheet by clicking on **Manage Forms**:

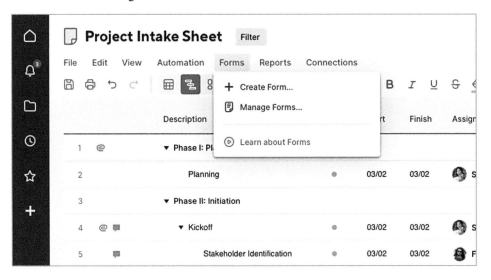

  ○ Click on the **Submit New Project** tile.
  ○ Click on the **Share Form** link in the top right-hand corner of the screen that comes up.
  ○ In the dialog box that pops up, click on the **Link** option:

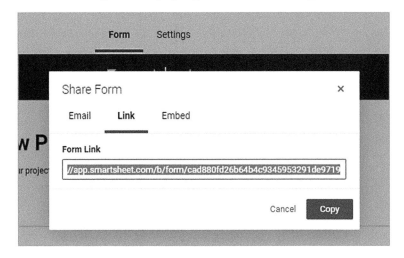

  ○ The form link appears. Click **Copy** and then paste this link into the Web Content widget we inserted into the dashboard.
❏ When all the above is done, a copy of the form appears on the dashboard and is ready to accept new proposals.

CUSTOMIZE PROJECT LEVEL INFORMATION

1. Modify the Project Plan Sheet

Use the project plan sheet to track and maintain critical data about a project.

- Project sheets in Smartsheet have dependencies enabled and include columns such as **Duration**, **Predecessors**, and **% Complete**.
- A standard project plan is provided as part of the template set which will automate the project timeline from the start date and will provide an estimated end date based on project tasks.
- This standard project plan is cloned for every new project when the project folder is copied.
- It is best to enable dependencies for projects with deadlines to ensure every milestone in your project is tracked, on time, and ultimately, meets your deadline.

Here are instructions to modify the key features of the project plan:

A. In the **Task Name** column, name the project phases in the parent (gray) rows.
B. Use the indented grandchild (white) rows in your hierarchy to enter tasks in the **Task Name** column.
C. Starting in row three, enter dates in the **Start Date**, **End Date**, **Target Start Date**, and **Target End Date** columns. This template uses the difference between the Actual End Date and the Target End Date along with Duration to determine the health of the schedule. At the beginning of your project, they should be the same for each row.
D. The other data on your ancestor and parent rows, including Start Date, End Date, % Complete, and Duration are auto calculated by the tasks below the parent row.
E. Attach documents or links to web pages in the rows of the **Attachment** (paper clip icon) column to keep all your project information and resources in one place.
F. Track the progress of your project by viewing the interactive Gantt timeline to see which tasks are complete (green), which are late (red), which are in progress (blue), and which are on hold (orange). Conditional formatting rules apply formatting automatically to rows or cells based on the values they contain.

2. Adjust Durations and Predecessors

Duration and **Predecessor** are two unique column types that exist in project sheets—refer to the screenshot below to do the following:

A. Set the duration of each task in the **Duration** column.

B. Set predecessors, or relationships between tasks, in the **Predecessors** column.

Start Date	End Date	% Complete	Duration	Predecessors
			Ⓐ	Ⓑ
12/19/19	**02/11/20**	**30%**	**39d**	
12/19/19	01/14/20	62%	19d	
12/19/19	12/25/19	25%	5d	
12/26/19	12/31/19	30%	4d	3
01/01/20	01/09/20	100%	7d	4
01/10/20	01/14/20	75%	3d	5
01/14/20	01/14/20	0%	0	6

3. Assign Tasks to Team Members

Assign tasks to individuals by adding their email addresses in the **Assigned To** column:

- A contact includes both the name and email address, which drives delivery of automated actions, alerts, reports, and more.
- Add contacts in the **Assigned To** column by individually creating a new contact, or adding an existing contact from your contact list.

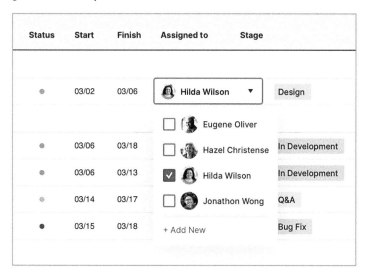

4. Adjust Alerts

As seen previously, automation is very useful in keeping team members apprised of project developments. For example, an automated alert workflow is a great way to let your team know they have new tasks to fulfill as soon as they are assigned. Here's how to implement the workflow:

1. Set the automated alert as shown on the following page by clicking on **Automation** and selecting **Manage Workflows** in the dropdown menu.

2. Then double-click on the workflow itself in order to edit the specifics of the Triggers and Conditions.

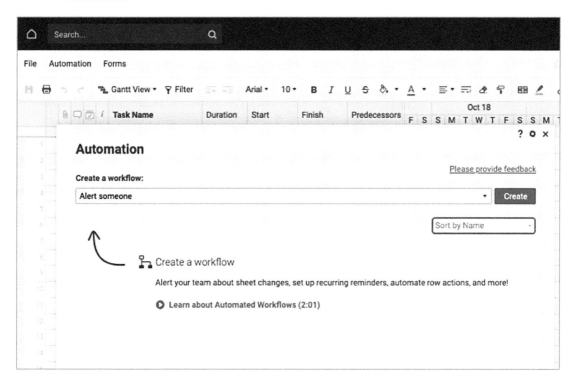

5. Recurring Reminders

An automated recurring reminder is a great way to save time and keep track of deadlines. The Recurring Incomplete Task alert will notify the contact listed in the **Assigned To** column every day when the end date is in the next three days and where the current status is On Hold, Not Started, or In Progress. Here's how to set it up:

1. Click on **Automation** and select **Manage Workflows** in the dropdown menu. Then double-click on the workflow to open the editor window.
2. To customize the workflow's schedule (trigger box), click on the dropdown that begins with **Every day starting on** and select **Run** once to trigger on a single date, or choose **Custom** to edit the recurrence schedule.
3. Customize the workflow conditions (condition boxes) to add criteria and then click **Save**.

6. Sheet Summary: View or Edit Your Project Summary Data

For those with a business or enterprise plan, this template set utilizes the sheet summary feature. The project plan sheet includes a pre-populated sheet summary that provides a standard, robust way to organize and report on project information in your sheet. Here you can see a quick recap of the status of tasks and the count of those at risk:

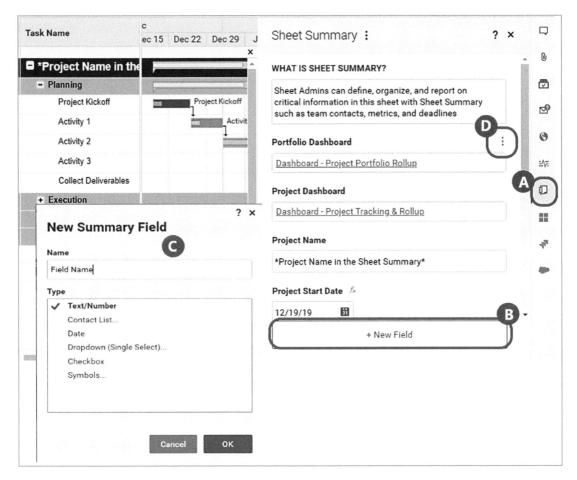

A. Open the sheet summary on the right panel to view or edit your project summary fields.
    • Notice that clicking the sheet summary icon will expand the sheet summary.
    • You can expand and collapse the right panel to stay in the context of your sheet or maximize your sheet real estate when you don't need to view it.
B. To add fields, click **+ New Field**.
C. Name your field and select the field type: Text/Number, Contact list, Date, Dropdown list, Checkbox, or Symbols.
D. To edit the field properties, hover over the right side of the field and click on the vertical **ellipsis (⋮)** to open the field options dropdown menu.

7. Update Status and Filters

After the task has been assigned, the task owner can update the status by selecting an option from a custom dropdown list in the **Status** column. If there are multiple owners, filters are an ideal way to help people cut through the noise.

1. On the project plan sheet, create a shared filter called **Tasks Assigned to Me**:

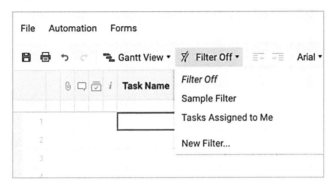

2. Anyone viewing the sheet can select that filter and see only their assigned items.
3. Click on the **Filter** button and select **Tasks Assigned to Me** to see tasks assigned to the current user viewing the sheet. You can also select any of the other filter options to perform other tasks.

8. View the Project Milestones Report

The project milestones report tracks all the critical project milestones by displaying any rows where the duration is equal to 0 (the definition of a milestone) and the Task Name is not blank. The information in this report also appears on the Project Rollup Dashboard. The screenshot below shows how to build this report and the choices to be selected under each column:

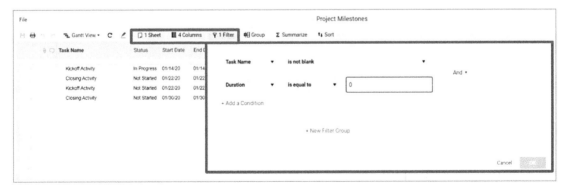

9. Use the Overdue Report

A task is automatically flagged as Overdue if the status is not Complete or Canceled and the End Date is in the past. This report surfaces all Overdue tasks in one view and displays them on the Project Tracking and Rollup Dashboard:

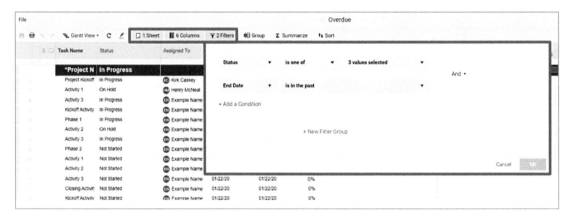

10. Schedule Health Column

Consider an indicator that would always show, objectively, if a particular milestone or deliverable within the project is late or on time. That would be very useful, especially when standardized across all milestones in a project and across all projects. Smartsheet has such an indicator available out of the box in the **Schedule Health** column which leverages several columns and formulas to produce an objective R/Y/G. Refer to the screenshot below and observe the following columns:

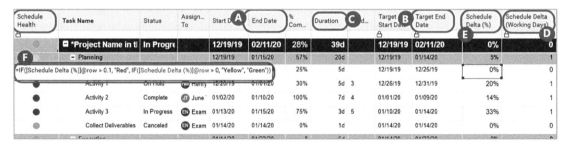

A. End Date: The actual end date of the task

B. Target End Date: Set at the beginning of the project as the planned end date of the task

C. Duration: The number of working days between the start date and end date

D. Schedule Delta (Working Days): Number of days +/− between the end date and the target end date

E. Schedule Delta %: This column measures the variance to the schedule as a percentage. It contains the following formula: =IFERROR([Schedule Delta (Working Days)]@row / Duration@row, " ")

F. Schedule Health: Uses the following formula logic rules: =IF([Schedule Delta (%)]@row > 0.1, "Red", IF([Schedule Delta (%)]@row : 0, "Yellow", "Green")

Here's how the R/Y/G is produced in the **Schedule Health** column:

- If the Schedule Delta % is greater than 10%, it's red for that row
- If the Schedule Delta % is greater than 0 but less than 10%, it's yellow for that row; these are tasks to watch as they could push the project to an unacceptable timeline
- If the Schedule Delta % is less than or equal to 0, it's green for that row and indicates the task is on schedule or faster

11. Project Rollup Dashboard

The Project Tracking and Rollup dashboard is the keystone for each project. It pulls together all the critical project information that needs to be tracked. Dashboards are made of different widgets that pull in real-time information from your sheets and reports. The next screenshot shows the dashboard, and the following bullets help customize it further.

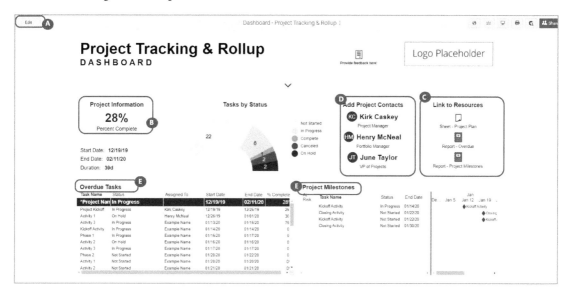

A. Click **Edit** in the upper left corner of the dashboard to begin customizing. Hover your mouse over any widget and select the pencil icon to start modifying the widget and its contents.
B. **Project Information** is a metric widget that summarizes key project data in your project plan.
C. **Links to Resources** is a shortcut widget that you can use to link sheets, reports, and other resources that reside outside of Smartsheet.
D. **Update Project Contacts** with information about your team.
E. Both **Overdue Tasks** and **Project Milestones** are report widgets, which display your live reports in your dashboard.

12. Share Your Project Tracking and Rollup Template Set

Sharing is the best way to collaborate with others involved in your projects. You can share your entire workspace with members of your department or share individual items within the workspace. Two important artifacts need to be shared:

- The intake sheet (so people can submit project proposals to include in the portfolio)

- The workspace can also be shared so project managers can operate within the folders of their respective projects

KEY CONCEPT: The features provided by Smartsheet are a very good fit for the purpose of portfolio reporting. Almost every conceivable need for reporting is met by this collection of widgets and the general functionality provided by the platform.

CHAPTER SUMMARY

In this substantive chapter, we began to apply the power of the Smartsheet platform to implement portfolio management. First, we listed the benefits of the portfolio reporting template set compared to building it from scratch. Next, we walked through the process of downloading the portfolio reporting template set from Smartsheet. We proceeded to install the portfolio reporting template set while explaining the components found in it. Next, we showed how to operate the portfolio reporting template set. Finally, while recognizing that every organization is different, we walked through the customization of the portfolio reporting template set.

8

PORTFOLIO RESOURCE MANAGEMENT AND IMPLEMENTATION WITH SMARTSHEET

INTRODUCTION

The people who actually work on projects are the most essential part of any portfolio. Without them, nothing can be achieved. In this chapter we cover the following aspects of resource management:

1. A discussion of why resource management may be the most important factor in managing a portfolio
2. The difficulties involved in keeping track of resources in a portfolio of projects
3. An approach that works in resource reporting
4. Implementing portfolio resource management in Smartsheet

> KEY CONCEPT: A portfolio's most important asset is the people (resources) that are working on the projects within the portfolio.

WHY IS RESOURCE MANAGEMENT SO IMPORTANT?

Resources, or the people working on the projects, are the "active ingredients" that make the projects go forward. They're also a precious and expensive ingredient—it costs a lot in terms of salaries and other compensation to keep people on board.

Resources are also an important metric in identifying the capacity in a portfolio. A limited amount of people means there can only be a certain number of productive hours that can be spent on projects. A good portfolio manager will recognize this upper limit of productivity and try to spend these hours in the best possible way on the most impactful projects. A portfolio where this upper limit is not even known will not be able to manage the productivity and output of the portfolio.

Therefore, it is important to use this expensive component in the best possible way. If the resources in a portfolio are not working on the right projects, little can be achieved. On the other hand, if the resources are all working on the most important projects, then the portfolio is on the right track to delivering value to the organization.

> KEY CONCEPT: Resource management is key to ensuring that people are working on the right projects and delivering value.

The Difficulties Involved in Keeping Track of Resources

Keeping track of portfolio resources is clearly vital to success. It could make all the difference between a productive portfolio and one that delivers little value. However, it can be rather challenging to actually do this. Before we explore the actual reasons, we need to understand how interconnected resource management is to the other components of portfolio management. If other components (for example, portfolio intake) are not functioning properly, it can be difficult to do resource management in an effective manner. Here are some of the practical difficulties encountered in keeping track of resources:

- **We don't have a unified list of projects**
    - If we can't pull together a standard unified list of projects, it is hard to get a complete picture of what people are working on.
    - This usually happens when the portfolio intake function is not working well. Projects are started without a review of the current workload of the resources.
    - As a result, there may be too many projects started when it is not feasible to do them.
    - This is actually a common problem—most portfolios have too many projects because no one has the complete picture of existing efforts.
- **We don't know who's working on what**
    - This problem is closely related to the previous one—without a complete list of projects, it is hard to get a complete picture of what people are doing.
    - Even if we do have a complete list of projects, it takes effort to track who's assigned to what project.
    - Knowing we have 25 people working on 50 projects is useless without additional information. For example, are 10 people working on one big project while the others are distributed across the remaining? This type of information is much harder to get.
- **We don't have a standard method of measuring effort**
    - There needs to be a standard way of measuring effort that is uniform across the entire resource pool.
    - For example, a person spending 50% of their capacity across a two-week project is the same as a person who spends 100% of their capacity on a one-week project. Similarly, there are many combinations of efforts and durations that all need to be measured with a uniform unit.
    - Without a uniform unit of measuring effort, it can be challenging to stay on top of resource management.
    - Few organizations have this type of measurement in place. At most, there may be a subjective description like, "I spend most of my time on these two projects, and the rest on other small projects."
- **We can't keep up with the changing effort estimates**
    - Resource management needs some prerequisites to work, but what makes it even more challenging is that resource allocation is never static—it keeps changing.
    - For example, a project manager could estimate that she will spend 20% of her time over the next three months on five projects. However, it may turn out that most of her time (say 80%) is spent on Project 1 and hardly any time is spent on Projects 2 through 5.
    - In this example, it would be a mistake to rely on the old estimate of 20% effort on Projects 1 through 5. The estimate needs to be updated in reality and then decisions can be based on that new information.

- **It takes a huge effort to compile the information from different sources**
  - ❑ Some organizations and teams put in a lot of hard work and use Microsoft Excel (typically) to organize resource management.
  - ❑ While it's possible, it takes a huge amount of effort and discipline to keep the data updated and valid.
  - ❑ Sooner or later, this process is discarded and resource management is no longer practiced.
- **Resource management is tied to tools like time sheets**
  - ❑ In some organizations, resource management is closely tied to tools like time sheet management.
  - ❑ The drawback of time sheets is that they are usually unpopular, and the users do not input high-quality data into these applications.
  - ❑ Another drawback is that since time sheets are *after the fact*, they are of little use in forecasting future effort estimates and the resource management output is not of much use in planning.

KEY CONCEPT: Several factors prevent resource management from happening easily. A careful effort is needed to ensure resource management is done right and in an effective manner.

RESOURCE MANAGEMENT: AN APPROACH THAT WORKS

Without thinking of a specific tool or platform, the following design pointers will always work in building a reliable project resource management system:

1. **Start with portfolio intake:** The key to successful project resource management starts with portfolio project intake (see Chapters 4 and 5 for an extensive discussion on portfolio intake). Here are the ways in which a well-designed intake process facilitates project resource management:
   a. **Eliminates under-the-radar projects:** By coming through a common (and standard) intake channel, all projects are known and will be included in resource planning.
   b. **Enforces mandatory resource-check:** Another advantage of coming through a standard intake form is that all projects will have to be assigned resources in a standard way—before assigning resources to a project, take stock of all other resource commitments in the standard set of metadata fields. Sometimes that means that some projects cannot be taken up immediately until resources are freed.
2. **Decide on a common template:** All projects need to work off a common template (see Chapter 3 for an explanation of how to build a basic project plan in Smartsheet). To this basic project plan, we can add a few columns to track effort (details next). Having a common project template also enforces a common way of accounting for resource estimates:
   a. **Effort estimates can now be stacked:** The data from projects which all follow a common template can be pooled or aggregated easily. What does that mean? As a simple example, all projects that have an "Effort Hours" field can be added to create a "Total Effort" number. A person with different effort entries in different projects can have them added to show projected total effort hours for the week.

3. **Roll up resource information to a common dashboard:** Showing all the resource information in one easy-to-understand interface is important. First, it lets people see everything in one place and that's not a small thing to achieve. Many organizations struggle to achieve this. But there are more advantages:

   a. **Seeing everything in one place lets people react:** People will act if they have visibility. Imagine there was one important resource who is fully allocated to five projects of medium priority. If your department leader now has a request from the CIO to expedite a new high-priority project, it's easy to ask this resource to offload those previous five projects (or delay them) and focus on the new high-priority one.

   b. **The resource dashboard is the *official place* to see what people are working on:** If your project is listed on the resource dashboard as one of your efforts, it is officially running. If it is not there, something's wrong and the situation needs to be fixed.

   c. **The dashboard makes it easy to grasp the state of the portfolio:** Portfolios take on too many projects. That's mainly because they don't realize that people are overloaded. A good resource dashboard will immediately make this clear, usually by showing that a resource is supposed to be working more than 40 hours a week—which is not sustainable. This useful information can be used to stop the blind addition of excess projects. The portfolio can now stop choking on the mass of projects and intelligent trade-off discussions can begin to happen.

> KEY CONCEPT: Regulated portfolio intake, a common project template, and a resource dashboard together form the foundation of robust portfolio resource management.

IMPLEMENTING RESOURCE MANAGEMENT IN SMARTSHEET

Smartsheet resource management offers visibility into team activity without the data entry pain or extra process normally associated with resource management tools. This delivers real-time information from the project sheets that are already being used to manage projects, in addition to the ability to drill down and get detailed views of user allocations. At a high level, here is the four-step process to implement resource management in Smartsheet:

- Step 1: Set up people on your account as resources
- Step 2: Assign people to tasks in various projects (who works on what)
- Step 3: Enable resource management
- Step 4: Set up a resource view and understand the data

Each of the above steps is explained in detail on the following pages.

> KEY CONCEPT: Being able to gather and display resource information as the people work on projects is a big advantage of the Smartsheet platform.

Step 1: Set Up Resources and Resource Viewers in Your Account with User Management

- Only people that have been added to your account can be tracked by resource management. This includes people who are licensed, unlicensed, invited, and active.
- To ensure that the right people are included in the account, a system administrator can use the **User Management** window to review, add, and manage users.

TIP: If somebody in your account does not need to create sheets, uncheck the **Licensed User** box when sending the invitation. This person will be invited to your account as a free member and they won't count against your user limit.

- To see how people are allocated across projects, you must be a designated **Resource Viewer**. Any system administrator can set this up in **Account > User Management**. (Note that you must be a licensed user to be a Resource Viewer.)
- If you would like to view resources, contact your Smartsheet system administrator.

Step 2: Assign People to Tasks in Various Projects (Who Works on What)

To assign people to tasks on your sheet, the sheet must contain a **Contact List** column. If it doesn't have this column, you can insert one using the following steps:

- Refer to the basic project sheet described at the end of Chapter 3. Click the dropdown arrow ▼ below a column's header and select **Insert 1 Column Right** or **Insert 1 Column Left**, depending on where you want to place the additional contact list column.
- The **Insert Column** window appears:

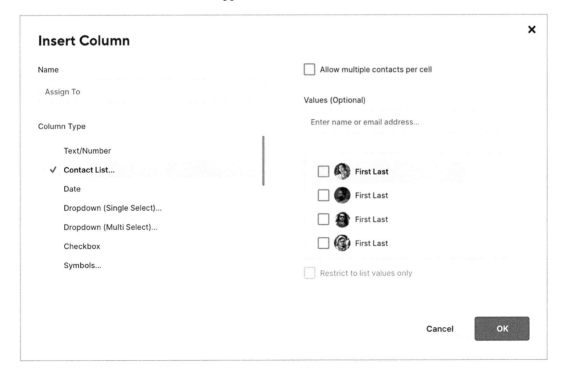

- Type the name of the column in the **Name** box (for example, type "Assigned To").
- Select the **Contact List** column type.
- If you have tasks that need to be assigned to multiple people, check the **Allow multiple contacts per cell** box.

By default, the allocation of a resource is 100%. However, it's rare for people to be allocated at 100% for one task. So, we need a column to track the specific percentage. To allocate a resource across two or more tasks, you'll need to create an **Allocation %** column:

- Insert a text/number column in your project. Name it "Allocation %" so that you know it will be used as the **Allocation %** column.
- Format the column properties to **percent (%)**.
- Start assigning people to tasks (see the **Assigned To** column):

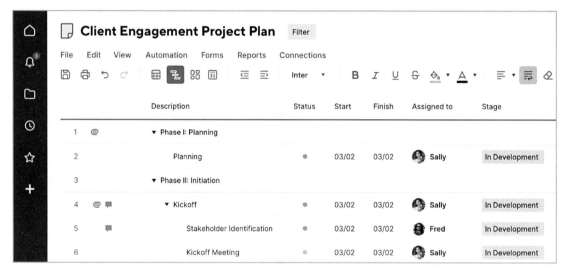

- Do this for all projects (go to every project sheet and allocate the resources to each task on that project as shown above).

Step 3: Enable Resource Management

- Click the dropdown arrow below any column header and select **Edit Project Settings**.
- Verify that the **Dependencies Enabled** checkbox is selected.

- From here, select the **Resource Management** tab. The **Resource Management** form appears:

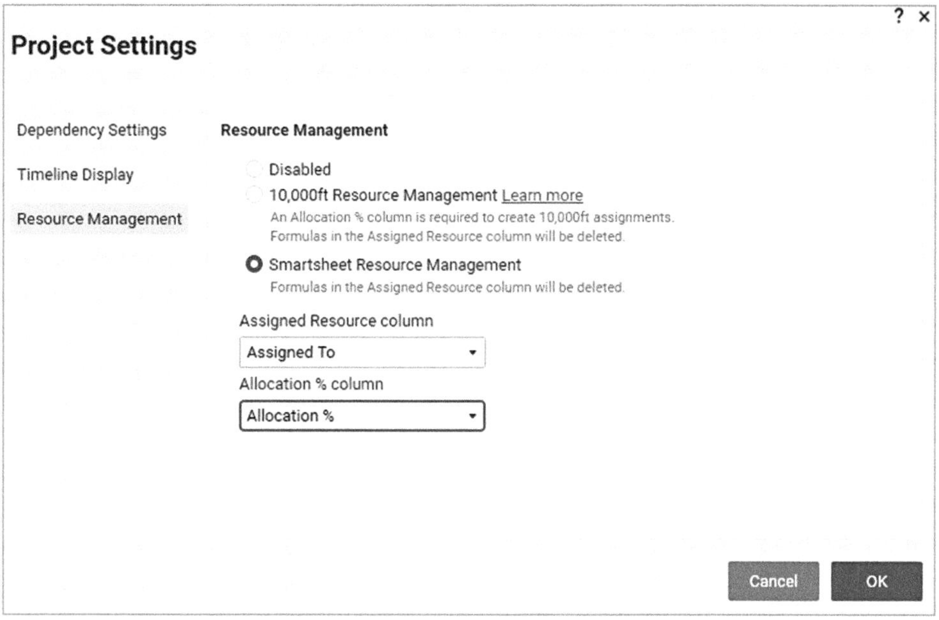

- Check the box for **Smartsheet Resource Management** and designate your **Assigned Resource** column by selecting the **Assigned To** column from the dropdown.
- In the **Allocation %** column dropdown, choose the **Allocation %** choice.
- Click **OK**.

NOTE: In the mobile application, you will be able to add one or more contacts to a **Contact List** column depending on which option was set on the desktop application; however, you cannot set this option from the mobile app.

Step 4: Set Up Resource View

There are 3 types of Resource View:

- Resource View by User
- Resource View by Project
- Resource View by Group

Each of these is explained below.

Resource View by User

Say you're the portfolio manager of the Launch Team Portfolio. As the portfolio manager, you will be most interested in seeing what the Launch Team portfolio resources (people) are working on currently. To show that resource view, here are the steps:

- Click the **Menu** icon (upper-left corner of the Smartsheet window) > **Home**.
- Right-click the **Resource Views** command and click **Create New View**.

- Ensure that **By User** is selected:

- Name the resource view "Launch Team."
- Select the people who are on the Launch Team and click **OK**.
- The Launch Team resource view is created:

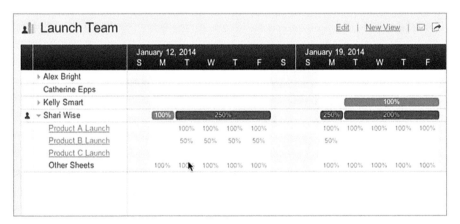

Points to Note:

- Notice that the allocation alert icon ♟ will be displayed next to any overallocated resource.
- Notice that in the time frame shown, the resource Shari Wise is overallocated and is also working on other non-Launch Portfolio projects.
- As the portfolio manager, this is useful information which should then be used to explore why Shari is overallocated and why her capacity is taken up by other projects not in the portfolio.
- Consider reassigning some of Shari's tasks to others.

Resource View by Projects

Assume you are still the portfolio manager of the Launch Team Portfolio. As the portfolio manager, you will also be interested in seeing who's working on the Launch Team projects. To show that resource view, here are the steps:

- Click the **Menu** icon (upper-left corner of the Smartsheet window) > **Home**.
- Right-click the **Resource Views** command and click **Create New View**.
- Ensure that **By Project** is selected.

- Name this view "Launch Portfolio Resource View."
- A list of projects in the workspace is shown. Select only the projects belonging to the Launch Portfolio—Project Launch One and Project Launch Two.
- That's it; the resource view is created and displays all the people working on the Launch projects.

Resource View by Group

Imagine there is a group of people in the organization who are needed in almost every project. Therefore, the portfolio manager must always monitor the workload of this group of key resources to ensure that they are not overallocated. The portfolio manager must also keep a close eye on this group to understand how much capacity they have remaining to take on additional projects or to swap out medium-priority projects for high-priority projects. Smartsheet offers an easy way to do this by defining and managing groups.

- First, we need to define a group. In the **Admin Center**, select the menu icon at the top left and choose **Group Management**. You're taken to the Group Management page.

- Select the **Create Group** button at the top right to display the Create Group panel:

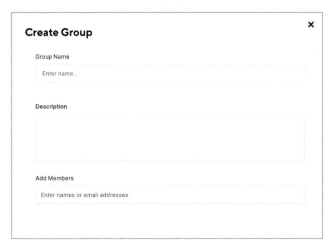

- Name your group (for example, "DBA Pool") and give it a description. Add an optional description and members.
- Select **Create**. The group will be added to the list and you will automatically be added as a member.
- Once the group is created, it can be edited to add members:

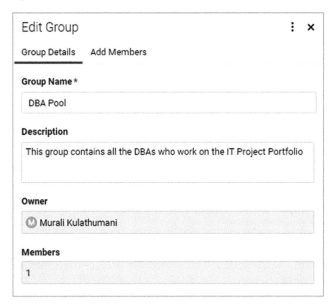

Now that we have the group in place, we proceed with defining a **Resource View by Group**:

- Click the **Menu** icon (upper-left corner of the Smartsheet window) > **Home**.
- Right-click the **Resource Views** command and click **Create New View**.

- Ensure that **By Group** is selected:

- Name this view "DBA Pool Resource View."
- Select the desired group **DBA Pool** that is shown. Click **OK**.
- That's it; the resource view of the DBA Pool is created and displays all the allocations of the people on the DBA team:

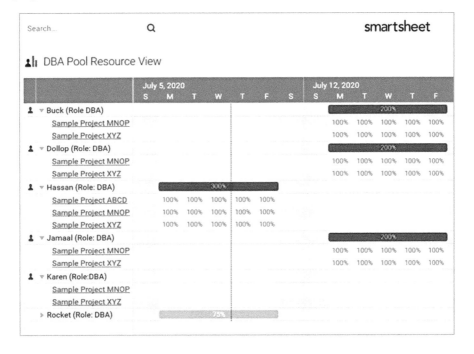

The previous screenshot is a useful tool. It shows that Hassan is overallocated this week while Buck, Dollop, and Jamaal are overallocated next week. The portfolio manager must find other people to take over these tasks so that no one is overworked and the portfolio keeps functioning well.

> KEY CONCEPT: There is almost always a resource crunch in portfolios. Finding this resource crunch and taking action to mitigate it is a huge success factor for the portfolio. Smartsheet enables this with some easy, out-of-the-box functionality.

TWO USEFUL WAYS TO DISPLAY RESOURCE MANAGEMENT VIEWS

The previous section covered how to set up resource views. Once that is done, you can see cross-project resource views in two places:

- From **Home** in the left panel
- From project-specific views from within project sheets

See Resource Views from Home (Navigation Menu)

1. Click the **Menu** icon (upper-left corner of the Smartsheet window) > **Home**.
2. Click **Resource Views**.
3. Select the resource view that you'd like to display.

From here, you'll be able to do the following:

- See a red icon on overallocated people and red bars on the overallocated days
- Expand each resource to see all the projects they are assigned to
- Click to open a project to resolve allocation issues
- Click **Edit** to view resources by project, user, or group
- Save a **New View** for a custom view of select people or projects

> NOTE: If a resource viewer is not shared to a project sheet where a specific resource is assigned, that resource viewer will see "Other" against that resource instead of the project name.

See Resource Views from a Project Sheet

- To open the Project Resource View for a sheet, switch to Gantt View, and then select the **Resource View** icon ![icon] in the upper-right corner of the Gantt View.

> NOTE: If you don't see the **Resource View** icon, contact your Smartsheet system administrator to become a resource viewer.

- It is useful to know if someone is overallocated even as we add them to a task in a project.
- A red allocation alert icon ♣ will alert you when people are overallocated in the project.
- As a resource viewer, you can click the allocation alert icon to open the **Project Resource View** which lists the sheets where resources in your project are assigned tasks.

The following example explains how the resource management view can help in real time while assigning resources to tasks.

1. As shown below, Hassan is overallocated as soon as he is allocated to a task (a red allocation alert icon ♣ appears). Click on the alert icon.

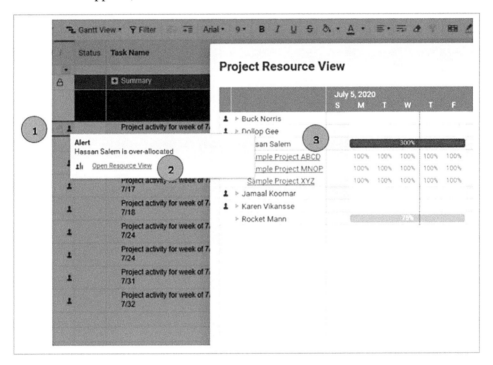

2. A pop-up appears stating that Hassan is overallocated (#2). Once **Open Resource View** is clicked, a **Project Resource View** window pops up.
3. In this view, we can see that Hassan is allocated 100% to three different projects in the same week, which is not feasible (#3).

The portfolio manager will need to resolve this resource contention by deciding where Hassan should spend his time. By solving such issues as they arise (in manageable chunks), resource contention is prevented and does not pile up to become a major problem for the portfolio.

KEY CONCEPT: By highlighting and resolving resource contention issues during resource allocation, much of the portfolio's resource management problems can be detected early and solved.

CHAPTER SUMMARY

We started this chapter by highlighting the people element of the portfolio and why they are vital to the whole mission—without them nothing can be achieved. We then proceeded to show that resource management may be the most important factor in managing a portfolio. Next, we discussed the practical difficulties involved in keeping track of resources in a portfolio of projects. From there we outlined a generic approach that works in resource reporting. Finally, we covered in detail how to implement portfolio resource management in Smartsheet and finished the chapter by describing how to apply the resource management view to facilitate the smooth working of the portfolio.

9

INTRODUCTION TO PORTFOLIO ANNUAL PLANNING

INTRODUCTION

Portfolio annual planning is the process of deciding, as an organization, which programs and projects to fund and execute in the next year. In some places, this might involve deciding what to do for the next two or three years. In others, this could be done twice a year, in which case it is called half-yearly planning.

Though the planning duration can vary, for our purposes in this book, we will call it *annual planning*. During this process, the whole organization brings forward the collective demand of the enterprise and puts it all on the planning table to be prioritized. In this chapter, we will cover:

1. The importance of annual planning
2. The different ways annual planning is beneficial to portfolio management

KEY CONCEPT: Annual planning is a must in all portfolios because it provides a glimpse of what is coming in the next year. This visibility is key to enabling the organization to decide what is most important to execute.

WHY IS ANNUAL PLANNING IMPORTANT?

Annual planning is a foundational requirement of solid portfolio management. Although this exercise is complex and time-consuming, a well-executed annual planning process can put your portfolio in high gear. The benefits of annual planning are interrelated and combine to deliver a comprehensive boost to the organization. These benefits are explored next.

Benefit 1: Priority Discovery

Most organizations deal with a large volume of projects. It's not easy to understand which projects are a priority for the organization as a whole. An annual planning exercise is valuable in "connecting the dots" from strategy to execution.

Benefit 2: Budget Discovery

What does it take to run a year of projects? How much money and/or resources will the organization need to execute on its strategic agenda? Annual planning provides these answers. How does it do that? By deciding which basket of projects to do, it allows the organization to start estimating the cost of these projects and then add them up to obtain a realistic budget.

Benefit 3: Project Discovery

In a large organization, information tends to fragment and distort; people simply don't know what other departments or teams are doing or planning on doing. Through the annual planning process, everybody is made aware of work other departments or teams are planning to do in the upcoming year. This discovery is valuable in several ways as explained next.

Benefit 4: Redundancy Elimination

Redundancy elimination is one of the big advantages of discovery. Project redundancy is the situation where two or more teams are attempting the same or similar projects and end up wasting resources. If this is known, these two teams could combine their efforts, one team could go do something else, or at the very least, they could negotiate a volume discount from a potential vendor.

There is also another type of redundancy—doing projects for systems that may be going away. For example, consider a department which is planning to do a project to write a series of reports for a particular system. As part of annual planning, it may be discovered that this system is obsolete, and it is no longer necessary or even feasible to develop reports for it. The department could therefore cancel the report-writing project and redirect the resources elsewhere.

Benefit 5: Project Sequencing

The next big advantage of discovering the demand in the organization is that it enables sequencing of complex efforts. When dealing with complex projects/programs, there is often a "correct" sequence to be followed in terms of which components to implement first. Also, it's hard to get all the budget, manpower, and bandwidth to do everything at once. By knowing the collective demand of the organization, the organization can arrive at this ideal sequencing of major projects.

Benefit 6: Project Greenlighting

Imagine a project that came through portfolio intake (see Chapter 4). It could take some time to understand where this project fits in the grand scheme of the organization. However, if this project has been reviewed and approved through a batch process earlier, execution can start immediately. That batch process is the annual planning process. And the process of *greenlighting* is defined as the accelerated approval of pre-vetted proposals known to be of importance. Why does this matter? In a large portfolio, it is likely that many proposals will be seen during the year and it is inefficient/time-consuming to perform a deep dive on each of them when initially presented. By reviewing the bulk of the organization's demand through an annual planning process, the projects which are vital to the company's strategic vision can be earmarked ahead of time and greenlighted when they are ready to be executed.

Benefit 7: Populating the Project Queue

Another advantage of the annual planning process is to maintain a project queue. In a typical portfolio there is always a chance that projects don't spend all the money they received for the year. In that situation it is always a good idea to keep a list of viable proposals which can absorb any leftover dollars that may get freed up due to underspend or termination of other projects. This list of viable projects that are waiting for resources is called the *project queue*. The annual planning process is how the project queue is created and populated.

Benefit 8: Rigorous Strategic Planning

Perhaps the biggest advantage of the annual planning process is that it reboots the strategic planning of the organization by sketching out a yearly journey to a strategic destination. It applies the blueprint of the strategic roadmap on top of the combined demand of the organization to identify which proposals are in line with overall corporate strategy. This is covered in greater depth in Chapter 15.

> KEY CONCEPT: Annual planning provides a host of benefits that generate tremendous value for the portfolio and all its stakeholders. When done right, annual planning is a strategic force multiplier.

CHAPTER SUMMARY

In this brief chapter we introduced the concept of annual planning and explained how it is foundational to a high-performing portfolio. We then examined the benefits of annual planning in detail—covering project discovery, project demand identification, project queues, and other aspects of the project portfolio. We finished this chapter by highlighting how annual planning is key to strategic planning. In the next chapter we'll see how we can get started with annual planning implementation using Smartsheet.

10

IMPLEMENTING PORTFOLIO ANNUAL PLANNING USING SMARTSHEET

INTRODUCTION

In the previous chapter we introduced portfolio annual planning and explained its importance as well as the benefits it offers to the organization. Ideally, every organization would like to execute annual planning and obtain these benefits. However, many, if not most, companies struggle to deliver on the promise of annual planning. This chapter will examine those factors in detail before proposing solutions to overcome these hurdles. In this chapter we will cover the following topics related to annual planning:

1. Examine the obstacles in performing annual planning
2. Explain how Smartsheet can be an effective vehicle for overcoming these obstacles
3. Explain the in-depth execution of annual planning through three passes
4. Outline a simple implementation of annual planning using the Smartsheet platform
5. List the key outputs of an annual planning exercise
6. List typical best practices that successful organizations have used in making annual planning work

KEY CONCEPT: Annual planning, when implemented correctly, is a vital activity with tremendous benefits.

THE OBSTACLES TO PERFORMING ANNUAL PLANNING

Before we get deep into the details of executing annual planning, it is important to understand why companies find this hard to do. By avoiding these missteps, the chances of success in this endeavor are significantly enhanced. The obstacles are as follows.

Obstacle 1: Choice of Platform

The overwhelming choice for most organizations is to use Microsoft Excel for portfolio execution. The limitations of this software become obvious very quickly in a complex exercise like annual planning. Microsoft Excel can (and does) fall short in many ways, causing lots of confusion and, ultimately, loss of confidence in annual planning.

Obstacle 2: Complex and/or Non-Uniform Process

In the absence of an active effort to spell out the process in a simple, consistent way, the teams within an organization tend to do their own thing in executing their annual planning deliverables. This, in turn, cascades the chaos.

Obstacle 3: No Trackability

Without a structured approach, annual planning tends to dissolve into long, "no-end-in-sight" process loops that drain and demotivate the organization. No one has any visibility into where the organization is in the cycle.

Obstacle 4: The Volume Problem

In most cases organizations are unprepared for the volume of projects they encounter during annual planning. Typically, this exceeds 100 projects—and this volume is overwhelming, especially when combined with the obstacles listed previously.

Obstacle 5: No Meaningful Outputs

Some companies struggle through the previously mentioned obstacles and perform annual planning at a significant investment of time and money. However, at the end of the exercise, there are no useful outputs from this exercise that can justify all the effort. Sometimes, the artifacts that may be produced are cast aside and are not referred to again until the next annual planning cycle. This creates a "why bother?" attitude in the organization leading to the whole exercise losing its efficacy.

> KEY CONCEPT: There are several well-known obstacles to successful annual planning. It is important to anticipate and mitigate these obstacles to ensure the benefits of annual planning.

HOW SMARTSHEET CAN BE AN EFFECTIVE VEHICLE FOR OVERCOMING THESE OBSTACLES

Annual planning is hobbled by several obstacles that prevent it from delivering on its benefits. The biggest obstacle may be the platform on which annual planning is performed. For most organizations, this platform is Excel. While Excel is simple and familiar, it is not an optimal choice for annual planning. In contrast, Smartsheet has many features which are a great fit for annual planning:

1. **Flexible platform:** Every organization's annual planning needs are different and the types of information captured and analyzed varies. With Smartsheet's flexible columns, the desired columns can be created rapidly to capture what is truly important.
2. **Ease of use:** User involvement is key to annual planning. If users are presented with a complicated data entry interface, they may not engage fully. Here's where Smartsheet's ubiquitous Excel-like interface is approachable for most users.

3. **Control of the data quality up front:** Data quality is a huge issue with annual planning. Often, the information capture is incomplete, and decisions made on such information is not particularly good. Smartsheet has a customizable data entry form that can ensure fields are mandatory where necessary.
4. **Visibility:** In a large, organization-wide effort like annual planning, visibility is the key to success. It is important to know which teams are doing what and how that affects others. Smartsheet has flexible reports and dashboards that make it possible to stay on top of this volume of data. Plus, there are configurable workflows that notify people of new project proposals in annual planning.
5. **Trackability with version control:** Annual planning is characterized by many iterations of the supplied data. Almost everything changes a few times—scope, budget, project names, etc. In this scenario, Smartsheet's built-in trackability of changes and audit trail capability are especially useful.

KEY CONCEPT: Several key obstacles to annual planning are eliminated using just the out-of-the-box features of Smartsheet. This enables speedy implementation and quicker value delivery.

THE EXECUTION OF ANNUAL PLANNING

At a high level, annual planning is done in three distinct iterations or *passes*. It is useful to break annual planning into passes as it helps the organization understand the process and keep track of the current status.

- **Pass One—Demand Gathering:** All the project owners participating in annual planning need to fill out a standard template. This is done to ensure that all the projects are captured and described in a uniform way.
- **Pass Two—Aggregation and Demand Analysis:** All the captured project demand data is aggregated, analyzed, and presented in views that enable the leaders to correctly decide on the priority of the projects.
- **Pass Three—Matching Demand to Supply:** There will always be more projects than we have people or money to do them. Somewhere, a line must be drawn. Projects above this line are the projects that will be executed over the next year. The rest of the project demand is preserved in a project queue so that if additional resources become available, they can be considered.

KEY CONCEPT: It's useful to structure the activity of annual planning into three distinct passes. This enables teams within the organization to understand where they are and what is happening.

Pass One of Annual Planning

As mentioned before, Pass One consists of gathering all the project demand in a standard template (the components of the template are explained in detail in the next section in this chapter). Here are the high-level steps in Pass One:

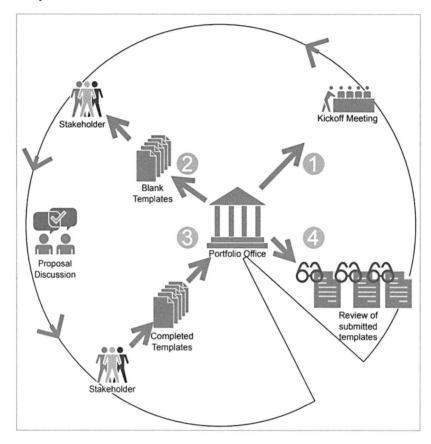

1. The portfolio manager typically starts Pass One by holding a kick-off meeting with all the department representatives and informs them that the annual planning is starting.
2. Then, the template is shared with the group and the important elements of the template are described so that everyone understands how to fill it out. The departments discuss internally what proposals to put forth as part of their demand.
3. The stakeholders fill out the templates accordingly and submit them back to the portfolio office.
4. The portfolio office reviews the submitted templates.

KEY CONCEPT: Pass One of annual planning is the stage where all the data is gathered—every project proposal is captured in a standard format.

Key Fields of the Planning Template

The planning template is the key document in the entire annual planning process. Here is a walk-through of the key fields found in the template:

- **Project Name:** The name of the project.
- **Project Description:** A concise description of what the project entails.
- **Program Name:** If the project belongs to a program, this field will capture it.
- **Project Manager:** Name of the project manager who will execute the project.
- **Project Sizing:** This field should have one of the following: Large, Medium, Small.
- **Continuing Project:** This yes/no field indicates if the project is continuing from last year or is a new project.
- **Executing Department:** Name of the department which would execute the project.
- **Assisting Departments:** Other departments whose participation is needed for this project. If no other department is needed, select N/A.
- **Project Owner/Customer/Stakeholder:** For whom are we doing this project? Typically, this field has the name of a senior business leader.
- **Stakeholder Department:** Name of the department to which the project owner belongs.
- **Project Priority:** This field describes how important this project is among all the other competing projects; typical values are High, Medium, and Low.
- **Project Justification/Benefits:** This field contains information on the benefits that would occur by doing the project. The field can receive a file upload.
- **Project Ranking:** This field is NOT added to the form but is added directly as a column to the sheet containing the list of projects and is filled in later to show the relative ranking of a project compared to the others. Each department may have to fill in the ranking field for their projects so that they can "draw the line" in Pass Three (described later in this chapter).

It is vital to capture these fields as accurately as possible to have an annual planning process that delivers value to the organization.

> KEY CONCEPT: It is important to use and enforce the above set of standard fields in annual planning because data quality can become a major obstacle without this standardization.

How to Implement Pass One of Annual Planning Using Smartsheet

1. First, create a workspace in Smartsheet and call it "Annual Planning Workspace" (for instructions on how to do that, refer to Chapter 3).
2. Go to the **Solution Center** and click on **Create**.
3. Click on **Form** and name it "Annual Planning Project Data Entry Form" when prompted.
4. Create all the form fields as listed in the previous section under "Pass One" (for detailed instructions on how to create and customize form fields, refer to Chapter 5).

5. This is how the "Annual Planning Project Data Entry Form" looks when the fields are created (not all the fields are shown as the form is rather long!):

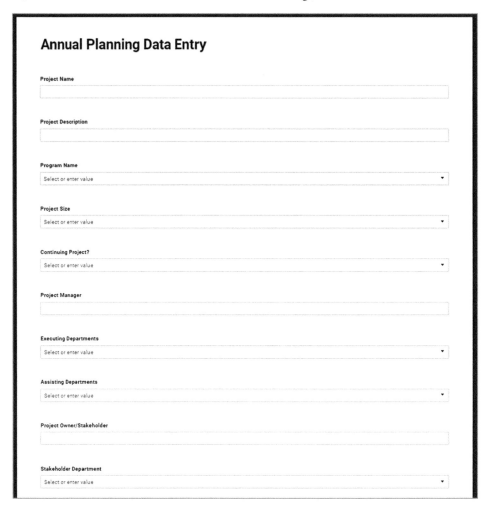

6. Click **File, Save** and then navigate to the Annual Planning Workspace location and click **OK**.
7. The next step is to distribute this form to everyone involved in annual planning. To do that, perform the following steps:
   a. Navigate to the "Annual Planning Data Entry form" sheet
   b. Click on **Forms** and then **Manage Forms**
   c. Click on the sole tile that appears to manage the form
   d. Within the form, click on the **Share Form** link that is visible in the top right-hand corner

e. A dialog box pops up:

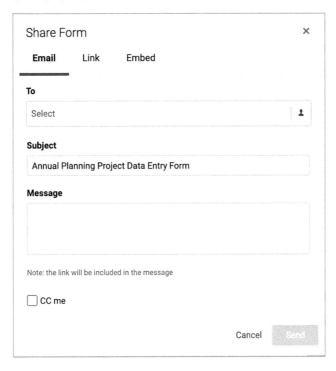

- Insert all the emails of the people participating in the annual planning activity in the **To** field.
- Include a message in the message field similar to "Please use this form to submit your project proposals for the annual planning activity that is under way."

f. Click **Send**.

Additional Fields in Pass One

1. As mentioned before, different organizations may find it necessary to collect different pieces of information during annual planning.
2. The basic set of fields is provided in the previous section and the portfolio manager can choose to add or remove fields from the form based on the organization's needs.
3. Whatever fields are added, it is recommended to adhere to the best practice of making the fields mandatory.
4. The following fields are considered advanced and will be explained at length in the next chapters:
   a. **Project Strategic Priority:** The contribution of the project to the strategic roadmap is described here. This is an important piece of information which needs to be sourced carefully to make optimal decisions in selection and funding.
   b. **Project Financials (Demand and ROI):** This field describes the total dollar demand of the project and the cost components of that demand. It also captures the expected return on investment (ROI).
   c. **Project Benefits:** This field spells out the benefits expected to accrue by executing the project.

KEY CONCEPT: Every organization needs to arrive at what data is important to capture during annual planning and then use that to determine what fields are present in the entry form.

Pointers for Success in Pass One

1. Before sharing the form and asking people to fill it out, provide guidance and examples showing project owners how to fill out the project fields (holding an annual planning workshop to walk stakeholders through the templates is a good idea).
2. Ensure that the standard name of the project is used and that this does not change. While it sounds obvious, experience has shown a lot of avoidable confusion created during annual planning by project names being inconstant during the various iterations (e.g., Website Redesign → Update Website → Remodel Intranet → Change Intranet).
3. Project description should be understandable to anyone even if they are removed from the domain and details.
4. All project fields should be mandatory. This eliminates the huge problem caused by incomplete data.
5. Wherever possible, the fields should be of the dropdown selection type to help standardization.
6. When filling out the Project Data Entry form, users should check the box at the bottom that says **Send me an email copy of my form submission** because this is then a unit of information that can be emailed between groups. The portfolio manager should also train users to click that box on the bottom as they submit proposals.
7. At the end of the form is a field for uploading a file. This file can contain information on the benefits that will occur by performing this project. It can also be used to show other related information to this project proposal. This one field can be left optional.

KEY CONCEPT: Adequate training incorporating the previous recommendations must be provided to users before the annual planning kickoff—this is the predominant factor that ensures success in annual planning.

Pass Two of Annual Planning

Pass Two of annual planning consists of aggregating all the demand that was gathered in Pass One and presenting it to the decision makers. If the project demand information was gathered using Excel, this task can be challenging because there is a need to sift through a considerable amount of material and then aggregate them to present to the executive decision makers in a concise manner. There could also be complex interconnections and duplicates in the collected project proposals. Using Smartsheet, however, Pass Two of annual planning is relatively easy to execute. The details are described as follows.

Execution of Pass Two

Aggregating the Gathered Information

In Pass One, all the participants in annual planning filled out their submissions using the Project Data Entry Form. All the submitted information is contained in the annual planning sheet. A sample is shown here:

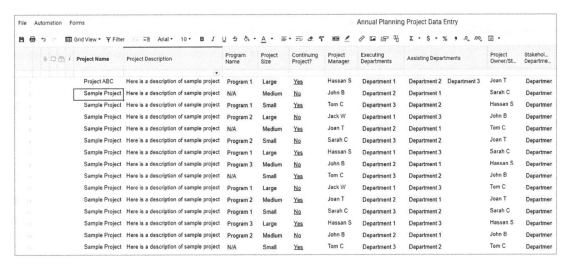

This is the major advantage of using Smartsheet for annual planning—the aggregation is automatically done. This would have taken a lot of effort if we were to use another tool, say Microsoft Excel, since the effort of aggregating several Excel files is significant.

> KEY CONCEPT: The major advantage of Smartsheet in annual planning is that it automatically aggregates submitted data which could be a significant effort with other tools like Excel.

The next task is to scrub the information to improve data quality:

1. Spot and remediate duplicate projects
2. Some project descriptions may be vague—these need to be fixed by the respective submitters
3. Program Name may need to be validated—for example, some people may have attributed their projects to the wrong program(s).
4. Validate the combo of "Project Manager & Executing Department"—for example, does John B. really work in Department 2 as the data shows?
5. Other data scrubs can be done depending on the kinds of data captured and the business rules in place.

> KEY CONCEPT: Despite adequate training, users tend to input bad data during annual planning, so it becomes necessary to scrub the data before making annual planning decisions.

Displaying the Aggregated Information

Annual planning yields a ton of data. It is not easy for an executive decision maker to assimilate all the data even if it is provided in list form that can be sorted. There are two vital *views* of the data that is useful to the organization:

1. **Aggregation Type 1:** Each department wants to see their own list of internal projects— projects that are owned and executed by that department. For example, the manager of Data Analytics wants to see the list of projects that was submitted by the team members in that department for the annual planning cycle.
2. **Aggregation Type 2:** Each department also wants to see a list of projects where other departments need input from their department. For example, the manager of Data Analytics wants to see the list of projects submitted by other IT departments that need the participation of Data Analytics.

Each department needs to account for both internal projects as well as projects that serve other departments. A department manager would like to see both their internal and external workloads before deciding on a resource split.

> KEY CONCEPT: There are two key data aggregation types that are useful in annual planning and together they offer important insights into project demand for each team within the organization.

Since an organization is typically composed of departments, all with their own list of proposed projects, we need to build a framework that can show the two views for each department.

Aggregation Type 1: How to Display Aggregated Annual Planning Data in Smartsheet

Smartsheet has a flexible report construct that lends itself very well for this purpose. Here are the steps to implement it:

1. Navigate to the Annual Planning Workspace that we just discussed.
2. Click **Create** and then **Report** in the pop-up box.
3. Name the report "Annual Planning 2020—Department 1's Projects."
4. Observe that the report is now created in the Annual Planning Workspace. To customize, click on the report.

5. The report opens:

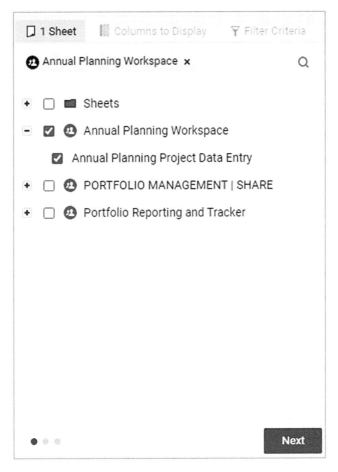

6. First, multiple workspaces appear as choices to report on. Since we are only interested in reporting on the annual planning projects, we just need to select the **Annual Planning Workspace** and then the **Annual Planning Project Data Entry** sheet under that. Click **Next**.
7. A list of columns appears as choices to select to include in our report—let's select all the columns.
8. Now we need to filter the rows. For this example, we are only interested in projects that Department 1 would *execute*. Here's how we filter for those:
   a. Click on **Filter Criteria** and then **Add a Condition**:

b. Click on **Select Field** and then **Executing Departments:**

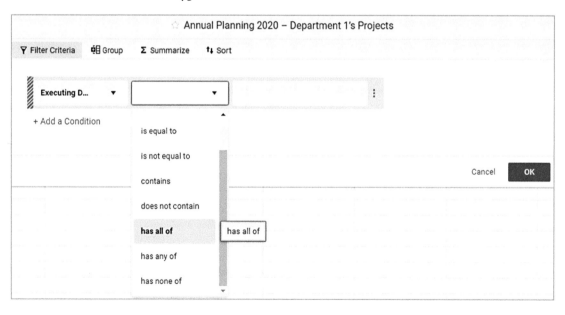

c. Click on **Select Type** and then **has all of:**

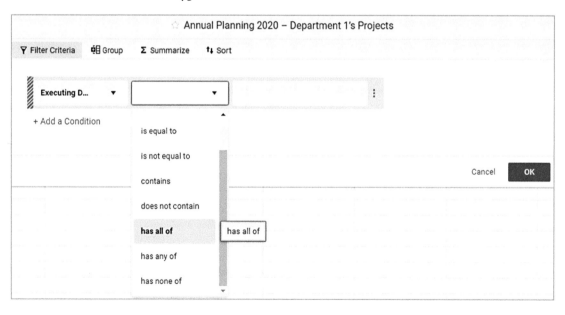

d. Click on **Select column option** and select **Department 1**:

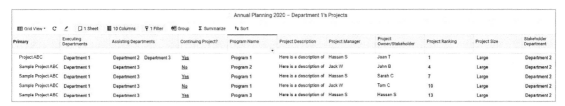

9. That's it! The report now shows all projects that are being executed by Department 1:

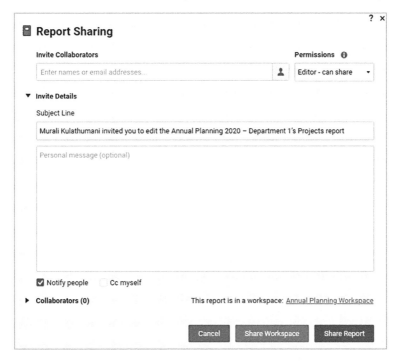

10. Click the **Share** button on the upper right of this report to get the following screen:

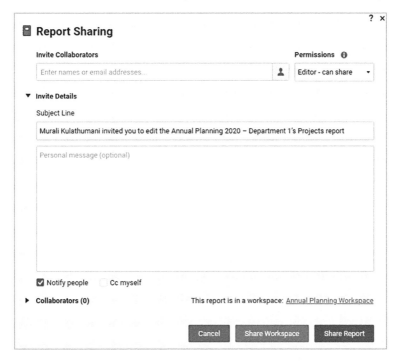

11. Enter the names of the Collaborators to make this report available to them. As people keep iterating through the annual planning process (adding/removing/editing projects), anyone who clicks on that report sees the latest information—another major win in annual planning.

All of these steps show how to display the project proposals for a particular department (Department 1 in this case). To complete this for all departments, multiple reports will have to be generated, but with one small difference:

- In Step 8d (page 145), change the **Select Column option** to **Department 2**, **Department 3**, etc.
- Continue the above pattern until there are separate reports for all the departments participating in annual planning.
- Share the reports with the annual planning team (whoever's involved with annual planning).

This concludes how to conduct Aggregation Type 1—the report that shows all the projects owned by a particular department.

> KEY CONCEPT: Aggregation Type 1 displays all the annual planning efforts owned by a particular department.

Next, we'll move on to Aggregation Type 2. As we mentioned before, each department (say Department 1) wants to see not only internal projects belonging to Department 1 (this is Aggregation Type 1) but also a list of projects where other departments need the input/participation of Department 1. This is typical of certain departments that function as shared services. For example, the manager of Cloud Infrastructure wants to see the list of projects owned by other IT departments that need participation (and expenditure of time/effort) by Cloud Infrastructure. This kind of aggregation of information during annual planning is called Aggregation Type 2.

Aggregation Type 2: How to Display Aggregated Annual Planning Data in Smartsheet

1. Navigate to the Annual Planning Workspace.
2. Click **Create** and **Report** in the pop-up shown.
3. Name the Report "Annual Planning 2020—Projects that need Department 1's participation."
4. Observe that the report is now created in the Annual Planning Workspace. To customize, click on the report.
5. The report opens.
6. First, multiple workspaces appear as choices to report on. Since we are only interested in reporting on the annual planning projects, we just need to select the **Annual Planning Workspace** and then the **Annual Planning Project Data Entry** sheet under that. Click **Next**.
7. A list of columns appears as choices to select to include in our report—let's select all the columns.
8. Now we need to filter the rows. For this example, we're only interested in projects that Department 1 would *assist* on. Here's how we filter for those:
    a. Click on **Filter Criteria** and then **Add a Condition**
    b. Click on **Select Field** and select **Assisting Departments** (refer to the screenshot from *Aggregation Type 1 Step 8b* on page 144 but notice a different field would now be selected).
    c. Click on **Select Type** and then **has all of**.
    d. Click on **Select column option** and select **Department 1**.

9. That's it! The report now shows all projects that are being assisted by Department 1:

Sheet Name	Primary	Executing Departments	Assisting Departments	Continuing Project?	Program Name	Project Description	Project Manager	Project Ranking	Project Size	Project Owner/Stakeh...	Stakeholder Department
Annual Plan	Sample Project ABC	Department 2	Department 1	No	N/A	Here is a descrip	John B	2	Medium	Sarah C	Department 3
Annual Plan	Sample Project ABC	Department 2	Department 1	Yes	N/A	Here is a descrip	Joan T	5	Medium	Tom C	Department 3
Annual Plan	Sample Project ABC	Department 2	Department 1	No	Program 3	Here is a descrip	John B	8	Medium	Hassan S	Department 3
Annual Plan	Sample Project ABC	Department 2	Department 1	Yes	Program 2	Here is a descrip	Joan T	11	Medium	Joan T	Department 3
Annual Plan	Sample Project ABC	Department 2	Department 1	No	Program 2	Here is a descrip	John B	14	Medium	John B	Department 3

Projects that need Department 1's Participation — Grid View · C · 1 Sheet · 11 Columns · 1 Filter · Group · Σ Summarize · Sort

10. Click the **Share** button on the upper right of this report to get the screen shown in *Aggregation Type 1 Step 10* on page 145.
11. Enter the names of the Collaborators to make this report available to them. As people keep iterating through the annual planning process (adding/removing/editing projects), anyone who clicks on that report sees the latest information.

All the above steps showed how to display the project proposals requesting input from a particular department (Department 1 in this case). To complete this for all departments, multiple reports will have to be generated as shown previously, but with one small difference:

- In Step 8d (page 145), change the **Select Column option** to **Department 2**, **Department 3**, etc.
- Continue the above pattern until there are separate reports for all the departments participating in annual planning.
- Share the reports with the annual planning team (whoever's involved with annual planning).

KEY CONCEPT: Aggregation Type 2 displays all the annual planning projects which need the participation of a particular department. The projects themselves are owned by other departments.

We just covered how to aggregate projects by department. Here are two other useful ways to aggregate projects during annual planning:

- Aggregate Projects by Project Owner/Stakeholder
- Aggregate Projects by Stakeholder Department

Although not shown in detail, the above aggregations are easy to do in Smartsheet by following the approach explained for Aggregation by Department.

The Annual Planning Portal

One best practice is to put hyperlinks to all the above aggregation lists on one dashboard and call that the **Annual Planning Portal**. This greatly facilitates annual planning because the biggest obstacle to this process is that people are often unsure about where to go and what to do. One dedicated Smartsheet dashboard that has hyperlinks to all the possible information is a huge step towards clarity and it provides the users with confidence in the annual planning process.

KEY CONCEPT: A Smartsheet dashboard dedicated to annual planning would be a great single-source portal for all the teams engaged in annual planning.

Pass Three of Annual Planning

After gathering all the information, it is finally time to make some decisions. It is well known that there will be more projects than resources. A line will have to be drawn, with those above the line going forward and those below the line going to backlog for the time being. So how exactly is this done? A basic approach is outlined below:

1. In Pass One, we collected the basic information for each project in a sheet called "Annual Planning Project Data Entry."
2. We now add an "Effort" field for each project—these fields capture the people-weeks of effort needed from each department for that project. Consider the following example:
   a. Project ABC is owned by Department 1 but needs collaboration/participation from Departments 2 and 3.
   b. All three departments go ahead and make a fairly good estimate of their respective efforts needed for Project ABC—see **Effort Department 1, 2, 3** columns:

Sheet Name	Primary	Executing Departments	Assisting Departments		Effort Department 1	Effort Department 2	Effort Department 3
Annual Plan	Project ABC	Department 1	Department 2	Department 3	12 wks	8 wks	6 wks

   c. Remember that these are "person-weeks." For example, if the project takes two people four weeks each, the total is $2 \times 4 = 8$ person-weeks of effort, just shown as 8 weeks.
   d. So, if these three departments decide to go forward with Project ABC, they each have committed 12 weeks, 8 weeks, and 6 weeks, respectively, from their resource pools.
      i. How do we estimate the amount of effort that is available in a resource pool?
      ii. A rough rule of thumb is that each full-time resource contributes 52 weeks of person hours each year.
      iii. Once vacation, holidays, and operational effort capacity are removed, a person may only have about 40 weeks of effort left (this varies from organization to organization).
      iv. Therefore, a small department with 10 people onboard has an annual capacity of 400 person-weeks available.
   e. Project ABC was ranked #1, so the departments next move to Project XYZ (Rank #2) and commit the hours needed.
   f. Eventually, the departments run out of capacity and that is where the *draft line* is drawn.
   g. It is not the final line because there will invariably be negotiations, reshuffling of priorities, adjustments to effort, etc. Plus, some departments may decide to overallocate, expecting future additions of staff or hiring consultants.
   h. Despite all that, the major advantage of this process is that departments become aware of their approximate capacity and understand how many projects they can realistically commit to doing.

i. The final step to the process above is to introduce an additional field called **Committed?** in the annual planning Project Entry sheet, with only **Yes** or **No** as the options. This records with finality the projects that will be executed during the year and allows everyone to see which projects are moving forward and which are not.

An overview of Pass Three is shown here:

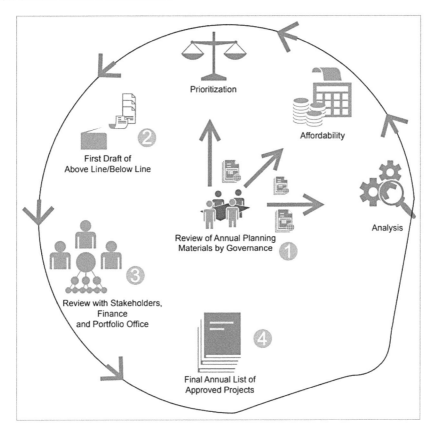

KEY OUTPUTS OF THE ANNUAL PLANNING EXERCISE

The annual planning exercise is considered successful if the following outputs can be generated:

- **Ranked list of projects:** A list of projects ranked according to importance—the higher ranking projects are approved and form the annual plan
- **Annual plan:** A list of projects that have been approved to go forward in the next year
- **Project description snapshot:** A brief explanation of what each project will accomplish, which department owns the project, and who is the project owner
- **Project dependencies:** Which projects depend on which mix of departments to be completed successfully

Additional outputs are certainly possible, but these outputs are considered as a basic requirement for any annual planning activity.

BEST PRACTICES FOR SUCCESSFUL ANNUAL PLANNING

1. Launch Annual Planning Exercise with a Comprehensive Workshop/Training

The success of the annual planning exercise is closely dependent upon meaningful participation by the organization. Participation in annual planning, in turn, is greatly facilitated by a comprehensive workshop that addresses all the questions surrounding annual planning. This workshop is also an appropriate venue to share and demonstrate how to use the various Smartsheet templates and other artifacts for the annual planning exercise. The workshop should also cover the timeline of the annual planning exercise. It's even more effective to archive this training session, along with relevant resources for later reference and use by the organization.

2. Follow Consistent Treatment for Existing Projects

Few portfolios start from a blank slate during annual planning. What should be done with existing projects? Should existing projects be prioritized along with new projects or should they be kept whole (funded for their full demand for the next year) and the remaining funds shared among new projects? Here are some recommendations:

- Existing projects should be included in the exercise but be given higher priority compared to new projects because of the money already invested in them—but only if the existing projects are performing well. If an existing project is underperforming, it should not be automatically elevated over new projects.
- If an existing project is significantly underperforming, annual planning could provide a venue to kill such a project.
- If an existing project is going forward into next year's annual planning, it is important to understand how much residual effort is left to complete the project.

3. Navigate Annual Planning with an Existing Enterprise Portfolio Management Tool

This whole chapter describes how to perform annual planning entirely outside of an project portfolio management (PPM) tool. But how does annual planning take place when the organization already has in place an established enterprise portfolio management tool? Based on the maturity of the organization, two choices are possible:

- Choice 1:
    - If the organization is comfortable working within the enterprise PPM tool, consider using the native scenario planning features of the PPM tool. This will work for only a few organizations since it requires a high degree of portfolio maturity. Most organizations find it daunting to use the enterprise PPM tool for annual planning.
- Choice 2:
    - Experience shows that the rank and file at most companies are more comfortable working on annual planning in an Excel-like tool such as Smartsheet.
    - In this case, orchestrate all the annual planning outside the portfolio tool (using Smartsheet, as explained in this chapter), and enter the final outputs into the enterprise PPM tool when annual planning.

4. Guard Against Bad Data and Hold People Accountable

The biggest problem during annual planning is that people will submit project data that is wildly inaccurate (imagine completely incorrect timelines, effort estimates, and benefits). In their defense, the project owners would say, "It's too far in the future to predict accurately. This is my best guess for now. Fund me so I can submit accurate estimates." The best defense against this is to periodically revisit the data and hold people accountable. In addition, a well-functioning annual planning process inspires confidence and reinforces the need for people to put forth estimates that are grounded in reality.

5. Preserve Annual Planning Continuity by Avoiding a Total Reboot Each Year

One of the biggest complaints about annual planning is that the organization seems to do a complete reset each year, learning nothing and using nothing from similar massive efforts in past years. It has frequently been compared to *boiling the ocean*—every year. However, it may not be necessary to do a complete new boil each year. A well-crafted process will allow for a more modest and easier effort each year because you are only managing the changes from year to year. Another huge factor in preserving continuity is to not change templates and approaches each year. Adequate change management should be in place where any changes each year are minimal and only what is truly necessary.

6. Ensure Follow-Through for the Annual Planning Exercise

Another frequent criticism of the annual planning process is that little if any follow-through is conducted regarding the artifacts seen during the process. In short, after the annual planning period finishes, things go back to how they were and the whole exercise seems to have been for nothing. This seems especially true for projects that did not get funded.

The only remedy for this situation is a conscious decision on the part of portfolio managers and their stakeholders to keep revisiting the carefully made annual plan and use it as a key input to drive portfolio decisions. For example, an effective annual plan will have a queue of solid project proposals that have been vetted and are awaiting funding—these should be the first place to invest any funds that become available during the year. At every possible opportunity, the annual plan should be demonstrated as the master plan which drives portfolio decisions. This serves to underscore the importance of annual planning to the rest of the organization and, in turn, drives increased participation.

7. Ensure the Link Between Strategy and Annual Planning

One of the characteristics of annual planning is that it shines a spotlight on the performance (or absence!) of the strategic planning function in the enterprise. A strategic planning process that is not grounded in the actual direction or roadmap of how the enterprise plans to transform itself will be found wanting when it is time to map project proposals to it.

The remedy for this situation lies in recognizing that effective strategic planning needs to be in place for annual planning and portfolio management to work. Well before the annual planning cycle starts, the organization needs to invest in the process and socialization necessary to produce a stable strategic plan that extends at least for the next few years. Having a well socialized plan in place along with advocates for each strategic priority will vastly simplify the annual planning process and succeed in matching proposals to key drivers of strategy. This is addressed in more detail in Section III—The Advanced Portfolio.

8. Preserve Each Year's Annual Planning Submissions for Reuse Next Year

Every annual planning exercise concludes with a sizable number of projects that did not get funded. These projects either need to try to get funding during the year or come back at the next annual planning exercise looking for funds. A significant number of projects do have to come back at the next year's planning session.

For those projects, it would be a much simpler effort if the various departments could access their previous year's submission (for any particular project), make some edits and updates, and then resubmit the same project for consideration at this year's annual planning exercise. To enable this scenario, the project office needs to make an active effort to capture all the submissions from the annual planning exercise and then make it available in an easy-to-navigate manner for all the stakeholders.

The Smartsheet approach described in this chapter is ideal for preserving last year's submissions and can easily be filtered by adding a field called "Annual Planning Year" which captures that year's information.

> KEY CONCEPT: Annual planning can deliver significant value to the enterprise but there are some nuances involved in running it effectively. The best practices listed above are gathered from implementations at several iconic companies and should be guideposts to any team setting up annual planning.

CHAPTER SUMMARY

Annual planning is a complex and time-intensive exercise. If executed well, it is a great enabler for a high-performing portfolio. To do it right, it must be easy to use and align well with the strategic roadmap of the enterprise. Annual planning also must be structured correctly to help the decision makers pick the right projects within the available sum of funds. In this chapter we began by exploring the importance of annual planning in some depth and covered the different angles in which it promotes the functioning of the portfolio. We then detailed the three distinctive iterations (passes) through which annual planning is performed. We covered data aggregation, compilation, and packaging practices and explained why these are integral to producing the right decisions from portfolio governance. We also detailed how to actually perform the three passes of annual planning using Smartsheet. We finished with a list of the key outputs of annual planning and best practices that have been proven to work in facilitating annual planning in various organizations.

SECTION III

Implementing the
Advanced Portfolio

SECTION III INTRODUCTION: THE ADVANCED PORTFOLIO

WHAT IS AN ADVANCED PORTFOLIO?

Up to this point in the book, we have been discussing the need for a portfolio and how to build a basic portfolio. As we saw over the past seven chapters, the *basic* portfolio will deliver significant capability to an organization that had no portfolio in the first place.

Portfolio management is a journey, and some organizations are ready to go to the next milestone in capability. These organizations have implemented a basic portfolio, seen its benefits firsthand, and are now looking to enhance this value proposition even further. That's where the *advanced* portfolio comes into play. The advanced portfolio takes the basic portfolio to another level, adding three key dimensions:

1. Money
2. Benefits
3. Strategic roadmap

In the next five chapters we examine what goes into the making of an advanced portfolio. We also examine how to implement these capabilities using Smartsheet.

11

BUDGET MANAGEMENT IN THE ADVANCED PORTFOLIO

INTRODUCTION

The essential function of a portfolio is to manage the budget allotted to it and produce the best outcomes with that budget. However, the management of portfolio funds can be a complex exercise that needs the portfolio manager to balance several factors. In this chapter we examine the following aspects related to portfolio funding:

1. Introduction to budgets—why use budgets in the portfolio?
2. Discussion of the annual funding cycle and the two types of investment dollars typically encountered in the funding cycle
3. The supply side challenges imposed by the annual funding cycle
4. The demand side challenges imposed by the annual funding cycle
5. A discussion of the best practices, including run-hot factor, allocation, release, and turnback features, to mitigate both supply side and demand side constraints
6. A discussion of different portfolio funding models commonly found in organizations

> KEY CONCEPTS: Portfolio budget management is a key function in advanced portfolios—it deals with managing the money spent in the portfolio to produce the best possible outcome.

WHY USE BUDGETS IN PORTFOLIO MANAGEMENT?

Before we get into the details of portfolio budget management, it's useful to examine why budgets are used in the first place. There are two broad approaches when it comes to the portfolio and money:

1. **The fixed cost/sunk cost approach:** This approach says that the portfolio/project teams are essentially *fixed costs*—that is, the organization has already committed to a certain (approximate) sum of money in hiring and maintaining the teams thvat perform the projects in the portfolio. Having committed to that money, the thinking goes, there is little to be gained by measuring how much money is being spent on each project. "We're doing this basket of projects for this total of $X million, let's just get it done," is sort of the motto here. It's also worth noting that keeping track of money is rather difficult if the basics (covered in the previous section) are not in place. This approach is suitable for portfolios that are just starting on the journey to advanced capability.

2. **The variable cost/measure the money approach:** This second approach believes that money is a valuable portfolio resource and worth tracking. It emphasizes that there is significant value in directing money towards successful projects and away from failing ones. To accomplish this, it is necessary to determine a framework to allocate money towards individual projects (the *project budget*) and manage the spend of this money (*project actuals*) through the year. When the project budget and project actuals are aggregated, they become the *portfolio budget* and *portfolio actuals*. The organizations that manage portfolio budgets tend to be more advanced in their portfolio capabilities and typically have some interface with the finance department within their company.

This chapter is geared towards organizations that want to implement portfolio budgeting.

THE ANNUAL PORTFOLIO FUNDING CYCLE

As we get into the details of portfolio budget management, it's useful to consider how the portfolio funding cycle works. Typically, a portfolio's allocation of funds for any given year is decided during the annual planning activity that occurs during the previous year. For example, the portfolio budget for 2021 is decided from the annual planning activity that usually happens at the end of 2020. As part of that activity, Finance sets aside a sum of money, divided into operating expenses (OPEX) and capital expenses (CAPEX). What are OPEX and CAPEX? Here is a basic definition: an operating expense, operating expenditure, operational expense, operational expenditure, or OPEX is an ongoing cost for running a product, business, or system.[1] Its counterpart, CAPEX, is the cost of developing or providing non-consumable parts for the product or system. For example, the purchase of a photocopier involves CAPEX, while the annual paper, toner, power, and maintenance costs represents OPEX.[2] For larger systems like businesses, OPEX may also include the cost of workers and facility expenses such as rent and utilities.

Therefore, the portfolio starts the year with an OPEX and CAPEX budget. The next task is to allocate these to various projects in the portfolio and manage their actual expenditures (commonly referred to as *actuals*) to stay within budget. The ideal end of the portfolio cycle entails finishing the year with as little variance to the budget as possible.

> KEY CONCEPT: OPEX and CAPEX are the two kinds of funds that need to be tracked and managed in portfolio budget management. The annual portfolio funding cycle is the yearly cadence of estimating and allocating these funds to the portfolio.

The Challenges in Managing the Portfolio Funding Cycle

The constraints encountered in optimizing portfolio spending during the year can be divided into two categories:

- **Supply constraints:** These are the cause of supply challenges, which refer to the consequences of actions and decisions taken by the portfolio manager in supplying funds to projects.
- **Demand constraints:** These are the cause of demand challenges, which refer to actions and decisions on the part of the projects which have an impact on the portfolio funding objectives.

Here is a list of the supply and demand challenges which the portfolio office needs to overcome to maximize the throughput of the portfolio in any given funding year.

Supply Challenge #1: Allocating Too Much Too Soon

Consider a situation where a handful of projects (say ten) were approved for funding during annual planning. Furthermore, consider that each of these projects had a projected demand of $1M for the year. If the portfolio decides to fully fund these projects in the beginning of the year, all the portfolio funds would be used. No funds would be available if an important new project appears for funding.

Furthermore, as seen in most portfolios, it is quite unlikely that the ten projects would spend according to their initial estimate (see Demand Challenge #1 below). At least some of them will underspend, leading to a surplus. This surplus may come late in the year, making it unusable. Thus, the supply decision of deciding to allocate all the requested demand may result in the portfolio funding fewer impactful efforts and falling short of its optimal output.

Supply Challenge #2: Allocating Funds Too Late

Consider an alternative scenario where the portfolio governance is wary of committing all funds too early. This wariness might result in a risk averse strategy where the portfolio tends to hold on to the money in anticipation of more projects approaching the portfolio for money. This may result in the portfolio office declining to fund some projects early in the year. However, there is a point beyond which there isn't enough runway in the year to execute, even if the project receives funding. By holding on to the money for too long, the portfolio might hobble itself by not being able to deliver as much impact as it otherwise may have.

Demand Challenge #1: Underspend in Approved Projects

Projects, even well-managed ones, tend to underspend relative to their budget in any given year (it's a separate problem that projects tend to spend more than their overall budget over the life of the project). The reasons for underspend include slow ramp-up, delayed availability of key resources, and faulty/optimistic estimation of work effort. The end result is that projects hold on to funds far too long into the year. Once it's finally realized that all the money won't be spent, a decision is then made to "return" the funds, but this is often done so late that this money is not usable in any practical sense in the portfolio. The portfolio then ends the year with a surplus, resulting in a surprise for Finance, and with the unused money representing decreased value attainment for the portfolio.

Demand Challenge #2: Overspend in Approved Projects

While projects in general underspend, there will always be those projects that spectacularly overspend their annual budgets. This causes a diversion of funds from other projects and/or reduced funds for new projects. Unless the overspend is caused by valid reasons, such as an expansion in scope (and, consequently, an expansion in benefits), this creates a less-than-optimal outcome for the portfolio, which is now unable to achieve as much as previously planned. An additional challenge for the portfolio manager is to communicate the impacts of the above challenges to portfolio governance, which is ultimately responsible for making portfolio decisions regarding funding. The portfolio manager needs to advise governance at every step to overcome these pitfalls and enable the portfolio to deliver maximum possible value to the enterprise.

> KEY CONCEPT: There are both supply-based and demand-based challenges in managing the portfolio funding cycle.

Best Practices to Optimize Portfolio Funding Decisions

As we saw in the previous section, it is almost an art to make the right funding decisions at the right time to get the optimal output from the portfolio. However, there are a set of best practices, which greatly increase the odds of success in getting the optimal throughput from the portfolio in any given year.

Best Practice #1: Allocation versus Release

Consider a project seeking $100K in funding. In a basic portfolio (or where there is no portfolio), this project would receive the $100K and that would be the end of it. This effectively removes $100K from the portfolio, and all the challenges mentioned before would apply—namely, the risk remains that the project may not spend the money and may come back at a later time looking to return it. Now, consider a situation where the $100K was earmarked/allocated but only $50K was released. This achieves the following:

- Removes $50K from the portfolio (but keeps track that a total of $100K is needed for this project) and prevents that money from being mistakenly committed to another project, which may lead to an overspend situation for the portfolio.
- Preserves $50K for potential deployment for high priority needs that may arise.

By this method, the entire sum of $100K is not locked up, and the risk of potential underspend is mitigated by holding on to the $50K for use on other projects. A secondary benefit of this best practice is that it compels the project to come back to portfolio governance for additional funds, during which time project performance and spend can be reviewed. It is harder to do that once all the funds have been released. Implementing this best practice provides the portfolio with an additional level of control in managing the flow of funds.

Best Practice #2: Managing the Run-Hot Factor

Consider a typical portfolio where the projects underspend their budget in any given year. A portfolio with a $10 million budget that distributes its funds fully to various projects may only see that $8 million of the money was used at the end of the year. Now, imagine that the portfolio, while still only having the same budget of $10 million, approves projects worth $12 million. Again, with the traditional underspend effect in place, the portfolio may only see $10 million of actuals at the end of the year, which is also the exact amount of money that the portfolio had to spend in the first place. Thus, by compensating for the underspend with an extra outlay of money, the portfolio ensured that all funds were deployed to maximum effect. This extra outlay is known as the *run-hot* factor and is a useful maximizing technique when there is a stable, reliable trend of underspend in projects. One note of caution: the spend must still be monitored throughout the year to ensure that the spending trend is controlled in line with the run-hot assumptions and that the portfolio does not spend beyond its budget.

Best Practice #3: Maintain a Queue of Viable Projects

A portfolio that conducts annual planning will typically produce a list of prioritized projects. The projects at the top of the list are funded until the budget limit is reached and the *line* is drawn. The projects below the line constitute the *queue*. The projects in the queue are still viable, useful projects but will need additional funds (beyond what was given to the portfolio initially) in order to execute. Now, consider funds becoming available during the year due to underspend in other projects. The queue provides a list of viable proposals which can then be immediately funded. Portfolios that do not have a queue will have to launch a hurried search for project ideas to deploy their unspent funds and may settle for less-than-viable options. What's more, the money will have to stay unused until a suitable project is found.

Best Practice #4: Use the Turnback Feature Actively

A project is not inclined to return funds on its own in a timely manner, even if it knows that the funds will not be used. There is a tendency to hold on to the funds, sometimes driven by the mistaken belief that the funds will be carried over into the next year. However, there is a term in portfolio management that denotes the return of funds from the project back to the portfolio reserve—*turnback*. The novel concept that allocated funds can be returned may itself be unknown in the organization. The portfolio manager needs to make everyone aware of this concept and why it is useful (to put unused funds to work while there is still time left in the year to deliver something tangible). The portfolio manager must monitor the spending of projects and actively direct projects with surplus to turn back funds which can then be deployed elsewhere.

Best Practice #5: Terminate Underperforming Projects

Not all projects perform well, despite the best efforts of the project managers. In fact, there are several studies/surveys that indicate that a high percentage of projects overall will underperform. If this is a prevailing trend in projects, why not use it to the portfolio's advantage? The portfolio should double down on winners (well-performing projects) and cut its losses (underperformers). The money saved by terminating underperformers should be reallocated to either projects that are on track that need more funds or reallocated to new, viable projects.

Best Practice #6: Deploy Earned Value Management (EVM)

One of the most powerful tools in managing a portfolio is EVM. EVM is an objective indicator that measures time and budget performance of a project in terms of concrete deliverables. It offers a high degree of predictability of a project's future performance based on its past performance. Although an extensive treatment of EVM is beyond the scope of this book, here's what EVM can do from a portfolio management perspective:

- Indicates if a project within the portfolio is performing on time and on budget
- Indicates if a project within the portfolio is holding on to more funds than it needs
- Indicates how much a project will cost at the end of the year with its current spending trend

Tracking and precisely delivering this information enables the portfolio manager to make correct decisions on portfolio funding and maximize the output of the portfolio.

Best Practice #7: Partner with Finance Closely

Finance is the source for all funds in an organization. A successful portfolio will partner with Finance closely and leverage that relationship to its benefit. Consider a situation where a portfolio takes advantage of a run-hot dynamic and funds projects in excess of its budget. Now, if the projects spend as planned (none of the projects spend less than planned) and they all perform well (no underperformers that can be terminated), this may actually create a situation where the portfolio runs a risk of spending beyond its budget. However, if Finance has been informed well in advance that this could happen at the end of the year, it may be able to direct underspend from another part of the organization and meet this potential overspend, while still balancing the overall organization's budget. Alternatively, consider a situation where the portfolio will close out the year with an underspend. If the portfolio can inform Finance of this possibility ahead of time, Finance can do the above mitigation in reverse—take the unspent funds from the portfolio and match it with overspend elsewhere in the organization, again resulting in a net neutral budget outcome for the organization.

Best Practice #8: Monitor OPEX and CAPEX separately

In organizations that differentiate between OPEX and CAPEX (most large organizations do this), there is an added challenge of ensuring that both OPEX and CAPEX usage is optimized and spent according to plan. Consider a project that is underspending its OPEX allocation by $100K and overspending its CAPEX allocation by $100K. Taken together, the two variances cancel out and show that the project is exactly on target and there is no problem to remediate. However, the reality is that the portfolio office has not one but two different problems to solve. The solution here consists of matching OPEX and CAPEX variance separately across the portfolio with the hope of canceling out as much as possible. In the event of irreducible variances, the only option left is to go to Best Practice #7, which is to work with Finance by giving them plenty of notice so they can try to mitigate the variance by looking for opportunities in the rest of the organization.

> KEY CONCEPT: These portfolio funding best practices are proven strategies for ensuring that the portfolio delivers the best possible outcome for the money spent in each funding cycle.

PORTFOLIO FUNDING MODEL

What are the ways in which a portfolio can be funded? There are a couple of models:

- **Centralized portfolio:** The portfolio is given a separate budget from Finance with the expectation that the funds will be disbursed to project proposals in line with the portfolio's objective. For example, consider a large enterprise with several portfolios—a functional portfolio, infrastructure portfolio, strategic portfolio, etc. The strategic portfolio would accept strategic proposals for funding whereas an infrastructure portfolio would only focus on proposals seeking to add infrastructure to the enterprise. This model creates a "strong" portfolio which is able to drive compliance with portfolio policies and procedures because the projects have to approach the portfolio for funds.
- **Distributed portfolio:** In this model, the departments already have the project funds given to them as part of their departmental budgets. The portfolio office only provides nominal oversight and a token approval to use funds that are already with the departments. This model creates a "weak" portfolio—the portfolio has little leverage over departments since they already have the funds. It is an uphill climb for the portfolio manager to screen proposals and insist on performance criteria for the projects.

> KEY CONCEPT: A portfolio's funding model can either be centralized or distributed based on how much autonomy is given to individual projects in the portfolio.

PORTFOLIO BUDGET MANAGEMENT IMPLEMENTATION USING SMARTSHEET

Solution Approach

Design a basic budget template in Smartsheet as shown in Figure 11.1, with the following features (alternatively, the Budget Management Template Set can be downloaded from Smartsheet which contains the sheet shown in Figure 11.1):

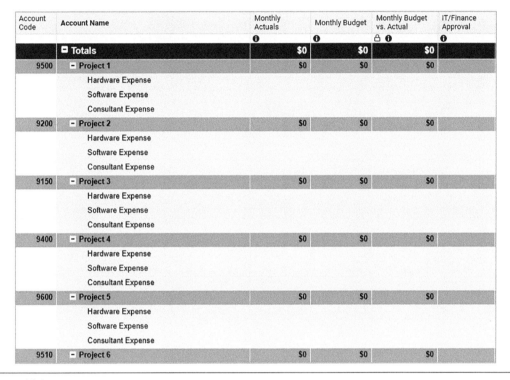

Figure 11.1

1. Every project's expenses are broken out into these categories of expenses:
   a. Hardware
   b. Software
   c. Consultant expenses
   (The above are just examples. An organization should create their categories after consulting with Finance.)
2. There are a few standard columns as explained below:
   a. Account Code
      i. This code is typically provided by Finance.
   b. Monthly Actuals
      i. This column is populated with the money spent this month for each project—this can be sourced from Finance.
   c. Monthly Budget
      i. This column is populated with the money expected to be spent this month for each project—this has to be populated by the project team.

      d. Month's Budget versus Actuals
          i. This is a comparison of the previous two columns.
      e. IT/Finance Approval
          i. This column tracks whether the amounts are approved.
          ii. It typically involves review by IT/Finance.

Figure 11.2 shows an example of what the budget template would look like when populated. This one shows the project budgets for the month of January. Similarly, for each month, there would be a sheet showing project budgets for that month. All of these sheets are combined into a master view as explained in the process below.

Account Code	Account Name		Monthly Actuals	Monthly Budget	Monthly Budget vs Actual	IT/Finance Approved
			❶	❶	🔒 ❶	❶
	⊟ **Totals**		**$1,094,038**	**$1,027,449**	**-$66,589**	
9500	⊟ Project 1		$163,319	$55,506	-$107,813	
		Hardware Expense	$48,446	$52,506	$4,060	Approved
		Software Expense	$2,237	$0	-$2,237	Approved
		Consultant Expense	$112,636	$3,000	-$109,636	Approved
9200	⊟ Project 2		$137,306	$167,984	$30,678	
		Hardware Expense	$118,172	$150,619	$32,447	Approved
		Software Expense	$1,073	$0	-$1,073	Approved
		Consultant Expense	$18,061	$17,365	-$696	Approved
9150	⊟ Project 3		$105,000	$96,000	-$9,000	
		Hardware Expense	$0	$0	$0	
		Software Expense	$105,000	$96,000	-$9,000	Submitted
		Consultant Expense	$0	$0	$0	
9400	⊞ Project 4		$164,434	$170,866	$6,432	
9600	⊞ Project 5		$185,015	$165,014	-$20,001	
9510	⊞ Project 6		$151,313	$203,640	$52,327	
9940	⊞ Project 7		$187,651	$168,439	-$19,212	

Figure 11.2

How the Whole Portfolio Budgeting Process Would Work

1. Before IT and Finance leadership approve the budget for a project, that project (say "Project 1") has to provide the composition of their budget by month and category.
    a. For example, Project 1 plans to procure consulting services (say Hadoop) for $100K in April and hardware (say Data Appliance) for $200K in May.
2. The details of the project are then added to the Project Expense Tracker budget template (see Figure 11.2).
3. Once a month, a budget review meeting is held to compare budget versus actuals for all projects.
4. The top-level report shown in Figure 11.3 pulls the finances of all projects (for all months) together in one place for easy review (this report can either be built from the ground up or downloaded as part of the Budget Management Template Set from Smartsheet).
5. The project actuals can be imported from whatever system Finance is using (Oracle, SAP, etc.).
6. At the monthly (or bimonthly) meeting, the portfolio governance body can get an idea of the following metrics:
    a. How each project is tracking to budget
    b. How the portfolio (all projects aggregated) is tracking to budget
    c. Which projects are not going to spend all their budget (and why)
    d. Which projects need more budget (and why)

Grid View ▾ C ✎ ☐ 1 Sheet ▦ 15 Columns ▽ 1 Filter ▦ Group Σ Summarize ↑↓ Sort

Portfolio Budgets Vs. Actuals

Project	January	February	March	April	May	June	July	August	September	October	November	December	YTD Actual	YTD Budget	Balance
Enterprise Portfolio	**$1,094,038**	**$1,299,904**	**$0**	**$0**	**$0**	**$0**	**$0**	**$0**	**$0**	**$0**	**$0**	**$0**	**$2,393,942**	**$7,900,000**	**$5,506,058**
Project 1	$163,319.00	$265,724.00	$0.00	$0.00	$0.00	$0.00	$0.00	$0.00	$0.00	$0.00	$0.00	$0.00	$429,043	$870,000	$440,957
Project 2	$137,306.00	$145,354.00	$0.00	$0.00	$0.00	$0.00	$0.00	$0.00	$0.00	$0.00	$0.00	$0.00	$282,660	$960,000	$677,340
Project 3	$105,000.00	$254,684.00	$0.00	$0.00	$0.00	$0.00	$0.00	$0.00	$0.00	$0.00	$0.00	$0.00	$359,684	$1,640,000	$1,280,316
Project 4	$164,434.00	$106,951.00	$0.00	$0.00	$0.00	$0.00	$0.00	$0.00	$0.00	$0.00	$0.00	$0.00	$271,385	$780,000	$508,615
Project 5	$185,015.00	$180,975.00	$0.00	$0.00	$0.00	$0.00	$0.00	$0.00	$0.00	$0.00	$0.00	$0.00	$365,990	$860,000	$494,010
Project 6	$151,313.00	$194,971.00	$0.00	$0.00	$0.00	$0.00	$0.00	$0.00	$0.00	$0.00	$0.00	$0.00	$346,284	$1,810,000	$1,463,716
Project 7	$187,651.00	$151,245.00	$0.00	$0.00	$0.00	$0.00	$0.00	$0.00	$0.00	$0.00	$0.00	$0.00	$338,896	$900,000	$641,104

Figure 11.3

> KEY CONCEPT: Using Smartsheet to construct a simple portfolio budget tracking system is the rapid way to start tracking the spend for each project in the portfolio.

LEVELS OF PORTFOLIO MATURITY

Level 1

- No concept of portfolio funding management—there is no awareness that portfolio throughput is a function of portfolio funding.
- No concept of turnbacks—money once allocated stays with project until year end, whether it is needed or not, creating an inefficiency.
- There may not be a practice of annual planning or a queue of proposals waiting for funding.
- Portfolio either funds too many projects or holds on to funds until too late into the year.
- No active monitoring of underspend or overspend (i.e., no attempt to achieve a "precision landing" at the end of the year).
- None of the portfolio funding best practices are observed, and the portfolio often finishes the year with significant overspend or underspend.

Level 2

- Basic awareness of portfolio funding management exists, even if only to avoid exceeding the portfolio budget at the end of the year.
- There may only be a limited awareness about maximizing portfolio throughput through portfolio funding best practices.
- Annual planning is performed, but a well-maintained queue may not be in place to exploit underspend from other projects.
- Awareness of turnback technique exists, although it may be used infrequently.
- Portfolio tries to manage funding by being cautious about approving too many projects in the beginning of the year.
- There may be some active monitoring of project spend, but no formal way to project year-end costs.
- Many of the portfolio best practices may be observed, but the portfolio may finish with a small overspend or underspend despite efforts to avoid variance.

Level 3

- Portfolio funding management is actively practiced with a view toward maximizing portfolio throughput.
- Annual planning is performed effectively, and a well-maintained queue is in place to exploit underspend from other projects.
- Awareness of turnback technique exists and is used where appropriate.
- Portfolio uses EVM extensively to forecast project spend, track underperformers, and highlight projects with excess funds.
- Underperformers are terminated after appropriate oversight and the funds are returned to the portfolio for redeployment.
- Portfolio uses most or all best practices for funding management and finishes with very little or zero variance to budget.

CHAPTER SUMMARY

Management of project funds is a central function of the portfolio and the various nuances around this topic were explored in depth. The chapter began with a discussion around the necessity of portfolio budgeting before introducing the annual funding cycle and the two types of investment funds, OPEX and CAPEX, that each need to be managed and disbursed by the portfolio office. This was followed by a detailed look at the various supply side and demand side challenges imposed by the annual funding cycle on the decisions of the portfolio office. We then moved on to a comprehensive discussion of best practices, including run-hot factor, allocation, release, and turnback features, to mitigate both supply side and demand side constraints. The different portfolio funding models commonly found in organizations were then discussed with the pros and cons of each model and we finished the chapter with a look at the various levels of portfolio capability.

REFERENCES

1. Maguire, D. 2008. *The Business Benefits of GIS: An ROI Approach, 1st Ed.* ESRI Press: Redlands, CA, USA.
2. Damodaran, A. 1999. *Applied Corporate Finance: A User's Manual.* John Wiley and Sons: Hoboken, NJ, USA.

12

PERFORMANCE MONITORING
IN THE ADVANCED PORTFOLIO

INTRODUCTION

Both in financial and project portfolios, there is a prime need to understand how the portfolio is performing. The fundamental reason for performance monitoring is to obtain an early warning of underperformance and course-correct to preserve the objectives of the portfolio. In addition to early detection of underperformers, a well-run portfolio also produces a slew of performance monitoring data that helps executives make optimal decisions for the portfolio. In this chapter we cover the following aspects of performance monitoring:

1. A discussion of why projects tend to go off-track and how this affects the portfolio
2. A listing of key portfolio indicators that need to be regularly tracked and reported on a periodic basis
3. A detailed list of different scenarios that are encountered during portfolio monitoring and prescribed actions to take for each scenario
4. An introduction to the enhanced monitoring list (EML)

NOTE: Although we saw a simple form of performance monitoring in the basic portfolio (Chapter 6), we need to revisit this topic in the advanced portfolio due to the introduction of the budgetary aspect (which was not present in the basic portfolio).

KEY CONCEPT: Portfolio performance monitoring, which is present in basic portfolio management, acquires added importance in advanced portfolios because of the budget dimension (funds management and tracking).

THE IMPORTANCE OF TRACKING PROJECT PERFORMANCE

Projects tend to deviate from the expected plan—that is a fairly common occurrence. However, it is important to spot and remediate this behavior because if several projects go awry, the whole portfolio will start underperforming. This is made even more compelling in the case of the advanced portfolio, where there is the added budgetary dimension. The prudent portfolio office will spot and correct underperforming projects before they lead to an underperforming portfolio. A less advertised function of portfolio monitoring is to terminate projects that are beyond remediation (this will be covered later in this chapter). Through performance monitoring, a portfolio manager can highlight the following:

- Which projects are or are not performing to plan?
- How are the off-course projects performing on cost and schedule?
- How is the portfolio performing as a whole; are the underperformers balanced out by a few overperformers?
- How is the portfolio performing on operation expenses (OPEX) and capital expenses (CAPEX)?

It is important to note that portfolio monitoring is a value-add activity only when portfolio governance is willing to act on the data.

> KEY CONCEPT: Portfolio performance monitoring is necessary to spot and remediate the inevitable occurrence of some projects going off-track and underperforming.

Key Portfolio Indicators that Need to Be Reported and Tracked

In Chapter 6 we covered project milestone reporting and performance tracking in detail. However, project milestone performance data is just one subset of portfolio performance data. There are other data that the portfolio manager needs to track and make available to governance. Here are the key types of data that governance would be interested in reviewing:

- **Overall portfolio budget:** This shows how much money has been allocated to the portfolio for the current year and should be broken out by OPEX and CAPEX.
- **Allocated funds versus remaining:** Of the total budget, how much has been allocated to various projects and how much is available for new projects?
- **Allocated versus released:** This compares the amount of money allocated to various projects versus the amount of money that has actually been released (refer to Chapter 11 for an explanation of allocation versus release).
- **Actual money spent by the portfolio:** This shows how much money has actually been spent by the portfolio, commonly known as *actuals*. Typically, a drill down should be available so governance can see actuals by project.

> KEY CONCEPT: These key portfolio indicators give a complete picture of portfolio health and all advanced portfolios are recommended to track these at a minimum.

In addition to the above, there are three other advanced indicators that are produced by earned value management (EVM). These are included here for completeness:

- **Cost performance of the portfolio:** This shows what the productivity is per dollar spent for the portfolio. Here are some additional thoughts on this piece of data:
  - A drill down should be available so governance can see cost performance by project. Sometimes, the cost performance of well-performing projects hides or masks the subpar cost performance of underperforming projects. The drill down helps triage the projects that are the biggest contributors to the cost variance of the portfolio.

- Portfolio cost performance is a useful high-level indicator that can be distributed to executive management to provide confidence that the portfolio is being well run. A trend can also be shown to substantiate how the various portfolio maturity efforts are helping to improve the cost performance indicator over time.
- **Schedule performance of the portfolio:** In some situations, timeliness is even more important than cost efficiency. This information shows what the schedule progress is per dollar spent for the portfolio. Here are some additional thoughts on this piece of data:
  - As seen in the cost performance data, a drill down should be available so governance can see the schedule performance by project. It may be the case that the schedule performance of some well-performing projects is masking the subpar schedule performance of underperforming projects. The drill down helps triage the projects that are the biggest contributors to the schedule variance of the portfolio.
  - Portfolio schedule performance is another high-level indicator that can be distributed to executive management to provide confidence that the portfolio is being well run. A trend can also be shown to substantiate how the various portfolio maturity efforts are helping to improve the schedule performance indicator over time.
- **Estimate to completion (ETC) versus allocated budget:** This indicator attempts to estimate how much more money is needed by each project before it is complete. Here are some additional thoughts on this piece of data:
  - The summation of ETC for all the projects in the portfolio indicates how much additional money is needed by the portfolio for the year. It is useful to compare this total with the funds still available to the portfolio.
  - If portfolio ETC is larger than the remaining budget, the portfolio is in danger of running out of money. The options are to either trim the spending rate of the projects or go to Finance and ask for more funds.
  - If portfolio ETC is smaller than the remaining budget, the portfolio is in danger of leaving money unspent. The options are to either take up new projects or inform Finance that the portfolio will be returning some money for potential redeployment elsewhere in the organization.

KEY CONCEPT: Although implementing EVM is an advanced undertaking, these EVM-based indicators can be valuable in providing an objective picture of portfolio cost and schedule performance.

Commonly Seen Performance Monitoring Scenarios

While monitoring the performance of projects in the portfolio, it is important to understand the possible situations that a project can find itself in. Each active project in the portfolio will fall under one of the following states:

- Project underperforming on cost, performing normally on schedule
- Project underperforming on schedule, performing normally on cost
- Project underperforming on both cost and schedule
- Project performing normally on cost and schedule
- Project overperforming on cost, schedule, or both

The above situations are explored in the next section.

Project Underperforming on Cost, Performing Normally on Schedule

Consider a project meeting all its milestones, but spending more money than planned. Is this worrisome? It depends—if the project seems to be getting things done on time, that is almost always a good thing. Many portfolio managers would not mind paying a little more in exchange for a strategic project being on track. However, this could become a problem if many projects in a portfolio start spending more than planned in order to stay on schedule. A prudent portfolio manager would calculate the ETC for every project and find out if the portfolio has funds to support that number (remember to sum up all the ETCs across projects to get to the final number). Beyond the affordability problem, it's worth investigating why the project is underperforming on cost. It could be a transient problem as the project may get the spending back on track in the next cycle. The portfolio manager should track if the project has an improving or worsening trend. In the case of a worsening trend, the project is moved to an EML (more details on this topic later).

Project Underperforming on Schedule, Performing Normally on Cost

Consider a project that is spending on track but not meeting its milestones as planned. This could be a problem because future spending could increase since milestones are not being met. The total money spent by the project could exceed the project budget. It could also be an issue where the project does not finish per plan and may need to stretch into the next year, taking up funds from next year's proposals. If several projects in the portfolio have this issue, the portfolio could face trouble down the road—there would be little money for new projects since most of the money is taken up by existing projects. Again, the solution is to monitor the trend of the projects having this issue and put the ones with a worsening trend on the EML.

Project Underperforming on Both Cost and Schedule

Consider a project that is neither meeting its milestones nor able to stay on track with its spending (it's spending more than planned). This is invariably a problem if it persists and is a symptom of serious trouble with either the planning or the execution of the project. Even a handful of projects like these in a portfolio is cause for concern for the portfolio manager and governance team. Put these projects on the EML if the issue persists beyond a monthly cycle.

Project Performing Normally on Cost and Schedule

A project that is delivering its milestones while spending is on track is every portfolio manager's dream come true. If most of the projects in the portfolio are in this category, the portfolio is well on its way to becoming a high-performing transformational vehicle. The key is to ensure that projects continue to perform and that any project going off course is immediately spotted and put back on track.

Project Overperforming on Both Cost and Schedule

Finally, imagine a project that is performing well on all fronts—meeting all planned milestones on time and seeming to be underspending. While on the surface this looks like a great situation to be in, there is something that still needs to be done. Consider that an overachieving project has more money than it needs, given its rate of spend. In most cases, projects in this situation are reluctant to return money because they may need it later. Now, imagine the situation that would arise if all projects held on to a little extra cash as insurance. The portfolio will have markedly less funds to allocate to new, viable proposals from the annual planning queue. Therefore, while it's good that the project is meeting milestones on time and under budget, the portfolio manager should direct such projects to return funds so they can be deployed elsewhere.

> KEY CONCEPT: Portfolio performance monitoring recognizes several well-known portfolio scenarios for which standard remedies are prescribed—it's important to know which scenario is occurring before mitigating.

THE ENHANCED MONITORING LIST (EML)

As stated before, one of the most predictable things in managing a portfolio is that projects will run into trouble and start underperforming on cost or schedule. This underperformance is of two types: the transient *noise* that tends to correct itself and the more stubborn *structural deficiency* that is harder to correct. Before it becomes obvious whether the project's problems are truly serious or solvable, there is a need to closely monitor the project. To facilitate this close monitoring, projects are designated as being on the EML. Typically, this consists of the following:

- An underperforming project is designated as a "monitored" project and is included in a special list of underperforming projects and programs (EML) that is reported to governance.
- Additional portfolio resources, including monitoring and support, are provided to all projects on the EML.
- Additional performance data on the EML projects are reported to the decision makers. This may involve drill downs to the milestone and even the deliverable level.

Typically, projects on the EML either get better or get terminated. A huge advantage of having the EML is that it provides a clear notice to projects to improve their performance or face termination. Having such a list in place increases accountability and generally *ups the game* across the portfolio.

> KEY CONCEPT: The EML is a useful construct for highlighting habitually troubled projects, which can then be actively assisted to show improvement.

LEVELS OF PORTFOLIO CAPABILITY

Level 1

- The organization does not understand the importance of project performance monitoring. Consequently, there isn't a standard way of reporting on project performance data. If project reporting is available, it may only be subjective.
- Few portfolio indicators are available, as seen below:
    - The portfolio may not follow an active allocation strategy. Therefore, it may be hard to estimate how much money has been allocated to projects and how much is left to be allocated.
    - The portfolio may not employ a strategy of allocation versus release and may simply release whatever is allocated. Therefore, it may not be possible to obtain allocation versus release as an indicator.

- □ Since project actuals may not be available, there may not be a way of showing the actual money spent by the portfolio as a whole.
- □ Because project actuals are not available, there is no way to show cost performance or schedule performance of the portfolio or of individual projects.
- □ ETC may not be tracked for each project and hence is not available for the portfolio either. Consequently, it may not be possible to show ETC versus allocated budget for the portfolio.
- The only project monitoring system in place may be the subjective red/yellow/green (R/Y/G) system, which could mean that there is no real information about project progress or milestone status. There is also no information about whether a project is overspending or underspending.
- The concept of an EML is unknown or the organization has not decided to implement it.

Level 2

- The organization understands the importance of project performance monitoring. Consequently, there is a standard way of reporting on project performance data. Although this may still be a subjective measure such as R/Y/G, it is applied in a uniform manner with many of the typical R/Y/G drawbacks mitigated.
- Several meaningful portfolio indicators are available and published, as seen below:
    - □ The portfolio office employs an active allocation strategy. Therefore, it is possible to estimate how much money has been allocated to projects and how much is left to be allocated.
    - □ The portfolio office employs a strategy of allocation versus release and does not release the entire allocated amount at once. Therefore, it is possible to obtain allocation versus release for each project as well as the overall portfolio.
    - □ Project actuals are available and compared to the approved budget. Some kind of spend plan exists and actual spend versus planned spend can be tracked. This also means that the actual money spent by the portfolio as a whole can be shown.
    - □ There is no way to show cost performance or schedule performance of the portfolio or of individual projects.
    - □ ETC may be tracked for each project, but since it is not backed up by an objective indicator such as EVM, the confidence in the ETC might be low.
    - □ ETCs for projects could be summed to show an ETC number for the portfolio. Consequently, it may be possible to show ETC versus allocated budget for the portfolio.
- The only project monitoring system in place may be the R/Y/G system, which could mean that there is no objective information about project progress or milestone status. There is also little confidence about whether a project is overspending or underspending.
- Although the concept of EML is known to the organization, it may not be possible to implement it without an objective indicator such as EVM being in place.
- Although some meaningful portfolio data is available as shown above, action may not be consistently taken in response to the data.
- There may be a comprehensive report on portfolio data and/or portfolio performance, however, it may not have look-ahead capability.

Level 3

- The organization fully understands the importance of project performance monitoring. Consequently, there is a standard, objective way of reporting on project performance data such as EVM in place. The presence of an objective measurement indicator removes a lot of the limitations seen in Levels 1 and 2.

- A full host of portfolio indicators are available and published, as seen below:
  - ◘ The portfolio office employs an active allocation strategy. Therefore, it is possible to estimate how much money has been allocated to projects and how much is left to be allocated.
  - ◘ The portfolio office employs a strategy of allocation versus release and does not release the entire allocated amount at once. Therefore, it is possible to obtain allocation versus release for each project as well as the overall portfolio.
  - ◘ Project actuals are available and compared to the approved budget. An EVM-backed spend plan exists and cost variances can be tracked. This also means that the actual money spent by the portfolio as a whole can be shown.
  - ◘ Since EVM is fully implemented, both cost performance and schedule performance of each project can be displayed. These measures can be aggregated to show the cost and schedule performance of the whole portfolio.
  - ◘ ETC is tracked for each project and is backed up by an objective system such as EVM. This creates a high confidence in the ETC number.
  - ◘ ETCs for the projects could be summed up to show an ETC number for the portfolio. Consequently, it is possible to show ETC versus allocated budget for the portfolio.
- Since EVM is the project monitoring system in place, objective information is available about project progress or milestone status. There are clear indications concerning whether the project is overspending or underspending.
- An active EML backed by EVM exists and serves as an effective measure to manage troubled projects.
- There is a governance body that has the political will to act on the strength of the above objective data.

CHAPTER SUMMARY

In this chapter we explored the essential components of portfolio data that need to be monitored. We saw how the advanced portfolio needs to monitor several key budgetary indicators beyond milestone data. We also addressed the core issues of monitoring project performance along with an analysis of the shortcomings of traditional reporting methods. We then detailed the most prevalent scenarios that projects encounter when monitored and what the portfolio manager needs to do in each of these scenarios. We also mentioned the possibility of using an advanced technique such as EVM to obtain additional insights into cost and schedule performance. Finally, we covered the EML and the need for portfolio governance to act on the gathered performance data and reviewed levels of portfolio capability from the portfolio monitoring perspective.

13

REBALANCING THE
ADVANCED PORTFOLIO

INTRODUCTION

The concept of portfolio rebalancing has its origins in financial portfolio theory, where rebalancing is the process of realigning the holdings of the portfolio. In this chapter we will cover the following:

1. Approach portfolio rebalancing by looking at the concept in financial portfolios
2. Adjust the concept of portfolio rebalancing for project portfolios
3. Define the fundamental need for project portfolio rebalancing
4. Describe portfolio scenarios where rebalancing is appropriate
5. Explore why it is hard to perform portfolio rebalancing
6. Consider an alternate view of rebalancing
7. Further our discussion of portfolio levels of maturity

> KEY CONCEPT: Rebalancing is a vital activity which helps the advanced portfolio adapt to changing circumstances.

PORTFOLIO BALANCING IN A FINANCIAL PORTFOLIO

The easiest way to approach the concept of portfolio rebalancing is by first illustrating how it works in a financial portfolio, since most people are acquainted with this type of portfolio. In a financial portfolio, rebalancing typically involves divesting some assets and buying others in order to maintain an original desired goal or benchmark, as in a retirement portfolio whose target asset allocation is a 1:1 mix between stocks and bonds. If the stock holdings grew because of solid growth during the period, it may wind up becoming 75% of the portfolio. The asset manager will then sell some stocks and buys bonds to return the portfolio back to the original target allocation of 50/50.

APPLICABILITY OF PORTFOLIO BALANCING TO A PROJECT PORTFOLIO

Does portfolio rebalancing apply to a project portfolio? Definitely, but in a markedly different way from how it applies to a financial portfolio. A project portfolio contains projects—not financial assets such as stocks and bonds. So, the concept of growth does not apply here; a project doesn't "grow" over time like a stock or bond. However, like a financial asset, a project can be considered a performing or non-performing asset. Here are some ways a project can be a non-performing asset:

- Project performance is consistently below par; not meeting cost or schedule expectations.
- A project is not delivering promised benefits.
- A project is no longer a strategic fit; strategic landscape changed after project was approved.

In this aspect, a project portfolio needs to adopt the mindset of an actively managed stock/bond fund which prizes returns above all. In a financial portfolio, all that matters is performance/returns. Losing positions (non-performing investments) are cut with alacrity and the funds are redeployed into other positions—new or existing. While the subject of project portfolio versus financial portfolio has been extensively debated, in this particular aspect, project portfolios would do well to emulate the financial portfolio model—cut the losses and let the winners run.

> KEY CONCEPT: The essence of project portfolio rebalancing is the same as financial portfolio rebalancing—to capitalize on well-performing projects and reduce the risk caused by non-performing projects.

THE FUNDAMENTAL NEED FOR PORTFOLIO REBALANCING

The fundamental need for portfolio rebalancing comes from a need to react to change. This change could come in many ways, such as a project turning out differently than planned or the strategic direction of the company could necessitate a pivot towards new projects. Other drivers of change could be a belt-tightening exercise, where the portfolio may be directed to execute a 10% budget cut, or a directive to self-fund a new critical priority. Change may not always be negative; there could be an availability of new surplus funds or certain projects may find that they don't need as much money to accomplish their objectives. Whatever the drivers of change are, a portfolio should always be in a position to exploit these drivers to its advantage.

> KEY CONCEPT: Portfolio rebalancing can be driven by a variety of scenarios—not all scenarios are negative and some are opportunities to overachieve.

THE PREREQUISITES OF PORTFOLIO REBALANCING

Portfolio rebalancing is hard to perform unless the following prerequisites are in place:

1. An enhanced monitoring list: A special list of underperforming projects and programs that receives additional scrutiny from governance.
2. A portfolio project queue: This queue is a collection of vetted projects that is waiting to be funded. These projects have a positive ROI and strategic fit but were below the *affordability line* during annual planning.
3. An objective system of measuring project cost and schedule performance, such as earned value management (EVM).

SCENARIOS WHERE PORTFOLIO REBALANCING IS REQUIRED

In the following paragraphs the most common portfolio rebalancing scenarios are explored.

Scenario 1: The Underperforming Project

As explained in previous chapters, the one predictable situation that a portfolio manager can expect to encounter is that of dealing with a project that is not performing to cost and schedule expectations. While some projects work through their challenges and fix themselves, others are not able to accomplish this and need to be put on an enhanced monitoring list (EML). Regrettably, there are bound to be projects that are not able to recover despite being on the EML. The only option left in that case is to terminate the project and redirect the remaining funds. How best to redirect the funds? Here are some options:

- Recall from previous chapters the need for maintaining a queue of validated projects that are ready for funding. This would be an ideal use for the funds freed up by terminating underperforming projects.
- Some existing projects may need additional funds. Recall in Chapter 11 the idea of *not* releasing all the funds requested by a project at one time. Such projects, which only had a partial release of the total funds requested, may now be asking for their additional funds. Provided that these projects are in good standing from a cost and schedule perspective, these become viable recipients of the funds made available by terminating underperforming projects with a deteriorating trend.

Scenario 2: The Famine

Another recurring situation that a portfolio manager has to contend with is the belt-tightening exercise. Due to the nature of the business cycle, portfolios are sometimes asked to give back a percentage of their budget to help cover a shortfall elsewhere in the business. Typically, portfolios deal with such requests by resorting to a percentage cut across the board where all projects are asked to share the pain equally. While this seems fair, in reality, this is suboptimal for the portfolio because not all the projects will be performing at the same level or will be at the same point in execution. Some projects might not even feel the loss in funds while others might be severely impacted if funds were reduced. Here are some options to approach this situation:

- Underperforming projects on the EML are good candidates for termination and recovery of funds, especially if the project's cost and schedule variance trend is worsening. If these projects are eventually going to get terminated, this might be a good opportunity to make that decision.
- Well-performing projects that seem to be underspending can give back funds without affecting their progress.
- Finally, if additional cuts are needed after the above two options, consider spreading the cuts across less strategically important projects and preserve the current level of funding for the critical, truly strategic projects.

Scenario 3: The Feast

A somewhat less frequent scenario to contend with for the portfolio manager is the sudden availability of additional funds towards the latter half of the year. A well-run portfolio will not normally have unused funds piling up as the year progresses because of the emphasis on optimal fund usage throughout the year. However, other portfolios within the organization might not have this rigor and might find themselves with more money than can be deployed. Alternatively, unspent funds from the rest of the organization might be looking for a home. Here is the advantage of having a well-run portfolio: *it is ready to take advantage of such funds made available by inefficiencies elsewhere.* Here are some thoughts for this situation:

- The importance of having a queue from annual planning makes all the difference here. With the availability of additional funds, these are prime candidates to receive funding. Note that it may be necessary to prioritize the queue to pick short-life/quick-win projects. The reason for this is that any excess funding is available for that financial year alone and should not be counted to continue into the new year. So, we pick projects that can get done quickly.
- Find projects that can be accelerated. EVM readouts indicate projects that could execute faster with more funding (projects that typically overachieve on schedule variance with the tradeoff of reduced performance on cost variance). Such projects would be great candidates for additional funding because the demand for funds would be reduced in the new year (since more of the project completion is being accelerated into this year).
- Invest in portfolio tools and capability enhancement. A well-run portfolio will always try to get to the next level of capability. The availability of excess funds would be a good opportunity to execute on these portfolio improvement plans and create a force multiplier effect for the portfolio.

Scenario 4: The Strategic Reset

Sometimes the organization will pivot in its strategic positioning. In a well-run portfolio, this will have a direct impact on what projects are being worked on—because of the direct link between the projects and the strategy being pursued. Therefore, the portfolio manager needs to be ready to take actions to reorient the portfolio to align with the new strategy. Here are some things to consider:

- The strategic roadmap will need to be recast and the existing projects re-ranked in terms of priority—with the help of priority advocates (see Chapter 15).
- A low-ranked project under the new strategic direction should be completed (if it is almost finished) or terminated so as to conserve funds and bandwidth for the execution of new projects ranked higher from a strategic perspective.
- In addition to the above, projects that were underperforming in the old strategic direction should also be candidates for termination to allow for redirection of funds and manpower to new projects.

In all the scenarios above, the common requirements are timely EVM reporting, robust annual planning, and a thorough strategic roadmap. Having these in place makes it straightforward to perform the course corrections needed as part of portfolio rebalancing.

> KEY CONCEPT: Portfolio rebalancing is vital to ensuring that the portfolio stays on the correct path despite some of the above scenarios occurring.

WHY PORTFOLIOS FIND IT HARD TO REBALANCE

Portfolio rebalancing is a great technique to ensure that the portfolio is always performing at its peak potential in delivering strategic value. However, it can be difficult to deal with unexpected change and many portfolio managers find it hard to maneuver around this topic. Next, we explore some reasons why.

Reason 1: Lack of a Venture Capital Mindset

A venture capital fund's mindset is to bet on many startups, hoping that some of them will pay off significantly and make up for those that fail. While all care is taken to vet the startup prior to funding, it still remains a speculative activity. Many startups fail and get terminated—this is the norm and all players are aware of it. This consequently creates a *win or die* dynamic where the winning startups receive funds at the expense of concepts rejected by the market. While it's true that a project portfolio has many constraints not typically faced by a venture capital fund, this win-or-fail-quickly mindset is something a portfolio would profit greatly by adopting. Projects are selected and planned with due diligence, but underperformers need to be quickly terminated, so that resources can be focused on existing successful projects and new ones. "Non-performing projects are at risk of termination" is the mindset that the rank and file needs to adopt.

Reason 2: Reluctance to Kill Projects

Organizations are reluctant to kill projects, even the obvious disasters. This *hesitate-to-terminate* mindset is one of the single biggest obstacles for a portfolio to reach its potential. Why? Quite simply, a portfolio has finite resources—both financial and human. Unless underperforming projects are terminated, there is no way to start new, promising projects. The only other way to start projects is to wait for projects to conclude on their own, which may take a long time, especially if there is no pressure to perform. It's a vicious circle that reinforces mediocrity and prevents a portfolio from rising to its full potential.

Reason 3: Lack of Data to Make the Right Decisions in Rebalancing

One primary reason why underperforming projects survive so long is that there is no objective measurement of performance. Using traditional ineffectual systems, such as subjective red/yellow/green, yield almost no value in spotting underperformers. Even after a project is visible to all as an underperformer, a lot of time is wasted waiting for the project to turn around. In other words, no one knows if a turnaround is working or even possible. Rebalancing in the absence of objective data is very challenging.

Reason 4: There Isn't a Queue of Viable Projects

Critical to the rebalancing concept is the availability of a queue—a list of viable replacement projects. However, few organizations have this queue ready, partly because having such a queue necessitates having a robust annual planning process, which is another capability that few organizations have.

> NOTE: You should begin noticing how portfolio capability dimensions are interlinked— getting to the next level requires many prerequisites, several of which are interrelated.

Reason 5: There Isn't an EML or *Kill List*

An EML or kill list is a great source for rebalancing opportunities. Projects on that list have landed there for a reason and in some cases are unable to get back on track in spite of enhanced support and review. However, few organizations have these lists. The main reason is a lack of objective data to designate projects as candidates for the EML, thus leading to a self-reinforcing cycle.

Reason 6: Rebalancing Is Political and Avoided as Long as Possible

In the absence of a performance-based mindset, a tradition of regular rebalancing, and objective data to make termination decisions, portfolio rebalancing becomes a political minefield. Stakeholders of underperforming projects are likely to push back hard at any moves to terminate their projects. Few leaders want to waste their political capital fighting these battles which seem arbitrary in the absence of well-established criteria.

> KEY CONCEPT: While portfolio rebalancing is a valuable exercise, there are a host of reasons why organizations find it hard to rebalance. A prudent portfolio manager needs to anticipate and mitigate these factors to enable rebalancing to occur.

AN ALTERNATIVE VIEW OF PROJECT PORTFOLIO REBALANCING

Based on the preceding discussion, it would seem that portfolio rebalancing is primarily concerned with *returns*—projects that deliver results continue to be funded and projects that don't are terminated to make way for more projects that promise to deliver. While this is how most portfolios want to operate, sometimes there are other considerations for why we would take a different approach.

Consider a diversified financial portfolio invested in a variety of instruments aimed at reducing risk/exposure while delivering promised returns to the investor. In contrast, a diversified project portfolio is aimed at meeting multiple objectives for the organization and correspondingly consists of different types of projects. If some of these projects are terminated as part of rebalancing, the portfolio may still be constrained to choose other projects of the *same type* it just terminated—it may not be at liberty to choose the next best proposal (financially). To illustrate, consider a diversified portfolio whose composition has 60% "Grow the Business" (GTB) projects and 40% "Run the Business" (RTB) projects. Imagine the Board of Directors has tasked the company leadership to maintain this mix of Grow versus Run. Suppose several GTB projects are underperforming and need to be terminated. The portfolio may have a steady queue of promising RTB projects waiting to begin. Can the portfolio then add a bunch of RTB projects and flip the portfolio composition mix to 60% RTB and 40% GTB? While advantageous, that may not be desirable from an organizational point of view. So, the organization may be constrained to pass over the promising RTB projects and fund the next GTB project in the queue as part of rebalancing.

Alternatively, governance may approve for now the funding of several RTB projects with compelling value propositions but may direct that the portfolio come back to its desired composition mix at the next balancing opportunity. There's no one correct way—each organization will have to consider the factors important to them and make decisions correspondingly.

> KEY CONCEPT: Although portfolio rebalancing can be returns-focused, there are situations where the rebalancing is driven by other considerations such as the need to keep a required mix of projects in the portfolio.

LEVELS OF PORTFOLIO CAPABILITY MATURITY

Level 1

- The organization is unfamiliar with the concept of portfolio rebalancing—it's unusual to terminate a project once it gets started.
- Organizational culture does not support rebalancing—projects just keep moving along regardless of relative importance to portfolio objectives.
- New projects are only able to begin with new funding or when existing projects complete.
- There isn't an objective assessment of project performance to support any rebalancing decisions.
- None of the prerequisites for rebalancing are in place, which makes any rebalancing activity sporadic and non-uniform.

Level 2

- An awareness of project rebalancing exists but it is not a well-grounded concept, hence, it is not done uniformly or comprehensively.
- Rebalancing may only be done at the end of the year and is usually driven by funding availability.
- If done during the year, rebalancing typically takes the form of across-the-board cuts necessitated by funding shortfalls.
- Rebalancing is unlikely to be driven by objective measures of performance such as EVM.
- Other prerequisites for productive rebalancing, such as EVM, an EML, and a project queue, may not be present.

Level 3

- Portfolio balancing is a well-known and embraced concept—rebalancing is done at regular intervals.
- There is an awareness and expectation of regular portfolio rebalancing and this is a driver for accountability and project success.
- To support rebalancing, all the prerequisites exist, namely EVM, an EML, and a project queue.
- Rebalancing also is taken into account during one-time events such as a portfolio funding reduction as well as a distribution of surplus funds.

CHAPTER SUMMARY

In this chapter we explored the vital activity of portfolio rebalancing, which helps portfolios cope with change. We approached the concept by looking at how portfolio rebalancing is done in financial portfolios. We then translated the concept of portfolio rebalancing to project portfolios and proceeded to describe the fundamental need for project portfolio rebalancing. We further explored portfolio scenarios where rebalancing is appropriate while also considering the real-life constraints that make it hard for portfolios to rebalance. We also considered an alternate view of rebalancing before rounding out the chapter with a look at portfolio levels of maturity.

14

BENEFITS REALIZATION IN THE ADVANCED PORTFOLIO

INTRODUCTION

What is the fundamental reason to execute a project? Quite simply, organizations execute projects for the benefits delivered by the project. A benefit is an outcome or end result that is advantageous to the organization. It could be to increase revenue, market share, or customer satisfaction; decrease cost; or optimize operations. Therefore, a high-performing portfolio is created by selecting projects that deliver tangible benefits to the organization.

However, that is harder to do than it appears. In reality, most projects that are funded simply do not have solid benefits that stand up to scrutiny. This is part of the reason most organizations consume huge project budgets without delivering much in return. Implementing a benefits management process is a hugely effective filter to screen out projects that won't actually deliver benefits. In this chapter we cover the following aspects of benefits realization:

1. Classify the different types of project benefits
2. Describe the need for a portfolio benefits management process
3. Describe the building blocks of the portfolio benefits management process
4. Describe the obstacles to benefits attainment and how to mitigate them

KEY CONCEPT: Advanced portfolios actively focus on benefits realization for the projects in the portfolio.

TYPES OF BENEFITS

Monetary Benefits

- **Hard return on investment (ROI):** This is typically either an actual reduction in costs or an actual increase in revenue. Hard ROI needs to be recognized as such by Finance and should be directly attributable to the project. This kind of ROI is most prized by portfolio managers and any project with a positive, verified hard ROI is a strong candidate for funding. Caution: it's rare to find projects with credible hard ROI benefits.
- **Cost avoidance[1]:** Cost avoidance refers to reductions that cause future spending to fall, but not below the level of current spending. Often, cost avoidance involves slowing the rate of cost increases. In other words, future spending would have increased *even more* in the absence of

cost avoidance measures. While sometimes attractive, projects whose ROI is cost avoidance need to be scrutinized carefully. A project that claims to avoid a future increase must be able to demonstrate a rising trend in costs that is then flattened due to the execution of this project. Caution: cost avoidance projects tend to have optimistic projections that may be hard to substantiate.

- **Soft savings:** These are typically created by measuring an increase in productivity or efficiency of an employee or process. It is not exactly a monetary benefit, but the increase in productivity can (and often is) translated into a dollar figure by converting hours saved into dollars. Soft savings usually are the bane of portfolio managers everywhere because most projects that are not worth doing often have benefits purporting to be soft savings.

Non-Monetary Benefits

Sometimes, the benefit of doing a project may be strategic or delivering a capability to the organization. It may also be aligned with delivering objectives that are important to the business. While some of these benefits can be quantified in monetary terms, at times the project may have to proceed on the basis of the non-monetary benefits. In that case, it is important to ensure that the non-monetary benefits are still worthwhile. It takes some planning and screening to ensure that the project's benefits, while non-monetary, are indeed aligned with the strategic roadmap of the organization. Sometimes, the business side of the company just wants certain projects done. In those cases, it is important to ensure that business sign-off exists before starting the project.

> KEY CONCEPT: While project benefits can be monetary or non-monetary, precise definitions of each type are recommended in order to prioritize among the projects if necessary.

THE PORTFOLIO BENEFITS REALIZATION PROCESS

The Need for a Portfolio Benefits Realization Process

- *Need #1:* People do not have a standard understanding of benefits—every project is "beneficial/worth doing" in the eyes of the respective project owner.
- *Need #2:* Without periodic review, the project benefits realized (if they are realized at all) have no relation to the benefits promised during project selection. Projects tend to exaggerate benefits during the proposal stage.
- *Need #3:* Projects are never going to self-regulate in terms of benefits delivery. There is a need for a mechanism to hold projects accountable for promised benefits.
- *Need #4:* The existence of a standard and periodically scheduled process to review all projects' benefits creates a climate of transparency and responsibility on the part of projects to deliver on their promises. This also creates a mechanism to spot projects that are unable to deliver.

> KEY CONCEPT: Without a portfolio benefits realization process, a portfolio could waste its resources with the non-valuable projects crowding out the valuable projects.

Building Blocks of a Portfolio Benefits Realization Process

#1: Uniform Taxonomy to Classify Benefits

The foundation of a successful benefits realization process is for all the stakeholders to speak the same language when it comes to benefits. This, in turn, makes it necessary for a document to describe the standard types of benefits that are used for that organization. Table 14.1 is a small sample of what the benefit taxonomy chart would look like. Every benefit category is derived from a strategic priority and further classified as monetary or non-monetary (monetary entries could be further divided into hard and soft). A description column is provided to capture additional nuances. The table needs to be completed and disseminated to business partners, as well as other functions such as Finance (especially to review the monetary benefits). Once everyone can agree that this document captures all the relevant benefit types, it serves as the benefit taxonomy chart (BTC). All proposals which promise benefits will then need those benefits to be classified according to this chart.

Table 14.1   Basic form of a benefit taxonomy chart

Strategic Priority	Benefit Category	Monetary/Non-Monetary	Description/Notes
Profit Growth	Increase in Sales	Monetary	
	Increase in Margin	Monetary	
Customer Service	High Availability	Non-Monetary	
	Customer Satisfaction	Non-Monetary	

#2: Mandatory Declaration of Project Benefits in Standard Form

Surprisingly, in most organizations, benefits are somewhat of an afterthought when project proposals are floated. In some cases, projects try to avoid talking about benefits by promising to provide benefit information afterwards. In other cases, projects create ad hoc, vaguely worded benefits that are not easy to validate or verify after go-live. The remedy for those situations is to make it mandatory for project proposals to choose benefits from the BTC. In other words, a project can only pick something that is already on the BTC—the project is not at liberty to make up their own benefit. The choice of benefits can then happen in two possible ways. During the annual planning process, the template that is filled out needs to contain choices from the BTC. Or, for off-cycle proposals, the intake process needs to be integrated with the BTC so that the proposals contain benefit information.

#3: Identification of the Earliest Time That Benefits Can Be Reviewed for Each Project

Projects tend to postpone benefit review until after go-live. In other words, they do not want to engage in any discussion about whether the promised benefits are materializing until it's a done deal (which is project go-live). At that time, it's mostly an academic exercise because the money has already been spent and there is nothing that can be done even if the project benefits are nonexistent. The approach of reviewing benefits after project go-live is contrary to the interests of the portfolio. A portfolio manager should seek to terminate projects that are not likely to deliver benefits and redirect those funds to existing projects with tangible benefits or to new projects with promising benefits. To enable this to happen, the earliest time benefits emanating from the project can be reviewed should be identified and this date or time period should come with project owner commitment.

#4: Secure Agreement about Project Benefits with the Project Sponsor

Project sponsors (typically senior executives) will often find their names attached to various proposals and may not really stand behind that proposal or even know it exists. This is especially true in the case of project benefits: rather generous promises can be made regarding benefits and the implicit understanding is that the project sponsor supports those claims. When the project completes, and the benefits are typically less than promised, it creates an awkward feeling all around. Some organizations deal with this problem in the following way: once the benefit projection is created for a project and some kind of validation/backup is established to support these projections, an agreement is created with the project sponsor listing the benefits and requiring the sponsor to sign off on them.

It is also typical for these agreement documents to have supporting statements from Finance and other business partners regarding the benefits. This is a good checkpoint for the sponsor to review and agree to the documents that purport to bear their name while promising benefits to the rest of the organization. It adds credibility that the benefits promised will be realized and is an indication that due diligence was performed.

#5: Ensure a Functioning Portfolio Benefits Review Council

A portfolio benefits review the council is a governance body that focuses on reviewing the promised benefits of a project. The functions of a benefits review council are:

- Periodically review benefit information of each project and compare to the promised level of benefits at the time of project approval.
- In case of significant variance (council to decide how much is significant), decide on whether to place this project on the enhanced monitoring list (EML), which we discussed in Chapter 13.
- For the projects that are on the EML due to under-delivery of benefits, continue to monitor benefits attainment and make a recommendation on an exit from the EML (return to normal status or termination of project).

The portfolio benefits review council is either part of the main portfolio governance council or is a subcommittee that reports to the main portfolio council. Some key points to the functioning of the portfolio benefits review council are listed below:

- Having this council in place helps greatly with tracking benefits for all projects. Now that there is a dedicated body that reviews benefits attainment (at least quarterly), the projects are compelled to treat this topic seriously—as opposed to the historical pattern of either ignoring benefits or making them up.
- For this council to be most effective, project benefits need to be reviewed well before projects go-live (see #3 listed earlier).
- Some organizations mandate that only projects that are bigger than a defined threshold should go to portfolio benefits review. This is done to ensure focus on the big-spend, big-impact items.

#6: Regular Report on the Benefits

If all the preceding steps are followed, the organization can reasonably expect to see a steady stream of validated benefits. The next logical step is to report on those benefits achieved by the portfolio. This has numerous benefits:

- Demonstrates the value of the portfolio to the business and other partner functions. This creates value substantiation during annual budget planning activities.

- Creates a culture where benefits are expected and celebrated as opposed to being an optional afterthought.
- Creates accountability for projects promising benefits and ensures projects will need to stand behind their original benefit projections.

KEY CONCEPT: Although it takes several components to successfully implement portfolio benefits realization, the dividends to the organization make it worthwhile.

Obstacles to Benefits Attainment

These next few paragraphs describe typical obstacles in the way of portfolio managers trying to implement a robust benefits attainment program for the portfolio.

Obstacle #1: Projects Avoid Mention of Any Benefits While Seeking Funding

One of the ways people try to defeat benefits realization is to not even provide the project benefits while requesting funding. Sponsors may claim that they don't have enough data to provide benefits until they receive funding to do the project. While there is some truth to the fact that it takes work to perform analysis on the impact and benefits of a project, it's a classic red flag for a project to request major funding or full funding without providing benefits. The prudent way of handling the situation is to provide a project with a standard minimal allocation of say 500 man-hours (this is a middle of the road estimate and would be adjusted as needed) to provide a comprehensive benefits statement. Second, funding must be contingent on the project integrating itself with the benefits realization process. This means that projects that do not appear for benefits review will have further funding withheld.

Obstacle #2: Overstated Benefits to Make Proposal More Attractive

Some projects promise vastly optimistic benefits that have no basis in reality. This is done to create a compelling value statement to increase the probability of funding. A remedy for the situation is to hold a formal benefits realization review (as described previously). At this review, a comprehensive look is taken at the actual benefits being delivered by the project as compared to the projections made at the time of funding. Periodic benefit reviews need to start well before the end of the project. A warning flag for underperforming projects is an inability to show any benefits before the complete end of the project. Such projects need to be revisited and the question of viability reconsidered.

Obstacle #3: Allowing Project Performance to Be a Proxy for Benefits Delivery

Some projects put forth their on-time, on-schedule performance as a proxy for benefits attainment. The point of view that's being advanced is along the lines of "The project is being executed well, so you can expect the benefits to be delivered as promised too." This is a fallacy because the project being well-run does not mean the outcome of the project will deliver the benefits. The project could execute on-time and on-budget and the end product could still deliver none of the promised benefits. The solution is still as outlined before—insist on early identification of benefits and also regular monitoring of benefits through the portfolio benefits review council.

KEY CONCEPT: While portfolio benefits realization delivers great value to the portfolio and the enterprise, there are obstacles that need to be anticipated and mitigated to enable the realization process to take root.

LEVELS OF MATURITY

Level 1

- No concept of benefits management.
- Project benefits are ad hoc and there is no standard framework to describe benefits.
- There is a wide disparity in project benefits—some projects show no benefits and are still approved.
- All benefits are lumped together. There is no distinction between hard and soft benefits or between cost avoidance and cost savings.
- Projects that actually have a potential to deliver hard benefits and cost savings are not favorably funded over others that have more modest benefits.
- Some projects have vastly optimistic benefits, which are never held to account.
- No standard benefits review process—any review is done in brief as part of a project postmortem.

Level 2

- An awareness of the need for project benefits exists but is not a well-grounded concept, therefore, it is not done uniformly or comprehensively.
- Some kind of standardization exists with regard to project benefits but there are many exceptions to the rule.
- No partnership with Finance and/or the business regarding validation of business benefits.
- Some disparity exists regarding project benefits—a few projects are still approved with slim or non-existent benefits.
- Some projects have vastly overstated benefits which are never held to account.
- There may be a standard benefits monitoring process but it usually happens after go-live and is ineffective in stopping projects which don't deliver benefits.

Level 3

- A strong awareness exists about the need for project benefits—it is well integrated into the whole project/portfolio life cycle.
- There is a standard benefits classification taxonomy and all projects are made to adhere to it.
- Projects that show potential hard benefits and actual cost savings are prioritized over other projects with more modest benefit profiles.
- There is a robust partnership with Finance and the business regarding validation of business benefits.
- All projects follow the benefits attainment process—no projects are allowed to proceed without a validated benefits statement reviewed by governance.
- There is a standard, robust benefits monitoring process that scrutinizes project benefits before go-live and is effective in stopping projects which don't deliver benefits. Projects with overstated benefits are held accountable to deliver those benefits.

CHAPTER SUMMARY

In this chapter we introduced the important topic of project benefits realization. First, we explored the two major types of benefits: monetary and non-monetary. We proceeded to outline the structure of a portfolio benefits realization process and reviewed the building blocks of the process. We then covered the typical obstacles in the way of portfolio benefits realization and how to handle these obstacles. We finished with identifying the benefits attainment capabilities at each level of portfolio maturity.

REFERENCE

1. The Cost Benefit Knowledge Bank, http://cbkb.org.

15

STRATEGIC PLANNING IN THE ADVANCED PORTFOLIO

INTRODUCTION

An organizational strategic vision seeks to transform the capabilities of the organization over time. The strategic vision typically seeks to enhance the positioning of the organization in the marketplace compared to its competitors and/or enable the organization to enter new markets. However, the strategic vision cannot execute in the real world without an aligned project portfolio. This chapter covers the following aspects of strategic attainment and the role of the project portfolio in enabling this journey:

1. Contrast strategic and non-strategic project portfolios
2. Introduce and explain the concept of the strategic journey
3. Explain the interaction and relationship between the strategic roadmap and the project portfolio
4. Describe the annual planning considerations of a strategic portfolio
5. Describe the intake considerations of a strategic portfolio
6. Explain why the strategic portfolio is typically an advanced portfolio
7. Describe the pseudo strategic portfolio

KEY CONCEPT: An organization needs to align its strategic vision to a project portfolio to achieve its strategic objectives.

STRATEGIC AND NON-STRATEGIC PORTFOLIOS

Imagine two portfolios: one portfolio (called a *strategic portfolio*) ensures strategic alignment before intaking a project while the second portfolio (called a *non-strategic portfolio*) does not check for that alignment. What would the outputs of these two portfolios look like? For the strategic portfolio, let's look at Figure 15.1 which shows a simple graph with two axes:

- The x-axis depicts a combination of time and money.
- The y-axis depicts the strategic capability/scale/capacity of an organization.

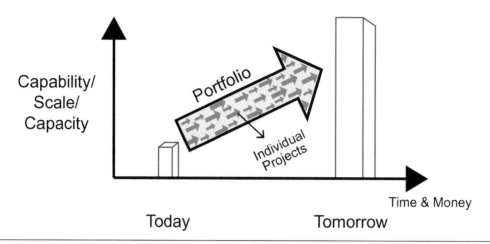

Figure 15.1   Graph showing growth in strategic capability over time when projects are managed in a high-performing portfolio

Figure 15.1 also shows the organization's modest strategic capability at the present (marked as "Today"). In this situation, we have a strategic portfolio which manages a stream of well-chosen projects that align with the strategic direction of the organization. When every project is aligned with a strategic component, the portfolio office can harness the transformative power of a portfolio and ensure that, over time, the organization will make significant strides on its strategic roadmap to achieve new capabilities, scale, and capacity. With the success of every project, the strategic journey takes another step forward. After a few years of execution, this new state of the enterprise's strategic capability in the future (marked as "Tomorrow" on the x-axis) is shown as the bigger tower representing enhanced capability and capacity.

In contrast, Figure 15.2 depicts the non-strategic portfolio. There is no check for strategic alignment performed before deciding to start work on a project. In this case, it is hard to predict the net effect of the projects toward achieving strategic goals, but it's much more likely that the net output over time will

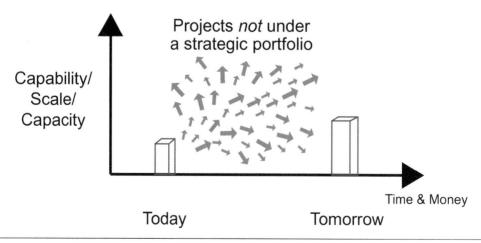

Figure 15.2   Graph showing growth in strategic capability over time when projects are *not* managed in a high-performing portfolio

be far more modest, as shown at the far right of the figure. While many projects are still completed successfully, there is little to no progress on the strategic journey because there is no link between strategy and the projects. The biggest risk from an executive's point of view is that there is no feedback or control concerning the pace of the strategic journey (explained next).

> KEY CONCEPT: A strategic portfolio actively manages the strategic alignment of its projects whereas a non-strategic portfolio typically does not worry about the strategic dimension of its projects at all.

FROM TODAY TO TOMORROW—THE STRATEGIC JOURNEY

The concept of growth is intrinsic to every organization and team. All entities have an impulse to transform—to become something greater and better in the future compared to their state today. But "transform to what?" is the key question that needs to be answered for an organization that is planning their strategic journey.

Let's examine what this would look like for an organization. Imagine a telecom provider company, First Telecom, has several strategic priorities: Priority A, B, C, etc. For example, strategic Priority A could be "Geographical Coverage," strategic Priority B could be "Digital Self-service Capabilities," while Priority C might be in yet another strategic area. Figure 15.3 shows the multi-year journey of strategic Priority A for First Telecom. The yearly milestones of attainment for that strategic priority are shown along the top. For example, the strategic Priority A for First Telecom in 2021 is "Achieve North America Coverage." Similarly, there are strategic priorities for years 2022, 2023, and 2024. Under each yearly milestone,

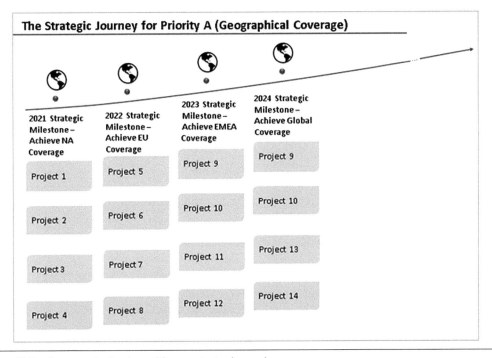

Figure 15.3   An organization's multi-year strategic roadmap

all the projects which contribute towards that year's milestone are shown. The takeaway is that all the projects directly under a yearly milestone contribute towards the attainment of that milestone. It's also understood that the yearly strategic milestone cannot be completed without the successful completion of all the projects underneath it. All these projects are managed under a strategic portfolio, which ensures that each project is aligned to that yearly goal before deciding to include the project in the portfolio.

It's also good to remember that sometimes projects can extend beyond one year to the next. For example, in Figure 15.3, Project 9 and Project 10 extend from Year 2023 to 2024. It is one more reason to keep all these projects in a portfolio that can track and manage the annual budget needed for such projects that extend for more than one year.

> KEY CONCEPT: The strategic journey of an organization describes how each of its strategic dimensions evolves over a multi-year journey.

THE STRATEGY/PORTFOLIO CROSSWALK

In the previous section we just established the following:

1. A strategic vision is necessary for the transformation of an enterprise/organization.
2. The strategic portfolio is necessary for the strategic vision to become a reality.

However, there are several challenges in making the strategic portfolio mirror the strategic vision, as shown below:

- In most organizations, the strategic roadmap is created and approved by senior executives while the projects are executed by project managers and mid-level staff.
- Project managers are familiar with the details of their specific project, but not the big strategic picture or how their individual project fits.
- So, when project managers are asked to choose the strategic priority related to their project, they are often not able to do it correctly.

To bridge the gap between the high-level strategic vision and the list of projects in the portfolio, we need an artifact called the strategy/portfolio decomposition crosswalk. It is typically in the form of a table (see Table 15.1) and is explained below:

- The first column of the table contains the organizational strategy. This is typically aspirational and high-level.
- This high-level aspirational strategy is then decomposed into a set of strategic priorities in Column #2.
- Column #3 contains the descriptions of these strategic priorities. Each strategic priority typically has a multi-year life, with different strategic milestones along the way (as previously seen in Figure 15.1).
- The strategic priorities in Column #2 are then subsequently decomposed into a set of actual project names (Column #4) with concrete scope, schedule, and budget. Every project rolls up to a strategic priority.

Table 15.1   Strategy/Portfolio decomposition crosswalk

High-level Strategy	IT Strategic Priority	Description of Strategic Priority	Projects Aligned to the Strategic Priority
Aspirational Strategic Vision for the Future	A	Geo-coverage	Project 1
			Project 2
			Project 3
	B	Digitizing the Organization	Project 4
			Project 5
			Project 6
	C	Operational Efficiency	Project 7
			Project 8
			Project 9
	D	New Markets and Products	Project 10
			Project 11
			Project 12

> KEY CONCEPT: The strategy/portfolio crosswalk is an artifact that establishes a defini-
> tive link between the strategic vision and individual projects in the portfolio that are
> instrumental in achieving that vision.

How to Use the Strategy/Portfolio Crosswalk

Although the strategy/portfolio crosswalk is a useful tool it cannot, by itself, solve the problem of mapping projects to the correct strategic priority. Even with the crosswalk, there are two common problems that persist:

- There are some project managers who willfully align their projects to a *hot* strategic priority to increase their chances of funding. (Some project owners like to feel that their project really matters to the organization by linking their project to an important or critical priority.)
- Even well-meaning project managers may inadvertently pick the wrong strategic priority to associate with their project because they just may not have all the context behind that priority.

To deal with the above issues, we have a function called a *strategic priority advocate* (SPA). The following are the roles and responsibilities of the SPA:

- The SPA owns a particular strategic priority of the organization's strategic journey.
- The SPA engages with the project owners and analyzes how/whether their project fits with that strategic priority (hence the term). For example, in Table 15.1, Project 1 has been found to be a valid fit under strategic Priority A. There may be other projects that were analyzed and found not to be a valid fit; therefore, they are not shown in the strategy/portfolio crosswalk.
- The SPA validates the strategic impact of a project proposal and assigns a relative score, if necessary. (Example: Project 1 could have a relative score of 9 versus Project 2 which could have a score of 7 as it relates to influencing the strategic priority. This becomes useful if several project

proposals are aligned to that priority and there isn't enough funding for all of them. In that case, the proposals with the highest score get funded first, creating the best possible impact for that priority with the available money).

> KEY CONCEPT: The strategic priority advocate is the point of contact who has ownership of decisions regarding that strategic priority, including which projects are aligned to that priority.

THE ANNUAL PLANNING CONSIDERATIONS OF A STRATEGIC PORTFOLIO

As we explained in Chapters 9 and 10, annual planning is the activity by which we decide which projects are worked on for the next year. For a non-strategic portfolio, the process is exactly as described in those two chapters. However, for a strategic portfolio, there are additional considerations for annual planning.

Consideration #1: Planning Template Form Changes

We covered the list of necessary fields that need to be in the annual planning template in Chapter 10. We now need to add a couple of fields to that list:

- **Project's Strategic Priority:**
  - This field is a dropdown on the Smartsheet form and is a mandatory field.
  - It contains choices that are officially approved strategic priorities.
  - The project proposal submitter needs to select a strategic priority.
  - Some project proposals won't have a strategic dimension, so "None" needs to be one of the choices, preferably the default choice.
- **SPA Validation:**
  - This field is a dropdown on the Smartsheet form and is filled out by the SPA.
  - It contains only these three choices:
    - "Approved"—This choice means that the SPA has reviewed the strategic priority selected for this proposal and approved it.
    - "Not Approved"—This choice means that the SPA has reviewed the strategic priority selected for this proposal and rejected it.
    - "N/A"—This choice is the default choice and simply means that there is no strategic priority applicable for this proposal.

Consideration #2: Project Proposal Review Process

With the help of the priority advocate, here's how the process unfolds during annual planning:

- The project owner fills out the annual planning template and selects a strategic priority choice (from the strategic priority field) that aligns with their project proposal.
- As part of Pass Two, the SPA reviews the strategic fit of every project proposal within their strategic priority. For example, the "Geo-coverage" SPA reviews all proposals that have selected "Geo-coverage."
- If a project proposal is indeed a fit within that priority, the SPA selects "Approved" in the SPA validation field. If it is not a fit, the SPA selects "Not Approved."

Consideration #3: Annual Planning Decision Making Using Strategic Impact

Imagine that there is a CEO/CIO directive to ensure that strategic transformation is driven forward through the annual planning activity. This could take one of the following forms:

1. Example 1: "Ensure that at least 50% of next year's projects are strategic."
2. Example 2: "Forecast the impact of chosen projects on the strategic journey."

These directives are impossible to execute when performing annual planning with a non-strategic portfolio—simply because there is no real connection between the projects and the strategy. However, when using a strategic portfolio, the following approaches become possible:

- Consider the preliminary list of approved projects in Pass Three of the annual planning process. How many of these project records have an approved strategic priority? That should inform how much of the proposed project activity for next year is strategic.
- The above insight is valuable and can drive actions such as strategic gap remediation; maybe the current list of projects is not comprehensive and needs to include more strategic efforts which can then be approved and tilt the balance towards strategic versus tactical.
- Another useful output is to compare the "ideal" strategic roadmap in Figure 15.1 with the "proposed" strategic roadmap created by the annual planning process. The ideal strategic journey is typically created a few years ahead with many assumptions. It is informative to take a blank version (minus the projects) of Figure 15.1 and put the proposed annual planning projects under the yearly strategic milestones to analyze how the actual picture is shaping up. The comparison between the *ideal* and *actual* is a useful output for executive management.

> KEY CONCEPT: Annual planning is closely connected to the strategic portfolio. Much of the activity during annual planning is intertwined with strategic considerations.

THE PORTFOLIO INTAKE CONSIDERATIONS OF A STRATEGIC PORTFOLIO

There are two ways a project gets into a strategic portfolio. One is through annual planning, which is a batch process that happens once a year. We just covered the strategic considerations of annual planning in the previous section. The other way projects get in is through the regular portfolio intake that happens throughout the year. The following are additional considerations of portfolio intake for a strategic portfolio.

Consideration #1: Portfolio Intake Form Changes

In Chapter 5 we covered the list of fields in a portfolio intake sheet for a regular (non-strategic) portfolio. We now need to add the following fields to enable this portfolio intake sheet for a strategic portfolio.

- *Project's Strategic Priority*
- *SPA Validation*

These are the same two fields that have been described in detail in the annual planning section.

Consideration #2: Project Proposal Review Process

With the help of the priority advocate, here's how the process unfolds during regular project intake:

- The project owner fills out the project intake form and selects a strategic priority choice (from the strategic priority field) that aligns with their project proposal.
- After the proposal is submitted through the project intake form, the SPA reviews the strategic fit of every project proposal within their strategic priority. For example, the "Geo-coverage" SPA reviews all proposals that have selected "Geo-coverage."
- If a project proposal is indeed a fit within that priority, the SPA selects "Approved" in the SPA Validation field. If it's not a fit, the SPA selects "Not Approved."
- As described above, the only function of the SPA is to verify or deny the linkage of the project proposal to the strategic priority. The rest of the project proposal review and approval is the same as described in Chapter 5.

> KEY CONCEPT: The portfolio intake of a strategic portfolio has to be modified to accommodate information that conveys how each project proposal has a bearing on the strategic roadmap.

WHY IS A STRATEGIC PORTFOLIO CONSIDERED AN ADVANCED PORTFOLIO?

In the previous paragraphs, we have analyzed at length all the features of a strategic portfolio. It is worth asking why a strategic portfolio is considered an advanced portfolio. In other words, why can't an organization that is just starting its portfolio journey just implement a strategic portfolio? Why is it recommended that an organization implement a basic portfolio and then proceed to building a strategic portfolio as an advanced step? To understand this, consider all the prerequisites that need to be in place for a strategic portfolio:

- A viable strategic roadmap/journey that has been endorsed by executive management.
- A formal strategy/portfolio crosswalk that is acknowledged and accepted by the entire organization.
- The existence of SPAs for each strategic priority.
- The ability and willingness of SPAs to execute the strategic validation duties for annual planning as well as project intake throughout the year.
- Finally, a mandate from executive management to tie the strategic journey to the portfolio.

This substantial list of prerequisites is not easy to attain for an organization that is just starting on its portfolio journey. So, the recommendation is for an organization to get the portfolio basics in place before attempting to implement a strategic portfolio, which is an advanced function.

> KEY CONCEPT: Only an advanced portfolio has the capabilities and process maturity needed to run a truly strategic portfolio.

THE PSEUDO STRATEGIC PORTFOLIO

A discussion about strategic portfolios would not be complete without a cautionary mention of the *pseudo strategic portfolio*. What's this unusual type of portfolio? Quite simply, it's a portfolio to which artificial strategic tags are applied on top of projects to try and create the impression of a strategic journey where there isn't one. Here's how it typically works:

- Annual planning is done as described in Chapter 10 for a non-strategic portfolio. There is no mention of any strategic attributes for any of the project proposals.
- After the proposals are screened, validated, and ultimately approved, an exercise is performed to apply strategic labels to projects after the fact. For example, a project named "Establishment of Dealerships in North America" would get a tag called "Geo-coverage."
- There are several drawbacks with this approach:
  - It is arbitrary to apply strategic labels to projects based on their names. Also, some project names are not descriptive enough.
  - With the above process, there is no scope for an SPA role to validate linkage between projects and strategy.
  - With the above process, the labels can (and often do) change year to year, thus defeating the purpose of a consistent multi-year strategic roadmap.

To summarize, a pseudo portfolio is a feeble attempt to tie a strategic roadmap to a group of projects without undertaking the actual steps to make it a meaningful exercise. Unfortunately, this practice is widespread although the "pseudo" descriptor would be missing from the portfolio title.

> KEY CONCEPT: In a pseudo strategic portfolio, there is no real link between the projects and the strategic roadmap. However, a typically weak matching process is performed to associate each project to the strategy without any supporting information or rigor.

SECTION IV

The Support Systems that
Decide Success

16

THE POLITICS OF PORTFOLIO MANAGEMENT

INTRODUCTION

There are few organizations, if any, that can claim to be apolitical. Political maneuvering is an everyday occurrence that we all deal with at the workplace. However, there is an extra dimension of politics to deal with when it comes to managing a portfolio successfully. The dynamics of portfolio management, with the attendant power to approve and terminate projects and control the spend associated with them, create a particularly fertile ground for political behaviors. In this chapter we explore the following aspects of politics as it relates to portfolio management:

1. Explore what contributes to the political nature of portfolio management
2. Discuss the behaviors associated with the politics of avoidance
3. Discuss the behaviors associated with the politics of deflection
4. Describe a comprehensive list of effective strategies to combat political maneuvering
5. Explore staffing strategies that enable the portfolio office to navigate the political landscape to the portfolio's benefit

WHY IS PORTFOLIO MANAGEMENT SO POLITICAL?

Portfolio management seeks to control how the resources of the organization are spent. It selects the right efforts to work on, and once selected, it reports on how those efforts are progressing. It also prescribes corrective actions when things are not proceeding according to plan—including termination of efforts and possible transfer of ownership of troubled projects. Each of the areas mentioned earlier is quite political, and therefore, portfolio management, the sum total of these areas, is bound to be very political too.

Portfolio management, when done right, could make or mar the careers of people in the organization. Imagine an executive who is adept at managing their projects and delivering on time and on budget. Such a person would do very well with a functioning portfolio, because their projects would be clearly shown as performing better than their peers. Quite soon, such an executive could create a track record within the organization as a dependable performer who can be trusted to deliver on their projects and would be a likely candidate for mission-critical projects and soon, other responsibilities.

However, consider another, more commonly found scenario—an executive whose team isn't quite as well managed. The odds are that their projects would not be as successful. Such a team would show up in a less-than-flattering light when the portfolio is managed well. It would then be apparent to all that this team is not quite delivering on their project commitments and would be characterized by cost and schedule overruns, possibly even project terminations. In a typical organization, most projects and their owners are performing less than optimally. Consequently, very few executives are willing to have portfolio management cast the harsh spotlight of accountability on their projects.

Another area where portfolio management affects the political fortunes of executives is in the approval to start new projects. In an organization where there isn't a functioning portfolio, people start projects with little oversight. Often, no one even knows that a particular project has begun and is consuming resources until well after the fact. While everyone is off executing their pet projects, there may be little alignment between these projects and the stated strategic objectives of the organization. This would work quite differently when a functioning portfolio is in place, along with a robust intake management process. Only the projects aligned with a strategic roadmap would get approved, thus restricting the actions of executives who would like to spend resources on other (nonaligned) initiatives.

> KEY CONCEPT: Portfolio management is political because it can show which project teams are effective and which are not.

THE POLITICS OF AVOIDANCE

As seen in the previous section, few people prefer to be under the *performance microscope* that a portfolio would put them under. Therefore, the first instinct of project owners is to entirely avoid being part of the portfolio and all of the procedures that go with the portfolio. This gives rise to a set of avoidance behaviors, such as:

1. **Refusal to participate in standard phase gates:** This typically unfolds as a request for exemption from portfolio procedures, such as going through the intake process. The most typical reason is that the project in question is *too critical* to be slowed down by going through the intake process.
2. **Refusal to use standard artifacts:** Project owners seeking to control the perception of their projects typically want to avoid the use of standard artifacts that may reveal the true status of their projects. This behavior manifests when the project owners insist on using their own nonstandard reporting templates, which may be vague or confusing. The typical reason given is often something like: "We don't want to waste time repurposing data from one format to another."
3. **Reluctance to be transparent:** Project owners who are practicing avoidance politics are reluctant to show the true state of the projects. The portfolio manager can expect them to resist (passively or actively) any portfolio procedure that would show the state of their projects; for example, milestone-based reporting. Along the same lines, they can also be expected to embrace (and refuse to discontinue) pseudo measures such as the arbitrary red, yellow, and green system of reporting.
4. **Aversion to governance:** Finally, project owners wanting to avoid scrutiny are typically averse to governance. As explained in Chapter 18, governance should review and approve schedule changes, major scope changes, funding releases, and funding turnbacks. The political project owner would want to avoid all or most of this oversight and continue to work independent of governance.

> KEY CONCEPT: The politics of avoidance can drive behaviors that try to evade the spotlight of performance evaluation, which is cast by following portfolio management processes.

POLITICS OF DEFLECTION

As explained in the previous section, the first instinct of project owners is to entirely avoid coming under the purview of portfolio management. But that cannot be a long-term strategy, for eventually the official policy would be to insist that everyone follow portfolio management guidelines. In that case, some project owners start adopting politics of deflection, such as:

1. **Complaining that the portfolio process is cumbersome:** This approach usually takes the form of blaming the new portfolio process for being unworkable—too many new steps, too many signoffs, and too much time taken to do it all. No matter how simple the process, the portfolio manager can expect an unfavorable comparison to the time when there was no process. "We'd like to follow the process, but it's simply unworkable," is the refrain adopted by the project team.

2. **Blaming the portfolio process for the slow pace of work:** This tactic tries to shift the blame to the portfolio process when the project fails to deliver on time or on budget. "Much of our time was spent on portfolio process overhead instead of doing the project work," is what the project owners want to convey.

3. **Projecting that the portfolio staff is inefficient/inept:** This rather malicious approach tries to undermine the portfolio process by attacking the credibility of the portfolio staff. Examples include blaming portfolio staff for missing data, not providing data to the staff on time and then blaming them for incomplete presentations, and various other underhanded tactics. "How can the portfolio team criticize our project for nonperformance when they are doing so badly themselves," is the strategy being adopted here.

KEY CONCEPT: Deflective behaviors aim to show the portfolio process itself as the cause of low performance.

PLAYING POLITICS VERSUS BEING POLITICALLY CORRECT

Given all the complex political tactics adopted by various stakeholders, how can the portfolio manager drive change and succeed in creating a high-functioning portfolio? A broad approach is outlined in this section.

The portfolio manager needs to slowly create an environment where it is no longer politically acceptable to come in with an underperforming project—in other words, bring about a transformation where being an underperformer is a bad exception and untenable. This creates a self-regulating mechanism where politics work in favor of projects that are performing well rather than provide cover for bad actors. Here are the strategies for the portfolio manager to follow in effecting a change in the political climate as it regards portfolio management:

- **Strategy #1—Acquire the mandate for change:** Without a powerful and clear mandate, the portfolio manager will not make much headway. The portfolio initiative needs to be accompanied by a public, prominent mandate—preferably from the chief information officer (CIO). This would signal the other stakeholders that this effort is backed by leadership and cannot be evaded or dismissed easily. The portfolio manager would do well to hold a series of meetings with all of the stakeholders and start by invoking the mandate. It would also help to announce that regular status meetings will be held with the CIO and/or executive management regarding the progress of the rollout.

- **Strategy #2—Seek a powerful patron:** Playing politics is a skill and some people are just not cut out for it. A portfolio manager may be very skilled at portfolio techniques but could also be a total novice at politics. The portfolio initiative is too important to be left to the mercy of political opponents if the portfolio manager is not political enough. What is to be done in that case? One solution is to have the portfolio manager report to a powerful, seasoned executive on a day-to-day basis. This executive should have direction from the CIO to *protect* the portfolio manager and preserve the mission of rolling out portfolio management to the organization.
- **Strategy #3—Roll out changes gradually:** One of the mistakes that portfolio managers make in rolling out changes is to *throw the book* at their organization—namely, they try to do everything that they've read in the latest portfolio management tome. This almost never goes well for the following reasons:
  - The problems are deep-rooted and need a comprehensive fix
  - There is a finite capacity for change in an organization and trying to do too much will overwhelm the people and processes that are already in place
  - Not everyone is invested in making the changes—some of them would like to keep the current state (low or no portfolio management), as it benefits them

Consequently, the *big bang* of change is met with a lot of resistance and may be used by some project owners to call into question the whole effort of portfolio management. The portfolio manager (and the initiative itself) may never recover from this body blow to their credibility. What's the remedy?

A more prudent approach would be to introduce changes slowly, starting with the most significant, useful fixes. For example, it may be more important to have all the work come through an intake queue than have everyone follow the same template for monthly project performance reporting. Once everyone is using the intake queue, the portfolio manager should move on to the next pressing change that needs to be rolled out. In this approach, change can be assimilated as it occurs in more limited portions. Any complaints can be redressed quickly, or the latest change can even be canceled/rolled back as the portfolio team regroups to address the complaints. The biggest advantage of a system of *creeping change* is that project owners cannot find anything objectionable to protest against.

- **Strategy #4—Divide and conquer:** The portfolio manager should take all care to prevent a chorus of complaints arising from the organization. If a critical mass of people begin to complain about the changes made by the portfolio management process, it will be hard for even the sponsors of portfolio management (e.g., the CIO) to shield the portfolio manager from criticism. It may be wise to adopt a *divide and conquer* approach, as described in the next paragraph.

When process changes are introduced as part of the new portfolio management process, it is inevitable that many people will complain. There will definitely be some stakeholders who don't want any change at all—it's impossible to placate such parties. However, not all of the complaining parties may have the same grievances. Some stakeholders may have concerns that can be remediated without much effort. A diligent portfolio manager would do their best to accommodate as many parties as possible, at least in the beginning stages of the portfolio rollout. This may mean going above and beyond in helping the project owners with portfolio artifacts, if possible. It may mean being available for questions in addition to the standard training and documentation. It may also mean being flexible in matters of formats and templates. By doing all of the above (and whatever else is necessary), the portfolio manager can blunt the criticism generated by a few aggrieved parties who just want the whole portfolio process to go away.

- **Strategy #5—Knowing when to adopt pull versus push:** Consider a setup where the project owners have their own funding and the autonomy to spend it on projects that they deem appropriate. Now imagine a portfolio manager tasked with bringing all these project owners into the fold of portfolio management, with the attendant restrictions on their autonomy. It's very hard for a portfolio manager to make any inroads into changing the behaviors and outputs in such a situation. It can be expected that the project owners would fight at every turn to hold on to their autonomy and try to undermine the portfolio effort in every way possible. What can be done in such a situation? An alternative situation is outlined in the next paragraph.

The previous approach can be characterized as a *push* situation, where the portfolio manager is attempting to *push* a new vision of how things should be run in the future—to an audience that is perfectly happy with how things are being run now. Consider a *pull* approach, where the project owners are compelled to come to the portfolio manager instead of the other way around.

A *pull* model fundamentally redefines the power vectors in the relationship between the portfolio and the project owners. In a *pull* model, the project owners are far more amenable to following portfolio procedures in the hopes of securing funding. Consequently, the probability of conflict is greatly reduced under a *pull* model. There will still be some political wrangling, but the portfolio manager holds much more power and can direct the outcomes in ways that are in alignment with the portfolio's success.

Therefore, a portfolio manager should recommend actions to executive management that enable the functioning of a pull model rather than a push model.

- **Strategy #6—Drive for systemic fixes, not spot solutions:** Imagine a system where all project activity (labor and purchase orders) are billed to a project code in the financial system. Furthermore, the project code is auto-generated when the project comes through the intake process and a flag is set after governance review. That's an example of a systemic flow that makes no room for exceptions—every project has to come through the intake process, be reviewed by governance, and approved in the system before money can be spent against it.

  Now consider another system where the portfolio manager has to approve *outside the system* through an email. Next, the project code is manually created and sent to Finance, who has to key it into the system before dollars can be spent against it. This is a recipe for confusion and an invitation for things to fall through the cracks, resulting in a backlash of criticism against the process. Wherever possible, the portfolio manager should focus on a *standard systemic flow* that addresses the needs of the vast majority of stakeholders. The flow need not be sophisticated or need expensive systems (consider Smartsheet for low cost and rapid startup), but needs to be usable and to *work right* most of the time. Any other approach is vulnerable to failure and will attract needless negative attention.

- **Strategy #7—Practice strategic neutralization:** In many organizations, there is usually one person who plays a prominent role in opposing change. This person significantly holds up the rollout of the portfolio by opposing any and all process changes because it may dilute their long-held role or power. This dynamic is usually made harder because this person tends to be *indispensable* or a powerful stakeholder themselves. How can the portfolio manager deal with this roadblock that prevents any progress from being made?

  In this situation the portfolio manager needs to appeal directly to the CIO and point out how the needs of one individual are blocking the progress for the whole organization. In a frank and confidential manner, the portfolio manager needs to recommend to the CIO that the *blocker* be reassigned to a role that prevents them from opposing the portfolio. Little can be done if the CIO is not receptive to this course of action. It is this author's observation that portfolio efforts have been delayed for several years in organizations by a single obdurate individual, and things only began to move once that person left.

- **Strategy #8—Always protect the portfolio office:** The portfolio manager must always be aware of the political nature of their work and be hypervigilant against political foes seeking to damage the credibility of the portfolio process. It's important to realize that not everyone is aligned with establishing a high-functioning portfolio in the organization. Consequently, it's best to have everything in writing and it's always good to have portfolio decisions disseminated after governance meetings.

    While the portfolio manager should endeavor to keep good relations with all stakeholders, the old adage of *trust but verify* would serve them well. In summary, the portfolio manager should be ready to provide proof or substantiation of all claims, especially as it relates to project performance and portfolio transactions.

- **Strategy #9—Anticipate problems and prepare to defuse:** Within a few cycles of the portfolio process, an astute portfolio manager can begin to predict the political actions of the stakeholders, especially ones that tend to be adversarial. As explained in a previous section, some political players seek to constantly evade and avoid while others try to deflect blame—the end goal is to defeat the portfolio system which affects their autonomy.

    In some time, the *habitual complainers* reveal themselves and tend to follow a predictable pattern of behavior. In such situations, the portfolio manager can preempt such behaviors by anticipating and taking advance action. For example, one common complaint following the rollout of a portfolio process is that *there was no training* or *no adequate training*. A smart move for a portfolio manager would be to attach a training guide, preferably with screenshots, to the email announcing the process change. To make their position more formidable, they would also conduct multiple sessions of training and note who attended (this info can be useful to show, for example, that the complainers did not attend the training despite multiple sessions being made available to them—or even that they received the training and are still complaining about the lack of training).

- **Strategy #10—Cultivate goodwill at every opportunity:** The portfolio manager needs to grab every opportunity to sow goodwill in the organization. This includes all of the following suggestions and more:
    1. The portfolio team needs to always be helpful in navigating the portfolio management process and templates. Irrespective of the training offered, it is inevitable that people will still have questions about what to do and how to go about filling out the templates. At times like those, it's never a good idea to ask, "Why didn't you attend the training?" What will be appreciated is the portfolio staff being helpful in the moment of need. The portfolio manager needs to convey the expectation of a service-oriented mindset to all of the portfolio staff—because ultimately, it will reflect on the manager alone.
    2. At least in the beginning of the portfolio rollout, there needs to be some flexibility in terms of templates and formats. It's important to choose battles wisely and it's almost never a good idea to be inflexible on the small things. This builds an image of the portfolio team being reasonable and easy to work with.
    3. Simple is good as far as the project owners are concerned. It must be kept in mind that they have complex responsibilities in addition to following portfolio rules, and doing less in the portfolio is more from their perspective.

    The cumulative result of cultivating goodwill is that the portfolio manager has a receptive audience while proposing additional process changes. It also creates a groundswell of support for the portfolio manager, which is useful when political foes want to attack the portfolio setup.

- **Strategy #11—Portfolio office should always super-communicate:** A portfolio manager can never communicate too much. At the same time, there are ways to over-communicate without being bothersome (such as spamming the organization with emails every hour). Consider the ways to super-communicate:

1. Have a "Portfolio Management Page" in SharePoint or Wiki (or whatever collaboration site the organization uses). This will serve well as a starting point for people to understand how the portfolio process works.
2. All updates to portfolio process and templates need to be broadcast in multiple channels. For example, a process update announcement is made in the SharePoint site and every email portfolio communication includes a link to the SharePoint site.
3. It needs to be easy and straightforward for stakeholders to find things on the portfolio SharePoint site or Wiki (or any other collaboration site used for organizational announcements).
4. Wherever possible, the portfolio office needs to offer to configure automated workflows using Smartsheet, enabling stakeholders to be immediately informed when something relevant changes on their projects.
5. It's very important to have a Frequently Asked Questions list on the SharePoint site that anticipates peoples' questions and redirects them appropriately.

Super-communication is a very smart political behavior to adopt, because it provides solid protection against the more serious complaint of: "The portfolio team never keeps us in the loop."

- **Strategy #12—Name and shame:** Some stakeholders are always trying to get an exception from following the process and having to do their part. Consider a project owner who is trying to wriggle out of creating a benefits statement for their project. In other words, they want to get the funding for a project without stating formally the benefits to be accrued by doing the project. Their end goal is to avoid providing a benefits statement that could then be held up as a comparison for what the project really provides by way of benefits at completion. Typically, they also want the portfolio manager to *provide cover* for them at the governance meeting by providing them with an exception. What should a portfolio manager do in such a situation?

  The portfolio manager should stop *buffering* such bad actors from adverse visibility and let them assume accountability for their situation or position. As discussed, the goal of the portfolio manager should be to make it politically unviable for bad actors to continue flouting portfolio procedures.

  In the example just quoted, the portfolio manager should ask the project owner in question to appear at the governance meeting and explain to the governance members why their ask is unaccompanied by the required artifacts (the portfolio manager should also advise the governance members in advance that this incomplete request is coming up for consideration and recommend not approving it).

  As the portfolio management procedures take hold, *name and shame* becomes a very effective strategy to compel all actors to observe correct policies and procedures.

- **Strategy #13—Build on the momentum:** The road to establishing a portfolio is long and winding, but the portfolio manager eventually overcomes all hurdles and the portfolio starts gaining traction in terms of visibility and results. The journey is far from complete though, when all the potential improvements in the capabilities of the portfolio are considered. Therefore, the momentum needs to be maintained and preserved. What are the political behaviors to adopt in building the momentum?

  The progress of the portfolio journey can be highlighted in the following ways to create a sense of successful transformation and momentum:

  1. Celebrate successes of the portfolio, whether they be successful launches of projects, benefits delivered to the organization, or any noteworthy accomplishment.

2. Celebrate project owners/managers who achieve portfolio benchmarks—such as on-time, on-budget project completions.
3. Describe the road ahead in terms of future capabilities of the portfolio to create a sense of *better things to come.*

The net effect of these activities is to create an impression of portfolio management delivering great value to the enterprise—this makes people want to align themselves with the portfolio team and comply with the policies and procedures.

> KEY CONCEPT: The portfolio manager needs a toolkit of political behaviors that collectively create a climate where it is mandatory to use the portfolio process.

THE EXPENDABLES

Rolling out a portfolio management process is quite a bruising political fight in most organizations. There are several players that are well entrenched in the current status quo and they can be expected to fight tooth and nail to oppose the new process that would directly impinge on their autonomy to select and run projects without oversight.

Few people would want to volunteer to step into the *hot seat* in those situations. Some executives and portfolio managers adopt a novel but expensive strategy to get change implemented while sidestepping the criticism and pushback that may come with it. That strategy is to hire a portfolio consultant who can be the *from-the-outside* face of all the tough decisions that need to be taken.

The consultant pushes through all of the painful iterations that need to be carried through and can finally leave once the system is stable and well accepted. A side benefit is that the consultant can be summarily terminated as a sacrificial offering in one of the political maneuvers if need be. Although this sounds somewhat cruel and mercenary, this practice is actually fairly widespread and is part of the reason why portfolio consultants bill at such a high rate.

There is always a risk in hiring a portfolio consultant. For example, an organization could hire a generic *Big 4* consulting firm (as opposed to a specialized portfolio management expert) and the result would be that much time and money could be wasted in paper-pushing optics while no real work is done in advancing the portfolio's capabilities.

> KEY CONCEPT: Sometimes it makes sense for an outside consultant to propose and implement the tough changes needed for portfolio management to effectively take root and function.

LEVELS OF PORTFOLIO CAPABILITY

Level 1

- Very political atmosphere, with spheres of influence carved out by respective players.
- Portfolio has almost no influence on the respective players—almost no one follows portfolio policies and procedures.
- Political considerations dominate in project selection and project performance readouts.
- It's almost impossible to make progress on portfolio process improvements.

Level 2

- Atmosphere still political, but there is an understanding that project performance supersedes politics.
- Most stakeholders follow portfolio policies and procedures, with a few exceptions.
- Strategic considerations dominate in project selection and performance, but some political jockeying exists.
- Some resistance to portfolio process improvements.

Level 3

- Political undercurrents in the atmosphere, but performance is paramount—there is a meritocracy of sorts.
- All stakeholders follow portfolio policies and procedures; it is politically incorrect to be seen as not following portfolio policies and procedures.
- Project selection and performance are driven by data and strategy considerations only.
- Portfolio process improvements are received well, as no one wants to be seen as holding up progress.

CHAPTER SUMMARY

In this chapter we examined the reasons as to why portfolio management is so intensely political and how the real-life constraints of organizational politics affect the implementation of a portfolio. We covered at length the types of politics that are played by various stakeholders and what their end game is. We then covered a list of effective strategies practiced by successful portfolio managers to blunt the opposition of stakeholders who are opposed to the mission of the portfolio office. The chapter closes with a discussion of staffing strategies that could shield the portfolio office from political blowback.

17

THE PORTFOLIO OFFICE

INTRODUCTION

When a portfolio starts getting large, structuring the portfolio office becomes necessary. The portfolio office is the face of portfolio management and is integral to the success of portfolio management as a function in the organization. In turn, the role of the portfolio manager is central to the portfolio office. In this chapter we explore the following aspects of the portfolio office:

1. The characteristics of an ideal portfolio manager
2. The strategies in staffing the portfolio office
3. The typical composition of a portfolio office
4. The ideal reporting structure and its place in the organizational hierarchy

DESCRIPTION OF AN IDEAL PORTFOLIO MANAGER

A portfolio manager needs to have a specific blend of skills to be effective. Unlike what some people think, an experienced project manager does not automatically qualify to be a portfolio manager. While the familiarity with projects definitely helps, there is more to being a portfolio manager than that. An experienced program manager, on the other hand, is more equipped to take up portfolio management duties. Why? A program is like a mini portfolio with the added complexity of having the projects in the program be interdependent of each other. Also, a program manager has to contend with financials, intake, and sequencing—all of which find parallels in portfolio management.

Another interesting aspect of the portfolio manager's role is the need to modulate role and tone depending on the audience—the portfolio manager needs to interact with a wide variety of people successfully in order to be effective. The following are some prime skills/capabilities that a portfolio manager needs to have in their repertoire.

Skill #1: Being Simultaneously Strategic and Tactical

One of the most important skill sets of a portfolio manager is the ability to toggle between the *big picture* and the *fine details*—namely, to see the woods as well as the trees when the occasion calls for it. The portfolio manager needs to grasp the big picture and be able to engage with the people who function at the big picture level—this includes decision makers, strategy formulation experts, as well as Finance, which is concerned with the bottom line. At the same time, the portfolio manager needs to be able to interact effectively with the project managers and program managers, who operate at a far more tactical level.

Skill #2: Being a Process Expert (and Knowing When to Abandon a Process)

Successful portfolio managers are almost always process experts. That's because they recognize the inherent efficiency in a streamlined process, which empowers people to do things the right way in tandem with the rest of the system. At the same time, portfolio managers design simple, lightweight processes that are realistic and workable for their target audiences. They know that process is always (only) a means to an end and should be as simple as possible. Truly outstanding portfolio managers also know when to suspend/abandon process in order to achieve the ultimate goal and are not dogmatic about following process.

Skill #3: Being Data Savvy

A portfolio generates a huge amount of data. The decision makers and other stakeholders are not necessarily interested in plowing through reams of data. It's up to the portfolio manager to read and understand all of the data, as well as being able to sift through the data for insights that then need to be communicated. This requires a fair amount of data savviness—not just being able to read data, but to actually understand what the data is saying.

Skill #4: Thinking Big + Thinking Small

The portfolio manager needs to always have the big picture in mind. Although we covered the need to grasp the strategic big picture, what is being conveyed here is the need to *think big* in all aspects of the portfolio—for example, the need to plan how to take the organization to the next level of portfolio capability. At the same time, the portfolio manager always needs to be in tune with what is feasible and practical on the ground—for example, he or she needs to carefully ponder whether the organization is ready to follow an earned value management (EVM)-based system or ready to undertake annual planning. A successful portfolio manager will always ensure that the little things are taken care of before aspiring to make the big moves.

Skill #5: Being a Credible Operator

While this skill is hard to define, it essentially comes down to being perceived as a credible, results-oriented person by the organization. In other words, the organization needs to have a high degree of confidence in the portfolio manager's competence and reputation in delivering results. This skill is integral to the role because the credibility of the portfolio manager is one of the factors that determines the success of proposed changes in portfolio process.

Skill #6: Being Financially Fluent

A portfolio manager's role is a semi-finance function. Central to the role is the ability to understand how funds are managed within the organization, the timetables of the finance calendar, how the organization classifies operating expenditures and capital expenditures, as well as the overall annual budget cycle and its cadence. In addition to all of this, a portfolio manager needs to interact frequently with the Finance team, and therefore, needs to be able to *speak their language*. Finally, the portfolio manager needs to be seen as knowledgeable in finance processes while conveying trend predictions to decision makers. All of this calls for a high degree of financial fluency.

Skill #7: Being Politically Savvy

Lack of political skills can completely thwart the progress of a portfolio manager who is otherwise skilled in all the aspects of the role. In fact, this one skill can overshadow all of the other attributes—a politically savvy portfolio manager will always find ways to get his or her agenda implemented. They also know when something is too risky to even attempt, and will bide their time to mount the right kind of attack to accomplish their goals. On the other hand, a nonpolitical portfolio manager will frequently find their efforts stonewalled and risk their continued viability in the organization when they try to press their viewpoints in politically adverse situations.

Skill #8: Possessing Project Management Expertise

While a project manager isn't automatically qualified to be a portfolio manager, it definitely helps a portfolio manager to have good project management skills. A portfolio is high performing only as a result of well-run individual projects. It is impossible for a portfolio to do well with multiple failing projects. Therefore, a portfolio manager has to be equipped with the skills to engage at a project level to understand if the project will fail and weigh down the overall portfolio.

Skill #9: Possessing a Customer Service Mentality

An important skill that is often overlooked while describing a portfolio manager's profile is that the portfolio manager needs to have a strong customer service mentality. Why is this skill so important? Let's consider—a portfolio manager seeks to modify organizational workflow by imposing many process steps and templates. While this is all being done to improve the overall organizational outcomes, it is still an inconvenience in the eyes of the stakeholders. Note that the whole business of portfolio management is seen very differently when viewed from the stakeholders' perspective!

For every change that is rolled out, stakeholders continue to ask many (and often the same) questions over and over again. To accommodate this user behavior pattern and ensure the ultimate success of the effort, the portfolio manager needs to have a customer service mentality to be able to field tedious questions. Having a customer service mentality doesn't just mean having a lot of patience—it involves keeping the stakeholder in mind and designing all changes with a view toward making things easier for the end-user stakeholder.

Skill #10: Possessing Strong Communication Skills

As with all knowledge industry endeavors, communication is a key skill in portfolio management, too. Portfolio managers have the added demand of modulating the same message to suit different audiences. For example, project managers need to be communicated to in specifics; at the same time, decision makers need the same data distilled in a format that lets them make the decisions; and finally, Finance needs an entirely different mode of communication.

Skill #11: Being a Salesman

A successful portfolio manager has to have elements of salesmanship, even showmanship in order to persuade the organization to stay on the portfolio journey. It's common for organizations to feel that they have achieved a lot just by getting to Level 1 capability in most portfolio facets. An organization needs a portfolio manager with good selling skills to convince management to continue investing both political and actual capital in getting to the next level. These skills would also come in handy for the portfolio manager to demonstrate the successful accomplishments of the portfolio office.

> KEY CONCEPT: The ideal portfolio manager needs to display several different skill sets to be successful. Some of these divergent skill sets are hard to find in one single person, thus creating the need for a multi-person portfolio office.

STRATEGIES IN STAFFING THE PORTFOLIO OFFICE

It's a tall order to find one person who possesses all of the skills a successful portfolio manager needs. Some of these skills are somewhat dichotomous and are unlikely to be found in the same person—for example, the ability to think big while also being detail oriented. Barring rare exceptions, big picture thinkers are typically averse to managing the details and vice versa. It may be more realistic to state that the previous list of skills are capabilities that need to be displayed by the portfolio office. That's why the portfolio office is made up of more than just the portfolio manager. How can the typical organization staff their portfolio office and ensure success? Coming up next are some of the proven strategies.

Strategy #1: Division of Competence

This strategy calls for different people in the portfolio office to play complementary roles, so that as a whole, the portfolio office is able to achieve the desired effectiveness. This works around the need for the portfolio manager to have all of the skills that are outlined in the previous section, which may be an impractical requirement to meet. How could this possibly work?

One way to make this possible is to have a director role (Director of Portfolio Management) and a manager role who reports to the director. The manager could conceivably focus on shoring up all of the tactical aspects of the portfolio office and follow ups with project and program managers, while the director could handle all of the senior stakeholders and be responsible for the portfolio office's direction.

Strategy #2: Outsourced Expertise

It's a full-time job to run the portfolio office in its day-to-day functioning and ensure that throughput is kept at an optimal level. However, the portfolio office also needs to continuously improve and get to the next level of capability in all dimensions. How can the portfolio office achieve this *quantum leap* while ensuring the normal operations are not disrupted?

One option is to hire outside help to put in place the arrangements to get to the next level. This may include, for example, consulting to design an EVM setup, along with the training to roll it out, as well as a website to ensure that people have resources to refer to.

Strategy #3: Political Support and Patronage

Perhaps the most important skill for a portfolio manager is to know how to navigate the political waters of the organization. Without this skill, the portfolio manager cannot prevail in their role and cannot get the portfolio office to where it needs to be. One way of overcoming this hurdle is to entrust the portfolio office role to a seasoned veteran of the organization who is political enough to weather the expected opposition while implementing the portfolio office. This person can then acquire team members who have the required portfolio management skills to actually start and run a portfolio.

Strategy #4: Strength in Numbers

This strategy creates momentum for the portfolio agenda by staffing the portfolio office with numerous personnel who can do much of the work for the stakeholders in an effort to eliminate pushback. For example, consider a situation where the portfolio office fills out the new project templates on behalf of the stakeholders, and then all that the stakeholders have to do is review the template and suggest changes. This would meet with much greater adoption and enthusiasm than, say, asking the stakeholders to fill out the new project proposal completely on their own. Similarly, for most other portfolio actions, the portfolio office can meet the stakeholders more than midway by doing much of the work.

> KEY CONCEPT: There are several strategies to staff the portfolio office—each strategy has its applicability according to the situation.

TYPICAL COMPOSITION OF THE PORTFOLIO OFFICE

What should the composition of a portfolio office look like? While it depends on the size of the portfolio, here is a starting point for the kinds of roles to keep in mind while designing the makeup of the portfolio office:

- A director of portfolio management—this should be someone who is typically a senior person with access to executive management. As mentioned before, this person needs to have the political wherewithal to push the agenda of the portfolio management office. This person also needs to be regarded as a credible and reliable partner who keeps their word and delivers results.
- A manager of portfolio management—this requires someone who is well versed in portfolio management and is willing to get involved in the details. This person needs to work closely with the director and provide them with the executive summary (with details as necessary) to convey to executive management.
- Finance role—this needs to be someone who is adept at finance processes and is able to manage the *money aspect* of the portfolio, including interfacing with Finance team members.
- Business analyst—this is someone who is comfortable with pulling reports, rearranging data, producing different views of the data as directed by the manager or director. This person would also own all of the portfolio data and manage the same.
- Project manager—this role is unusual in a portfolio office, but is sometimes seen. This role would provide project management guidelines to the other project managers. This role could also function as the process expert and point of contact for the other project managers.
- Web content management—this role can manage all of the voluminous data being generated by the portfolio operations, maintain the website, and make changes to the website as necessary. This role also needs to be responsible for storing and retrieving historical data for later reference.
- Communications—this would be a role to manage the messaging that comes out of the portfolio office. This person would be responsible for communications regarding the governance schedule, the annual planning timeline, and deadlines.
- Portfolio coordinator—this should be someone who can manage the numerous meetings that need to happen as part of the portfolio operations. This would include scheduling monthly governance meetings, template update meetings, rollout meetings for new portfolio changes, and training sessions for annual planning.

It needs to be kept in mind that this is just a listing of roles/functions that need to be in place for the portfolio to run effectively. More than one role could be done by the same person: for example, the web content management, communications, and portfolio coordination role could be performed by the same person, unless the portfolio is so massive that it makes sense to have a dedicated person filling each of the roles. Also, the director and manager role could be combined, as the situation permits.

> KEY CONCEPT: An effective portfolio office has several different functions that are typically filled by a team of people with complementary skill sets.

PORTFOLIO OFFICE'S REPORTING STRUCTURE

Where should the portfolio office be in the organizational hierarchy? A few broad outlines are provided here, with the understanding that the specifics would vary by organization.

1. The portfolio office needs to have unfettered access to the CIO in order to communicate important decisions that need to be made. See Chapter 19 for more on the close interaction between the portfolio office and the CIO.
2. As mentioned several times, the portfolio needs political power to carry out its role. Where it reports could play a major role in signaling the political clout of the portfolio office to the rest of the organization.
3. From a reporting standpoint, the portfolio office could report directly to the office of the CIO or it could report to a role such as vice president of shared services, who in turn would report to the CIO.

> KEY CONCEPT: The effectiveness of a portfolio office is determined by its place in the organizational structure and is optimized by reporting to a powerful executive who reports to the CIO.

LEVELS OF PORTFOLIO CAPABILITY MATURITY

Level 1

- The concept of a portfolio function is absent—projects are essentially run independently by the respective project managers. A portfolio office, if present, has little power and impact.
- There is little awareness of a portfolio office's value in the organization.
- Sometimes there may be an approximation of the portfolio function, which may only involve one person collecting readouts from all the projects and presenting this status to leadership.
- There is no central management of the portfolio's funds.
- Management does not know how the projects are doing beyond what is self-reported.

Level 2

- The portfolio function exists but is insufficiently defined.
- While there is a portfolio manager, the other supporting roles may not be present, causing the portfolio office to operate at a reduced capacity.

- The portfolio office oversees the execution of projects, but its responsibility is limited due to the basic nature of its capabilities.
- The portfolio office does not have access to executive management and only provides read-outs of basic value.
- The portfolio office is not able to carry out funds allocation based on project performance.

Level 3

- A well-defined portfolio function exists with all of the necessary roles that enable the portfolio office to offer a full range of services to the organization.
- The portfolio manager is ably supported by auxiliary roles in the portfolio office.
- The organization recognizes and accepts the role played by the portfolio office.
- The portfolio office oversees the execution of projects in all aspects.
- The portfolio office has access to executive management and provides meaningful recommendations.
- The portfolio office is able to direct resources to the most important strategic activities.

CHAPTER SUMMARY

This chapter covered the team that actually drives the mission of portfolio management forward—namely, the portfolio office. We began by exploring the characteristics of the ideal portfolio manager and the difficulty of finding all of those characteristics in a single person. From that introduction, we went on to describe the strategies that are effective in staffing a portfolio office. We further covered the composition of an ideal portfolio office before detailing the ideal reporting structure and place of the portfolio office in the organizational hierarchy. We concluded the chapter with a description of the levels of maturity for this portfolio capability.

18

PORTFOLIO GOVERNANCE

INTRODUCTION

In an ideal world, only the right projects would present themselves for funding, get funded quickly, and then proceed to deliver all of the promised benefits while executing on time and on budget. In the real world, almost none of those things happen. That's where portfolio governance comes in and tries to steer the actual course of events closer to what should ideally happen. This chapter explores the following aspects of governance as it relates to portfolio management:

1. Define governance and explain the role of governance in portfolio management
2. List the modes of operation of portfolio governance and distinguish between the modes
3. Explain the functions of governance under the routine portfolio operation mode
4. Describe the artifacts produced under the routine portfolio governance mode
5. Explain the functions of governance under the annual planning portfolio operation mode
6. Describe the artifacts produced under the annual planning portfolio governance mode
7. Describe the role of support systems in enabling portfolio governance to occur
8. Explore the ideal composition of portfolio governance
9. List the factors for portfolio governance success

WHAT IS PORTFOLIO GOVERNANCE?

Formally, governance is defined as the establishment of portfolio policies and continuous monitoring of their proper implementation by the members of the governing body of an organization. It includes the mechanisms required to balance the powers of the members (with the associated accountability). In the case of portfolio management, the primary duty of the governance body is to maintain and enhance the performance and viability of the portfolio.[1]

Portfolio governance is also used to refer to the team of senior leaders who carry out portfolio governance functions as previously defined. These leaders bear responsibility for the success of the portfolio and are empowered to make decisions about the portfolio, both tactical and strategic. They also have ownership of the direction of the portfolio.

> KEY CONCEPT: The effectiveness of a portfolio is determined by the presence of a governance body which is empowered to make tough decisions.

TWO FUNDAMENTAL MODES OF PORTFOLIO GOVERNANCE

For discussion purposes, two modes of portfolio governance have been identified:

- Routine portfolio governance: The context for this mode of operation occurs during the whole year—focused on the current year.
- Portfolio governance during annual planning: The context for this mode of operation occurs during annual planning, which is basically planning for the next year. Annual planning is covered extensively in Chapter 10.

The details of these two modes are addressed separately in the next section.

ORCHESTRATION OF ROUTINE PORTFOLIO GOVERNANCE

Functions of Governance

The following functions are carried out by portfolio governance as part of the routine, year-round operation.

Function #1: Review of Current Portfolio Finances

The portfolio governance body convenes periodically to review the portfolio. One of the key functions during each session is to review the current state of the portfolio finances. Key assessments include the following:

- Is the portfolio spending as planned? Both underspend and overspend are undesirable.
- Has the portfolio allocated enough funds to projects? Again, a balance is needed here because either too much or too little will create a suboptimal scenario.
- Does the portfolio look like it will end the year on budget or within a small variance? It is important for portfolio governance to be aware of how the year-end scenario is shaping up and start taking corrective actions.

Function #2: Approval of New Projects

A key activity that portfolio governance needs to perform is the approval and funding of new projects. In doing this activity, a delicate balance needs to be maintained: Appropriate proposals that are in line with the portfolio's mandate need to be approved as soon as possible, but questionable proposals need to be reviewed and blocked from proceeding. The key to achieving this balance lies in the application of project approval criteria as shown here:

- **Strategic fit:** How is this proposal a fit for the goals of this portfolio?
- **Cost:** What does this cost in terms of operating expenditure (OPEX) and capital expenditure (CAPEX)—by quarter, by year?
- **Strategic roadmap impact:** How does this project relate to our strategy? What capabilities will this project add to our strategic roadmap?
- **Benefits:** What is the return on investment (ROI)? Are the benefits soft (productivity savings, etc.) or hard (revenue, actual cost reduction in the general ledger, etc.)?
- **Resources needed:** What are the estimated resource requirements for this project?
- **Opportunity cost:** What is the cost of not doing this project? (This is good to have in case the proposal is not approved for funding.)

To enable portfolio governance to make the right decision, the fields listed above need to be populated and vetted for accuracy by the portfolio office before being presented to governance for a decision.

Function #3: Review of Project Performance

Portfolio performance ultimately depends on the performance of each project. Therefore, project performance is a key activity that needs to be undertaken by portfolio governance at every periodic session. Here is the key factor that influences speedy and effective reviews of project performance:

- **Subjective performance data versus objective performance data:** Objective performance data is strongly preferred over subjective performance data for the purposes of project performance review by portfolio governance. Apart from the obvious advantages of making decisions based on objective data, there is the added advantage of objective data lending itself to sorting and ranking in a manner that allows portfolio governance to focus on the most essential projects in need of attention. Objective performance data allows portfolio governance to triage their efforts in an optimal manner.

Function #4: Decision to Kill Projects

It is a fact of project management that some projects with serious performance problems cannot be remediated and have to be terminated. Other projects may be performing as planned but the anticipated benefits of the project may not be occurring, creating a need to terminate the project (see Function #5). Sometimes projects need to be terminated because of changing priorities or strategic direction. In all cases, portfolio governance has to make the decision to terminate a project after reviewing all the previous information. After portfolio governance makes the decision, the portfolio office records the decision and implements the same. It needs to be reiterated here that for any kind of performance-related action on a project, it is vital to have an objective performance measurement system (e.g., objective red/yellow/green).

Function #5: Decision to Approve Change in Project Parameters

Projects are dynamic entities whose parameters cannot be predicted with certainty at the beginning of the project. Therefore, it's quite common for projects, even well-performing ones, to request an authorized change in scope, schedule, or budget parameters. It's a function of portfolio governance to approve these changes and the responsibility of the portfolio office to ensure that those changes are made part of the project's record.

Function #6: Review Benefit Delivery of Projects

The purpose of undertaking projects is to obtain the benefits promised by the projects. However, a significant proportion of projects fail to deliver the promised benefits. Hence, it is the duty of the portfolio governance body to monitor the delivery of benefits as promised and take corrective action if the benefits are not to be found. There needs to be a portfolio benefits realization process that is managed by a portfolio benefits review council (PBRC). This council is the working body that goes through the details of the benefits of various projects and then presents the readout of these benefits (along with recommendations of courses of action) to portfolio governance. It's up to portfolio governance to decide whether to proceed with the recommendations. The actions that portfolio governance takes are recorded by the portfolio office and followed up on to ensure execution.

> KEY CONCEPT: The portfolio governance body needs to perform the above functions regularly to have a working portfolio.

Meeting Frequency

How frequently does a portfolio governance body need to meet for the purpose of routine governance? Although it is a function of the combined availability of a group of senior people, the minimum recommended meeting frequency for routine governance is monthly. In the case of large portfolios, the monthly meeting may have to be long enough to accommodate all of the projects that have transactions at the session. An alternative is to hold more frequent sessions of smaller duration.

Artifacts of Routine Portfolio Governance

There are two important artifacts of the routine portfolio governance meeting:

1. The portfolio governance deck
2. The portfolio governance decision letter

These two artifacts are covered in detail in the next sections.

The Portfolio Governance Deck

The portfolio governance deck basically consists of the portfolio materials that are compiled by the portfolio office for review and decision by the portfolio governance body. The following are the three main components that should be in each meeting's deck.

Component #1: Portfolio Financial Performance Data

Portfolio financial performance data describes how the portfolio is doing from a financial perspective. Typically the following data is included while describing portfolio performance:

- **Overall portfolio budget:** This data shows how much money has been allocated to the portfolio for the current year. This needs to be broken out by OPEX and CAPEX.
- **Allocated funds versus remaining:** Of the total budget, how much has been allocated to various projects and how much is available for new projects?
- **Allocated versus released:** This data compares the amount of money allocated to various projects versus the amount of money that has actually been released.
- **Actual money spent by the portfolio:** This data shows what has actually been spent—the actuals—by the portfolio. Typically, there is a drill-down that should be available so governance can see the actuals by project.
- **Cost performance of the portfolio:** This data shows what the productivity is per dollar spent.
- **Schedule performance of the portfolio:** This data shows what the schedule progress is per dollar spent.
- **Estimate to completion versus allocated budget:** This data indicator attempts to estimate how much more money is needed for each project need before it becomes complete.

Component #2: New Project Proposals for Approval

New proposals that need approval and funding are included here for review and decision by portfolio governance. In order to facilitate a speedy decision, the following data should accompany each proposal, as pointed out in Chapter 4 (Introduction to Portfolio Intake and Assessment):

- **Strategic fit:** How is this proposal a fit for the goals of this portfolio?
- **Cost:** What does this cost in terms of OPEX and CAPEX—by quarter, by year?

- **Strategic roadmap impact:** How does this project relate to our strategy? What capabilities will this project add to our strategic roadmap?
- **Benefits:** What is the ROI? Are the benefits soft (productivity savings, etc.) or hard (revenue, actual cost reduction in the general ledger, etc.)?
- **Resources needed:** What are the estimated resource requirements for this project?
- **Opportunity cost:** What is the cost of not doing this project? (This is good to have in case the proposal is not approved for funding.)

While only summary data regarding the proposals are needed for the portfolio governance review, the details substantiating the aforementioned information should be available in the Appendix (described under Component #3).

Component #3: Appendix with Raw Data

It needs to be remembered that all of the data shown in the first two components of the portfolio deck are summary data that are meant for quick review by the portfolio governance members. However, the members may want to dive deep into certain items to understand the details before coming to a decision. For completeness, all the raw data (from which the summary data is derived) is stored in the appendix. The raw data consists of the following:

- Details underlying portfolio actuals (for Component #1)
- Details underlying new project proposals (for Component #2)

To make navigation easy, it is recommended that hyperlinks be embedded in the main body of the deck which when clicked upon would jump to the relevant section in the appendix.

> KEY CONCEPT: Regular production of the portfolio deck (in any format) ensures predictability and reportability in portfolio transactions.

The Portfolio Governance Decision Letter

Each time portfolio governance meets, there are many decisions to be made. Potentially every item listed on the portfolio governance deck could result in a decision. Therefore, there is a need to create a format where all of these decisions can be recorded and disseminated. This is where the portfolio governance decision letter comes in. This is a document that contains all the decisions that were made by portfolio governance at a particular session. This document is then disseminated within the organization to ensure visibility to the decisions contained therein.

> KEY CONCEPT: Producing and archiving the portfolio governance decision letter enables a historical reference for key decisions over a multi-year period.

Relation to Other Governance Bodies

As mentioned before, portfolio governance is composed of senior people whose time is at a premium. One way of mitigating this executive availability constraint is to divide some of the governance load among other parties. This arrangement will typically take the following forms:

- **The portfolio subcommittee:** This is a subordinate body to portfolio governance and has been granted oversight authority within limits. For example, the subcommittee could approve new project proposals up to a nominal amount of $100K. The subcommittee could also review other components of the portfolio governance deck and make recommendations for portfolio governance's consideration. For example, the subcommittee could review the performance details of projects and recommend that some of them be placed on the enhanced monitoring list (EML). Alternatively, they could recognize the improving trend of certain projects already on the EML and recommend that these be taken off the EML. The advantage of this arrangement is that the subcommittee can spare the time to go through the details and then make appropriate recommendations for final approval by the main body (portfolio governance). To make this arrangement functional, there needs to be a trusted working relationship between the main body and the subcommittee.
- **The benefit review board:** One of the big challenges in portfolio management is ensuring that projects deliver on their promised benefits. Benefits realization management practices need to be in place to ensure that benefits are delivered as promised. One of those benefit management practices is the regular functioning of a PBRC. The PBRC reviews benefits in detail and then makes recommendations to the portfolio governance body. For example, consider a project that is not delivering benefits as planned. The PBRC reviews this project as part of its review of all benefit-bearing projects and makes a recommendation whether to terminate the project or not. This recommendation is supplied to the portfolio governance body, which then has to make the final decision to terminate the project.

ORCHESTRATION OF ANNUAL PLANNING PORTFOLIO GOVERNANCE

Functions of Governance

Annual planning is the exercise to comprehensively analyze the organization's demand for the next year and decide which proposals to fund. The following functions are carried out by portfolio governance as part of the annual planning activity.

Function #1: Authorization of the Annual Planning Exercise

The portfolio governance body authorizes the portfolio office to kick off the annual planning exercise. Before socializing changes to templates and processes with the rest of the organization, the portfolio office first previews the same with the governance body for their approval. After portfolio governance provides their approval, the portfolio office proceeds to launch annual planning activities—such as the planning workshop—where the new templates and process changes are socialized.

Function #2: Validate the Strategic Roadmap and Strategic Priorities for the Coming Year

Before the annual planning year can start, portfolio governance needs to review and validate the strategic roadmap. Figure 18.1 shows the strategic multi-year roadmap for Dimension A. Similar to this roadmap for Dimension A, there are other roadmaps for the other strategic dimensions. Prior to embarking on gathering the demand data from the organization, the following is required from portfolio governance:

- Confirmation that the set of strategic dimensions is valid for the annual planning activity

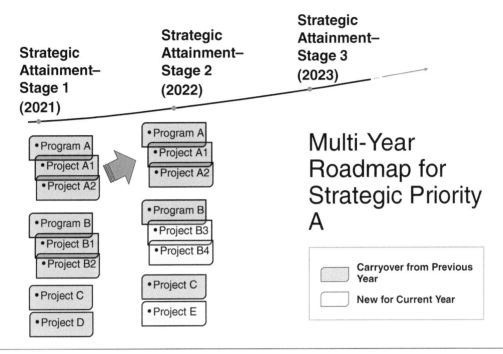

Figure 18.1   Strategic multi-year roadmap for Dimension A

- Confirmation that all projects need to align themselves to one or more strategic dimensions to be included in the annual planning exercise

This function is very important because the whole exercise of annual planning needs to be in alignment with the strategic roadmap of the organization. By confirming the strategic priorities ahead of the annual planning effort, portfolio governance sets the stage for the rest of the exercise.

Function #3: Review Aggregated Annual Planning Data

The first step in annual planning involves the collection of demand from all the stakeholders in the organization. The second step is to compile this demand data into an aggregated form for easy analysis. It's the portfolio governance's role to review this data and make key decisions on whether a certain project is above the line or below the line. One of the key artifacts for portfolio governance to review is the bubble chart shown in Figure 18.2. This bubble chart shows how all the demand gathered during annual planning is distributed from a cost/risk/benefit perspective.

Review of the bubble chart is necessary to decide which projects offer the best cost/benefit/strategic value ratio and factor that decision into the final *above-the-line/below-the-line* determination.

It also falls to portfolio governance to review how the mass of collected demand aligns to various strategic dimensions—for example, certain priorities could be oversubscribed while others may not have sufficient projects that identify as belonging to those undersubscribed dimensions. In that case, portfolio management has two decisions to make:

1. Decide which of the projects aligned to the oversubscribed dimensions should get funding. For example, if 15 projects are aligned to Strategic Dimension A, portfolio governance should decide if all 15 would get funded (leaving less money for other strategic dimensions) or if only some of the 15 should be funded—and if so, which ones.

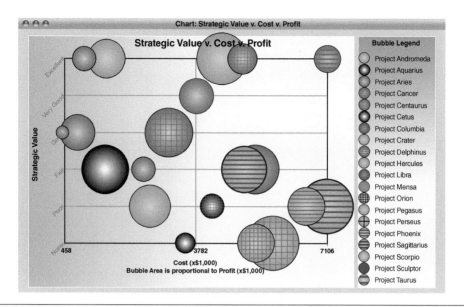

Figure 18.2   Bubble chart showing the distribution of annual planning demand

2. Decide what should be done to mitigate the undersubscribed dimensions. For example, if only two projects are aligning themselves to Strategic Dimension B, it may not be enough to achieve the required transformation in that dimension's multi-year journey. Portfolio governance needs to decide if they will direct certain project owners to make changes in their submission or make new submissions that mitigate the gaps.

Finally, portfolio governance may need to review the templates associated with each project to get more in-depth information about each project, as necessary. After reviewing all of the oversubscribed and undersubscribed dimensions, portfolio governance needs to decide on the ranking of the projects. This ranking information is provided to the portfolio office, which then publishes a ranked list of projects comprising the annual planning demand.

Function #4: Supply Demand Matching

Most organizations start the annual planning exercise with a preliminary budget number that represents the total amount of money available to fund projects in the new year. The challenge then is to maximize the value delivered to the organization within the constraints of this budget number. When it is found that the aggregate demand exceeds the supply of funds, it is then a function for portfolio governance to determine what needs to be done to bridge the gap between supply and demand, which is addressed as follows:

- Portfolio governance first reviews the available funds along with the demand of the top-ranked projects and determines what's above-the-line (funded) versus below-the-line (unfunded).
- The implications of not funding certain projects (also known as the *cost of not doing*) is discussed among the portfolio governance body and shared with the organization and other stakeholders as appropriate. The aim is to determine if the present above/below line proposal creates unacceptable risk to the organization.

- Typically, some relief is obtained from Finance in the form of additional funds, which makes it possible to squeeze in a few more projects above the line. Portfolio governance will need to make the decision about which projects should get these funds and get above the line.
- Alternatively, if no additional funds become available, portfolio governance may decide that funds need to be carved out of existing above-the-line projects to provide for a few below-the-line projects. Portfolio governance also needs to decide which projects need to pare down their demand and by how much.
- After some jostling and rearranging, a final configuration emerges that portfolio governance needs to make official as the annual planning list. In the context of this final list, the portfolio office updates the strategic roadmaps (Figure 18.1) for all the dimensions to show *funded versus unfunded* projects so that portfolio governance fully understands the impact of the funding decisions to the strategic roadmap.
- The below-the-line projects are turned into a queue that can absorb any new funds that may become available during the year. Portfolio governance reviews and approves the *queue* and confirms that these projects will be first in line for any new funding that becomes available.

KEY CONCEPT: A functioning governance body is integral to successful annual planning.

Meeting Frequency

How frequently does a portfolio governance body need to meet for the purpose of annual planning governance? Although the name *annual planning* denotes once a year, in reality, the annual planning exercise takes several months to successfully accomplish. Therefore, it is appropriate to plan for several sessions of portfolio governance to transact the necessary actions for annual planning leadership. Since the earlier constraint of availability of a group of senior people still applies, some organizations prefer to hold a few combined sessions where both the annual planning activity and the routine governance activity occur. Given the difficulty of holding long sessions with the limited availability of executive members, one mitigation strategy followed by different organizations is to circulate annual planning materials for offline review by the portfolio governance members. Only the final decisions need to be included in the live session.

Meeting Artifacts

Before we explain the list of meeting artifacts involved in the annual planning governance, it needs to be remembered that these artifacts are created and reviewed in a progression of time and are not all present at one meeting. (This is in marked contrast to routine portfolio governance, where the governance deck and the decision letter are featured at every session.) In other words, the first annual planning meeting may involve just a review of the annual planning materials package, which consists of the unranked list of projects, multi-year strategy roadmap, and the bubble chart. Once portfolio governance has had a chance to review these artifacts and articulate a preliminary priority, the portfolio office is able to create and table the next artifact (preliminary ranked list of projects) for discussion at the next session, and so on until the final annual planning list is created. Here is the combined list of the artifacts used as part of the annual planning exercise:

1. Unranked list of projects
2. Multi-year strategy roadmap
3. Bubble chart

4. Preliminary ranked list of projects
5. Above-the-line/Below-the-line determination list
6. Final annual planning ranked list of projects

Relation to Other Governance Bodies

Annual planning is characterized by the need to analyze huge amounts of demand data in order to arrive at the optimal mix of projects to fund for the next year. Although the portfolio office distills the mass of data into a few concise artifacts—such as the annual planning materials package—it is still a time-intensive task that the senior executives who comprise the portfolio governance body are confronted with. One way of dealing with this situation is to divide some of the governance load among other parties. This arrangement typically takes the following forms:

- **The portfolio subcommittee:** This is the same subordinate body that was seen earlier as part of the routine portfolio governance. The subcommittee works under the authority of portfolio governance and has been granted oversight authority within limits. The subcommittee would go through the annual planning demand data and make requests for changes or clarifications. It may challenge some of the data that does not stand up to scrutiny. It may even come up with a suggested ranking, which would then be approved (with modifications, if necessary) by the portfolio governance body. The advantage of this arrangement is that the subcommittee can spare the time to sift through the mass of data generated by annual planning demand gathering and ensure that all of the data is correct and dependable for portfolio governance to make decisions. An added advantage is that the subcommittee can make appropriate recommendations for final approval by the main body (portfolio governance). To make this arrangement functional, there needs to be a trusted working relationship between the main body and the subcommittee.
- **The strategic priority advocates:** The priority advocate is someone who is the steward of a particular strategic priority. The roles and responsibility of the priority advocate are described as follows:
    - The priority advocate owns a portion of the strategic roadmap and has been designated as the point person for that strategic priority of the organization's strategic roadmap.
    - The priority advocate engages with the project owners and analyzes how/whether their project fits with that particular strategic priority (hence the term *priority advocate*).
    - The priority advocate validates the strategic impact of a project proposal as documented in the annual planning template and assigns a relative score, if necessary. (Example: Project A1 could have a relative score of nine, whereas Project C could have a score of seven as it relates to influencing the strategic priority. Alternatively, strategic impact (to the same specific priority) can be described as high/medium/low).
    - It's worth noting here that there may be several priority advocates, each responsible for a particular priority in the strategic roadmap.

Portfolio governance relies heavily on the priority advocate to ensure that the whole annual planning exercise is strategically meaningful. The priority advocate ensures that projects are really aligned to the strategic priorities and provides portfolio governance with the confidence to proceed on that basis to make the right decisions. Finally, after the conclusion of the annual planning exercise, the priority advocate updates the strategic roadmap with new projects that fit within the priority and get funded as part of the annual planning.

EXPLORING GOVERNANCE COMPOSITION

Is governance essentially a case of managing by committee? Traditionally, a committee structure of leadership is associated with deflection of responsibility and lack of accountability. One could make a case that it would be more effective for the portfolio to be run under a single point of leadership—which does happen in many places. However, the corporate trend points toward *participatory democracy*—a group of leaders getting together to make decisions that work for all of them, hold them accountable, and still achieve the desired impact on the ground. Therefore, the predominant structure for portfolio governance tends to be a team of people.

Another reason governance composition needs to be more than one person is to ensure representation of all of the stakeholders' interests. An information technology (IT) portfolio might have its governance body consist of all of the CIO's direct reports, ensuring that the portfolio works for all of IT and not just engineering, for example. It's also a good idea to include business representation in the portfolio governance body because the ultimate purpose of a portfolio is to serve the interests of the business.

SUCCESS FACTORS FOR GOVERNANCE

Governance is successful when all (or most) of the following concepts hold true.

#1 Governance Members Have a (Significant) Stake in the Portfolio's Functioning

Sometimes organizations will have governance members who are not directly related to the portfolio's main body of work. Such people, while well meaning, are simply not driven enough to demand optimal output from the portfolio. They are also not very insistent on taking the portfolio to the next level. Their lukewarm interest in the portfolio's capabilities and throughput translates into a suboptimal functioning for the portfolio.

#2 Governance Members Have the Mandate to Make Hard Decisions

As the saying goes, the buck stops with the governance as far as the portfolio is concerned. The portfolio governance members need to be able to make hard decisions, such as:

- Saying *no* to bad projects—not even starting them
- Terminating bad projects that are beginning to underperform
- Validating projects if they are indeed delivering benefits as promised
- Rebalancing the portfolio as needed

#3 Governance Is Empowered with Tools and Data

For governance to work, they need to be provided with the right tools and data about project performance so they can make the right decisions. That's precisely why there is a strong need to provide governance with clear, objective data. In the absence of such a system, even a motivated and empowered governance team is prevented from making the right decisions.

#4 Governance Members Are Coachable in Portfolio Theory

Governance members must recognize that portfolio management is a science and that there is opportunity for their portfolio to evolve in terms of capability. Consequently, they should be coachable/receptive in understanding how to function in a way that enables the portfolio to get to the next level. I have found that portfolios work best when governance understands how to integrate new tools or new techniques to aid their decision making.

> KEY CONCEPT: Governance bodies can only be effective in enabling portfolio function when the success factors described above are aligned.

CAUTIONARY NOTE ABOUT GOVERNANCE

Having a governance body in place is a great thing for a portfolio, as long as the governance body actively monitors the portfolio and makes the right decisions. At the same time, governance bodies would do well to guard against becoming the *masters of the tea ceremony*. Imagine a portfolio with regularly scheduled governance meetings, with all the trappings that go with it—that is, well-prepared meeting materials, followed by detailed meeting minutes and documented decision letters. Does this always result in a well-functioning portfolio? No, it doesn't.

An indicator of the portfolio's success over the years can be measured using the portfolio's performance over the course of a multi-year journey. A high-performing portfolio should show an increasing trend in cost efficiency and schedule efficiency over the years. This increasing trend is only possible when the portfolio governance is willing to make the hard decisions of terminating bad projects, funding the right projects, and being an effective steward of portfolio funds and output.

Surprisingly, many portfolios are reluctant to tackle the politically harder task of actual governance and instead settle for observing the outward appearances—much like an elegant tea ceremony that transacts no real business. In this kind of situation, the only way to ensure that governance is effective comes from executive vision at the top.

LEVELS OF PORTFOLIO CAPABILITY

Level 1

- The organization has a limited understanding of the importance of governance. Consequently, there is little governance overseeing the portfolio.
- Due to the limited footprint of governance, it may not be possible to draw a distinction between the different modes of governance (such as routine mode and annual planning mode).
- If governance exists, its role may be limited to a cursory review of project performance as opposed to a comprehensive review of portfolio health indicators.
- There may not be defined artifacts generated by routine portfolio governance.
- There may not be other defined bodies—such as the benefit review board—that can complement the function of governance. Consequently, governance may have to perform those functions or do without them.

- Few or none of the success factors of governance are found.
- At this level, governance is symbolic and not really delivering meaningful direction or value to the portfolio.

Level 2

- The organization has a good understanding of the importance of governance. Consequently, there is governance oversight over all the major areas of the portfolio.
- There is a clear distinction between the different modes of governance (such as routine mode and annual planning mode).
- Governance's function covers a review of project performance as well as a comprehensive review of portfolio health indicators.
- There is a clear definition of artifacts generated by routine portfolio governance as well as annual planning portfolio governance. These artifacts are widely used and circulated.
- The function of governance is complemented by related bodies such as the benefit review board and a portfolio subcommittee.
- Some success factors of governance are present, helping the governance body to function better. Governance may still not be able to terminate underperforming projects in a prompt manner.
- At this level, governance is present and serving a useful function to the portfolio, although much more optimization is possible.

Level 3

- The organization has a highly evolved understanding of the importance of governance. Consequently, there is governance oversight over all of the major areas of the portfolio.
- There is a clear distinction between the different modes of governance (such as routine mode and annual planning mode).
- Governance's function is comprehensive and covers both a review of project performance as well as a detailed review of portfolio health indicators.
- There is a clear definition of artifacts generated by routine portfolio governance as well as annual planning portfolio governance. These artifacts are widely used and circulated.
- The function of governance is complemented by related bodies such as the benefit review board and portfolio subcommittee.
- All success factors of governance are present, creating an optimal environment for portfolio governance to function. Portfolio governance is able to perform the difficult task of terminating underperforming projects in a timely manner.
- At this level, governance is not only present but also optimized. It effectively performs its primary role of providing direction and oversight, thus creating the conditions for a high-performing portfolio.

CHAPTER SUMMARY

In this chapter we explored the vital role of governance in creating a high-performing portfolio. First, we defined portfolio governance and then listed the modes of operation of governance. We also covered at length the typical functions of governance under the routine portfolio operation mode as well as the annual planning mode. Next, we explored in detail the artifacts created as part of the two modes of operation. We also covered the ideal composition of portfolio governance and explored the pros and cons of committee structure. We then looked at the success factors that enable portfolio governance to succeed in carrying out its mission of providing direction to the portfolio. The chapter expressed a cautionary note that advises how to ensure that a portfolio does not devolve into a ceremonial body, then concludes with a listing of the levels of maturity in this key portfolio capability.

REFERENCE

1. *Definition of Governance,* http://www.businessdictionary.com/definition/governance.html.

19

HOW THE PORTFOLIO OFFICE
INTERACTS WITH THE CIO

INTRODUCTION

More than ever, the office of the chief information officer (CIO) and the portfolio office are connected in a symbiotic relationship in modern organizations. This chapter will cover the following topics to illustrate this two-way dependence:

1. Explore how the CIO's mandate has a direct impact on the portfolio
2. Demonstrate how the CIO is the biggest beneficiary of a high-functioning portfolio
3. Demonstrate how the CIO is also the biggest enabler for a high-functioning portfolio office
4. Enumerate the services the CIO can expect from the portfolio in addition to a list of actions the CIO can take to empower the portfolio

Although this chapter mentions the CIO as the primary executive of interest, it may be a good idea to substitute CxO in place of CIO. The reason for this is that projects are no longer found just in IT and are common in other organizations that report up to other executives (hence the catch-all "CxO").

A CIO'S MANDATE

A CIO's mandate is essentially that of a change agent. The CIO is expected to effect a change for the better in systems, performance, and capabilities of the organization. However, this mandate is not without constraints—the biggest one being a time horizon within which the CIO is expected to move the needle or move out of the role. The time-tested way to effect change is through a well-managed portfolio of projects—a project being a temporary endeavor that results in an end product/capability/service.

Therefore, it is essential for a CIO to have or create a high-functioning portfolio. Without such a mechanism in place, the bad projects will crowd out the good, slowing down enterprise transformation to a crawl and ultimately leading to a loss of confidence in the CIO's leadership. To avoid this negative spiral, the CIO needs to put every possible resource into supporting the portfolio office.

> KEY CONCEPT: A CIO's mandate is strategically connected with a portfolio in that these two are interdependent.

HOW THE CIO IS THE BIGGEST BENEFICIARY OF THE PORTFOLIO OFFICE

Benefit #1: Portfolio Office Can Help Define the Strategic Transformation Journey in Concrete Terms (and Call Out When that Is Not Done)

Although every CIO starts with a lofty strategic vision, there must be a concrete description of what is sought to be achieved and how to get there. That document is the strategic roadmap and that, in turn, can be decomposed into more tactical units of achievement. The portfolio office relies heavily on an accepted strategic roadmap to carry out much of its function. Conversely, the portfolio office is among the first entities to notice and call out (politics permitting) the absence of a strategic roadmap. This in itself is a big help for the CIO—the realization that there is not a credible strategic roadmap that forms the basis of the CIO's strategic transformation vision. Although it is not the primary function of the portfolio office to come up with a strategic roadmap, the portfolio office can be a very effective partner in the effort. Furthermore, the portfolio office can ensure that the strategic roadmap is usable and grounded in reality, thus avoiding the usual trap of the strategy becoming *credenzaware*.

Benefit #2: Portfolio Office Can Help Choose the Right Projects (and Block the Wrong Ones)

Once a strategic roadmap is created and agreed to by all stakeholders, it forms the underpinning for all projects being considered for execution. In other words, only those projects need to be taken up that are in accordance with the roadmap and will take the vision forward. The portfolio office is the gatekeeper that manages the intake process and ensures that incoming projects are vetted before execution. Without this function of the portfolio office, the CIO is likely to be blindsided by projects that waste time and money while contributing little to the strategic agenda. The best time to stop a bad project is at the very beginning, which is what the portfolio office does through intake management.

Benefit #3: Portfolio Office Can Help Decide Whether to Terminate Underperforming Legacy Projects

Most CIOs have to contend with legacy projects that they inherited from previous management. Some of these projects are performing as planned and are not a problem. Often, however, these projects are long-running debacles and may have played a role in the previous CIO's departure. Once inherited, tough decisions remain as to whether this project should be kept alive in order to avoid writing off the millions already spent in the years past—or whether there is a risk of throwing good money after bad in trying to salvage these projects. Here is where a competent portfolio office can save the day and provide the right recommendation to the CIO. First of all, the portfolio office would get past the simplistic analysis of *sunk cost versus cut losses* and proceed in the following way:

- Does the legacy project still fit the new strategic roadmap as currently agreed by all stakeholders?
- What has been the strategic attainment of the legacy project until this point? How does this compare to the promised strategic attainment?
- If the project has been running for a while, has it already delivered some benefit? How do the delivered benefits compare with the promised benefit statement?

If the project clears all of the above hurdles, the portfolio team would also create an analysis for the project that determines the following:

- Is the project performing to plan while staying on track with budget and schedule?
- Is the trend worsening or getting better?
- Extrapolating to the future, what will the project cost when it is finally done?

With all of the previously mentioned data and analysis, the portfolio office can deliver a detailed, data-supported recommendation about keeping legacy projects and prevent the CIO from the twin dangers of:

1. Terminating a viable project
2. Not terminating an unviable debacle

Benefit #4: The Portfolio Office Can Call the CIO's Attention to Trouble before It's Too Late

The bane of most CIOs is that people who report to them do not bring them bad news until it's almost too late to do anything. In the defense of people who report to the CIO, many of them are not sure about the true status of projects and the transformation effort themselves. There are a whole host of factors that prevent the true status of projects from being visible to stakeholders (including the CIO, who is ultimately accountable for the success of the strategic transformation).

This is where the portfolio office offers an early warning that may save the larger transformation effort. By using a Pareto approach, the portfolio focuses on the few projects that are in need of executive intervention. Not only does this focus executive attention where it is truly needed, it also does so in a timely manner, where the executive still has room to maneuver (for example, replacing the current project manager on a troubled project with a more seasoned veteran might correct the project's trajectory before more time and money are lost). By taking quick, effective action on the few projects that need it, the overall transformation effort is kept on track. The portfolio office enables this corrective feedback loop by accurately focusing on the trailing projects.

Benefit #5: The Portfolio Office Creates a Project Meritocracy that Supersedes Politics

Every organization has its own kind of politics and the CIO has to find a way to execute the strategic transformation agenda within that political framework. As detailed in Chapter 16, the political behaviors adopted by various players (in most organizations) serve to either obscure the visibility of true project performance or evade oversight by governance. Prevailing rules of political correctness allow subpar execution to be hidden until the damage is obvious to all and beyond recovery.

However, the portfolio office, when supported by the CIO, can create an environment where the true performance of projects is visible to all. The portfolio office creates transparency, which puts underperformers on the defensive and accelerates either recovery or termination. Over time (within a year, in most cases), there is a sort of meritocracy in place in which underperformers find it politically unviable to operate for long. This self-regulating mechanism is a huge catalyst to the eventual achievement of the strategic transformation effort—underperformers will either actively try to improve or bow out.

Benefit #6: The Portfolio Office Can Give the Governance Body a Framework to Operate Within

In organizations that are advanced enough to have knowledgeable and empowered governance bodies, there remains a final hurdle—the governance members do not have actionable data. What is actionable data? It's objective, quantitative data that enables decision making with a high degree of confidence.

Instead, governance is often fed reams of paper that hold pseudo tracking information—such as the red, yellow, and green system of reporting—or extensive, often subjective, verbiage describing status. Such information wastes the time of governance and camouflages the true problem projects. Therefore, although the CIO looks to the governance body to provide effective oversight of the portfolio, the governance members are unable to deliver on that expectation for lack of actionable data.

The portfolio office can remedy this situation through objective project performance indicators that replace pseudo performance data, such as subjective red/yellow/green. It also provides drill-down capability and trend information, as well as the basis for assessing whether or not turnaround efforts are working for underperforming projects. Taken together, this provides the governance body with a solid basis to make sound decisions, and furthermore, enables them to govern by exception—in other words, spend time on the projects that need it.

Benefit #7: The Portfolio Office Can Orchestrate Annual Strategic Planning for the CIO

Without annual planning, the organization is at a distinct disadvantage in optimally matching supply and demand. Furthermore, annual planning eliminates redundancy and promotes much needed conversation about program alignment, prioritization, and dependency. The various artifacts created during annual planning help the organization make the right decisions about aligning demand with the strategic roadmap. In short, annual planning is a vital prerequisite to enabling the strategic transformation effort of the CIO.

The portfolio office is the body that owns and delivers annual planning. It works through the templates, the data gathering rounds, and orchestrates the multiple passes involved in the planning activity and finally provides the analyzed information to the decision makers (including the CIO) for the right projects to pick for the year. This exercise vastly clarifies the picture of what the organization seeks to achieve and how that picture is directly related to the strategic roadmap. Furthermore, it creates a *queue* of vetted projects that are next in line to receive funding when it becomes available.

Benefit #8: Provide Concrete Feedback on Strategy Attainment

A fairly surprising gap in most organizations is that there is no mechanism to measure strategy attainment. There is a lot of effort spent on strategic planning, but a puzzling lack of feedback on how that journey is actually progressing. Sometimes there is a descriptive assessment, often filled with jargon, that does not really help provide a sense of *how much is complete* and *how much is yet to go* in terms of the strategy roadmap. This is a huge handicap to the CIO, because unless the difference between *actual progress on the strategic roadmap* and *expected progress on the strategic roadmap* is known, how can corrective actions be taken in a timely manner?

> KEY CONCEPT: A functioning portfolio provides a whole host of benefits that are quite useful for the office of the CIO.

HOW THE CIO IS THE BIGGEST ENABLER OF THE PORTFOLIO OFFICE

Earlier in the chapter, we saw how the portfolio office provides the CIO with a host of benefits, both tactical and strategic. At the same time, the portfolio office is heavily dependent on the CIO for support.

The portfolio office needs a powerful patron from whom it derives its power—and that patron is the CIO. Here are the prominent ways in which the CIO can enable the portfolio office to reach its potential and deliver all of the discussed benefits back to the CIO.

Enabling Action #1: CIO Needs to Equip the Portfolio Office with a Mandate

The portfolio office needs to be given a clear, public mandate to effect all of the changes it needs to make in the organization. This mandate is key to the portfolio office claiming the role of a change agent. The CIO needs to provide this mandate in a clear, public way and periodically reinforce the mandate. The CIO can also clearly set the tone with public celebrations of the portfolio's successes.

Enabling Action #2: CIO Needs to Fund the Portfolio Office with Resources

The portfolio office needs resources to achieve its full potential. It may include all of the following:

- Hiring a seasoned portfolio manager
- Funding for staffing a small team, potentially temporary staff
- Funding for portfolio consulting services to jump start the effort
- Software licenses for portfolio software
- Training the organization on new portfolio processes
- Change management, including *how-to* content for a website

Enabling Action #3: CIO Needs to Provide Political Cover to the Portfolio

It is a certainty that the portfolio effort will face opposition from some stakeholders who would prefer the status quo. There may also be missteps on the part of the portfolio team as they attempt to effect the necessary changes. In all of these situations, the CIO needs to come out strongly in support of the portfolio team. The CIO needs to signal to the organization that the portfolio office has CIO support and that the portfolio agenda is not one to be sidelined. There also needs to be an implicit (or explicit) message that stakeholders trying to thwart the portfolio implementation will be held accountable. This may involve one or more high profile terminations of stubborn players whose refusal to comply with portfolio guidelines may threaten to derail the entire effort.

Enabling Action #4: CIO Needs to Be Accessible to the Portfolio Office

Consider a situation where the portfolio office has a mandate, and all of the necessary resources. Can the CIO leave the portfolio office alone and expect all the strategic transformation to happen? No, of course not.

While an empowered portfolio office can do a lot of good by itself, the transformative power of the portfolio lies in this closed loop: Gather Data → Analyze Data → Detect Deficiency → Advise CIO → Get CIO Decision → Perform Correction → Gather Data.

The CIO (or their proxy, governance) needs to be available to receive the advice from the portfolio office and agree to the recommendation so that the portfolio office can *Perform Correction.* The CIO needs to act on the advice provided by the portfolio office for the loop to work. To ensure that this happens, there needs to be an arrangement for the portfolio office to have a regular touchpoint with the CIO.

Enabling Action #5: CIO Needs to Appoint Governance Body that Works

The current portfolio trend is for a body of senior, empowered people, collectively called *governance*, to function as the proxy for the CIO and provide oversight to the portfolio. This also optimizes the CIO's time, since governance can filter out the noise and make decisions on behalf of the CIO. However, as frequently seen in many organizations, governance can fall short of the mark and become more like an ineffective *country club* body. When that happens, governance members shy away from making the tough decisions. Other pitfalls include a disinterested governance body or one that doesn't feel adequately empowered. The CIO needs to address these problems in order to prevent the portfolio from falling into dysfunction. First, the CIO needs to appoint governance members that are motivated, knowledgeable, and willing to shoulder the responsibility of providing oversight to the portfolio. Second, the CIO should try to get portfolio training for the governance members—this is overlooked all too often and the portfolio suffers as a result. Third, the CIO needs to review the effectiveness of governance periodically and be willing to cycle out members for whom the role is not a good fit.

> KEY CONCEPT: The office of the CIO can be one of the biggest enablers of the portfolio function.

LEVELS OF PORTFOLIO CAPABILITY MATURITY

Level 1

- The CIO and the portfolio office are isolated from each other, other than the issuance of periodic reports.
- The strategic transformation roadmap is poorly defined, if it exists at all.
- If a strategic transformation roadmap exists, the portfolio office has little or no input on the artifact.
- The portfolio office is not empowered by the CIO to choose the right projects and block the wrong ones.
- The portfolio office has no say in recommending termination of underperforming legacy projects that continue to occupy organizational resources.
- The portfolio office has no connection to the CIO that enables early communication of projects that are going awry.
- The portfolio office is not empowered to create a meritocracy that can supersede politics.
- The portfolio office is not empowered to carry out annual planning.
- The portfolio office is not allowed to play a role in measuring strategic attainment in objective terms.

Level 2

- The CIO and the portfolio office have some contact, but it is sporadic and nonuniform.
- A strategic transformation roadmap exists, even if it is not complete and detailed.

- The portfolio office does not own the strategic roadmap—it may have a limited role to play in the review and consumption of the roadmap.
- The portfolio office has input about project intake but still may not be fully empowered by the CIO to choose the right projects and block the wrong ones.
- The portfolio office may recommend the termination of underperforming legacy projects, but these recommendations may not be acted upon at all times.
- The portfolio office is able to communicate to the CIO about projects going awry; however, the CIO office may not always take the necessary action.
- The portfolio office is not able to create a meritocracy that can supersede politics.
- The portfolio office is able to carry out annual planning, but it may not be optimized.
- The portfolio office is able to play a limited role in measuring strategic attainment in objective terms.

Level 3

- The CIO and the portfolio office are in regular contact and aware of each other's perspective.
- A complete, detailed strategic transformation roadmap exists; it is well socialized and maintained/updated regularly.
- The portfolio office owns and maintains the strategic roadmap—it also plays a major role in the organizational review and consumption of the roadmap.
- The portfolio office has complete control over project intake and has been empowered by the CIO to choose the right projects and block the wrong ones.
- The portfolio office has the CIO's backing to recommend and follow through on the termination of underperforming legacy projects.
- The portfolio office has a hotline to the CIO office to communicate about projects going awry; the CIO office is responsive to such notifications and provides the portfolio office with the necessary support to remediate the situation.
- Through objective project performance data and effective governance, the portfolio office is able to create a meritocracy that can supersede politics.
- The portfolio office is empowered to orchestrate effective annual planning each year.
- The portfolio office is able to play a major role in measuring strategic attainment in objective terms.

CHAPTER SUMMARY

This chapter explored the critically important relationship between the CIO and the portfolio office. We first explored how the mandate of the CIO creates a direct dependency with the portfolio. We then discussed at length how the CIO is the biggest beneficiary of the portfolio office. We went on to illustrate how the CIO is also the biggest enabler for an optimally functioning portfolio office. We elaborated on this theme by listing all of the services that the CIO can expect from the portfolio office. Next, we listed all of the actions that the CIO can take to empower the portfolio. We concluded the chapter with the indicators found at each level of this portfolio capability.

20

HOW THE PORTFOLIO OFFICE INTERACTS WITH FINANCE

INTRODUCTION

Portfolio management can be thought of as a semi-finance function. The whole endeavor of portfolio management focuses on managing significant sums of the organization's money toward improving the company's capabilities and ensuring that the spending of money stays on track. Therefore, it is quite logical that successful portfolios have a close relationship with Finance as well as support from that function in their organization. In this chapter we explore the following aspects of the relationship between Finance and the portfolio office:

1. Explore interface points between Finance and the portfolio office
2. The different roles that Finance plays in complementing the portfolio office's function and ensuring strategic success
3. The benefits that Finance derives from the portfolio office

INTERFACE POINTS BETWEEN FINANCE AND THE PORTFOLIO OFFICE

The *touchpoints* between Finance and the portfolio office are multifaceted and illustrate how tightly these two functions are bound together.

Touchpoint #1: Guidance about OPEX and CAPEX

Capital expenditures (CAPEX) and operating expenditures (OPEX) are two different categories of business expenses.[1] CAPEX are the funds that a business uses to purchase major physical goods or services to expand the company's abilities to generate profits. These purchases can include hardware (such as printers or computers), vehicles to transport goods, or the purchase or construction of a new building. The type of industry a company is involved in largely determines the nature of its CAPEX.

OPEX result from the ongoing costs that a company pays to run its basic business. In contrast to CAPEX, OPEX are fully tax-deductible in the year they are made. As OPEX make up the bulk of a company's regular costs, management examines ways to lower them without causing a critical drop in quality or production output. Sometimes an item that would ordinarily be obtained through CAPEX can have its cost assigned to OPEX if a company chooses to lease the item rather than purchase it. This can be a financially attractive option if the company has limited cash flow and wants to be able to deduct the total item cost for the year.

In a few cases, it is straightforward to distinguish between OPEX and CAPEX; however, in most cases, guidance from Finance is needed to decide whether it is OPEX or CAPEX. Having this guidance and partnership in place is strongly recommended because it could make a major difference in classifying project spend correctly and could potentially save the organization millions in tax management.

Touchpoint #2: Partnership During Annual Planning

Annual planning is a comprehensive exercise to plan next year's activity. As part of this activity, all of the known demand is gathered and prioritized. This demand is then compared against the available funds and the *affordability line* is drawn where the funds run out. The projects above the line get approved for funding and the projects that are below the line are placed in a queue for future consideration. Finance has two important roles to play during an annual partnership exercise:

1. During the gathering of demand, input from Finance is essential to categorizing that demand as OPEX or CAPEX. This is important in order to get a true picture of demand and avoid surprises later in terms of mismatch between supply and demand. (Consider a situation where the organization realizes later in the year that much of its annual CAPEX demand was actually OPEX, which is now scarce to find.)
2. During the *drawing of the affordability line*, Finance needs to specify how much funding is available for the portfolio next year. This is usually a by-product of the larger financial planning exercise that is done for the whole company. Finance can also advise if any extra funds can be found for strategically important projects which might fall *below* the line.

Touchpoint #3: Benefit Management

There needs to be a standard taxonomy on benefits that all stakeholders can agree to follow. Finance's input is crucial when it comes to defining what the different kinds of project benefits are. In the case of hard benefits, Finance needs to sign off that those numbers are valid and are expected to make a difference on the balance sheet. This formal screening by Finance goes a long way in avoiding benefit inflation by project owners.

During benefits management, Finance needs to be on the governance body that reviews benefit performance and compares it to what was promised at the start of the project. As the steward of the organization's money, Finance is expected to take a hard line and recommend terminating projects that are not delivering benefits per plan.

Touchpoint #4: Reporting Actuals on Projects

One of the most vital services performed by Finance is to ensure that the portfolio office has visibility to the actual spend by each project per month. This data is crucial for the portfolio office to make decisions regarding the project. Only Finance can authoritatively produce this *official* information directly from the financial reporting systems. This data is then used for portfolio performance monitoring.

Touchpoint #5: Managing Underspend and Overspend

Sometimes a portfolio will, despite best efforts, either overspend or underspend its budget. Sometimes this may even happen for valid reasons—a strategically important project within the portfolio may discover additional scope worth doing that costs more money but is ultimately beneficial to the organization. In these cases, a close working partnership with Finance may save the day—Finance has visibility as to the spending trend of the rest of the organization and may be able to arrange for a way to match the portfolio over/underspend with a corresponding under/overspend in another area of the organization. For this arrangement to work, the portfolio needs to also give Finance sufficient advance notice of an anticipated over/underspend at the end of the year.

Touchpoint #6: An Authoritative Voice on Governance

Finance is an essential part of portfolio governance and must be represented in all key decisions regarding the portfolio. Sometimes Finance needs to exert its role as the steward of the organization's funds and ensure that the right decisions are made in the portfolio. This is key in terms of terminating bad investments and not approving funding for projects that do not have strong benefits or return on investment.

> KEY CONCEPT: Finance and the portfolio office have several touchpoints that underscore the mutually interdependent relationship between them.

A SYMBIOTIC RELATIONSHIP

As we just saw, Finance extends many services to the portfolio office that are integral to the smooth working of the portfolio management function in the organization. However, this is a mutually beneficial relationship—a well-run portfolio provides Finance with the assurance of managing project spend in a responsible manner. Predictability in project spend is generally prized by Finance because any adverse surprises in this area (or any other area, for that matter) creates a problem for Finance in managing the overall financial picture for the enterprise.

Finance can also be a major beneficiary of a well-implemented portfolio budget tracking system. When portfolio performance and spend trends (as a sum of individual projects) can be objectively captured, Finance can use this information to become ready for year-end surprises in under/overspend.

The foundation for this symbiotic relationship needs to come from executive management, typically in an arrangement worked out between the leaders of information technology and Finance—the chief information officer and the chief financial officer. This understanding is then translated to mid-level management support between Finance managers supporting the portfolio manager.

HOW FINANCE BENEFITS FROM THE PORTFOLIO OFFICE

- **Benefit #1**: Without an effective portfolio office to manage projects, Finance would have to deal with projects running wild in terms of both overspend and underspend. The biggest benefit that comes with an effective portfolio office is the predictability of spend of projects and to a certain extent, an ability to control the spend.
- **Benefit #2**: A portfolio office is able to exert control to ensure that funds are being well spent. It is possible to show the multi-year trend in how the organization is getting more efficient at spending money to achieve project objectives. Such an objective indicator of money being well spent would be of interest to Finance leadership in their ongoing role of managing the organization's money.
- **Benefit #3**: The portfolio office monitors the performance of projects and takes a closer look at projects that are not performing well. If an underperforming project does not recover and continues to show a deteriorating trend, the portfolio office will move to terminate the project. Such prompt action is necessary to ensure that bad projects do not crowd out the good projects

and waste the organizational resources. Finance relies on the portfolio office to make these hard decisions and ensure better use of the organization's funds.

> KEY CONCEPT: Finance benefits in several ways from the presence of a functional portfolio and, therefore, is vested in the portfolio's success.

LEVELS OF CAPABILITY MATURITY

Level 1

- There is no concept of partnership between the functions of the portfolio office and Finance.
- The organization may not have an effective framework to treat OPEX and CAPEX differently.
- Even if the organization classifies OPEX and CAPEX separately, Finance may not offer sufficient support to the portfolio office in distinguishing the two classes of funding.
- There may be little partnership between the portfolio and Finance during annual planning. This translates into a situation where project demand and funds supply have no relation to each other, and results in diminished confidence in the utility of the annual planning exercise.
- There may not be any coordination between the two functions on benefit management. This results in projects making promises of generous benefits without any basis to back them up.
- In the absence of an effective partnership with Finance, the portfolio office may not have a standard, systemic method of obtaining project actuals. This greatly hampers the function of the portfolio office.
- Due to the lack of communication and partnership between the portfolio office and Finance, there may not be a view to anticipate and control overspend and underspend at the end of the year.
- Finance may not be represented on the portfolio governance body.
- Portfolio budget tracking may not be in place. Therefore, there is no way for the portfolio office to create objective performance data indicators to share with Finance.
- Due to lack of alignment between the two functions, there may not be mid-level management support (such as a Finance manager dedicated to supporting the portfolio office).

Level 2

- There is awareness of the need for partnership between the functions of the portfolio office and Finance. Accordingly, the two functions endeavor to coordinate and align wherever possible.
- The organization has an effective framework to treat OPEX and CAPEX differently at all levels, including project spend. Finance offers authoritative guidance and support to the portfolio office (and projects) in distinguishing the two classes of funding.
- There is an effective partnership between the portfolio office and Finance during annual planning. Therefore, project demand and funds supply are managed to be within range of each other, and this arrangement creates confidence in the utility of the annual planning exercise.
- There is coordination between the two functions on benefit management. This results in projects being held accountable for promised benefits.
- Due to the partnership with Finance, the portfolio office is able to depend on a standard, systemic arrangement of obtaining project actuals. This significantly helps the function of the portfolio office.

- Due to the coordination between the portfolio office and Finance, there is some visibility regarding the anticipated overspend and underspend at the end of the year.
- Finance is represented on the portfolio governance body.
- Due to alignment between the two functions, day-to-day support is available at mid-level management (such as a Finance manager dedicated to supporting the portfolio office).

Level 3

- There is awareness of the need for partnership between the functions of the portfolio office and Finance. Accordingly, the coordination and alignment between the two functions are optimized to a high degree.
- The organization has an effective framework to treat OPEX and CAPEX differently at all levels, including project spend. Finance offers authoritative guidance and support to the portfolio office (and projects) in distinguishing the two classes of funding.
- There is an optimized partnership between the portfolio office and Finance during annual planning. Therefore, project demand and funds supply are matched to a close degree, and this arrangement creates confidence in the utility of the annual planning exercise.
- There is coordination between the two functions on benefit management, with Finance taking a leadership role on the benefits review council. This results in each project's benefit statement being screened for viability before the project is approved and the project then being held accountable for promised benefits.
- Due to the partnership with Finance, the portfolio office is able to depend on a standard, systemic arrangement of obtaining project actuals. This significantly helps the function of the portfolio office.
- Due to the coordination between the portfolio office and Finance, there is heightened visibility to anticipated overspend and underspend at the end of the year.
- Finance is represented on the portfolio governance body and weighs in on all key decisions.
- Portfolio budget tracking with actuals is comprehensively implemented in the organization. This provides an objective basis for the partnership between Finance and the portfolio office.
- Due to alignment between the two functions, day-to-day support is available at mid-level management (such as a Finance manager dedicated to supporting the portfolio office).

CHAPTER SUMMARY

This chapter detailed the vital partnership between Finance and the portfolio office. We first explored the multiple interface points between Finance and the portfolio office and illustrated how tightly the functions are woven together. We then listed all of the different benefits that the portfolio office receives from partnering with Finance. To show the symbiotic relationship between the two functions, we went on to explore all of the benefits that the Finance office receives from working with the portfolio office. We concluded the chapter with the indicators found at each level of this portfolio capability.

REFERENCE

1. *Investopedia, The Difference between CAPEX and OPEX* (http://www.investopedia.com/ask/answers/020915/what-difference-between-capex-and-opex.asp).

21

PORTFOLIO ROLLOUT AND CHANGE MANAGEMENT

INTRODUCTION

While it's one thing to launch portfolio management in a small department, it's a completely different ballgame when launched in a larger organization-wide context. Many organizations launch portfolio management with lots of fanfare but there is little adoption or observed throughput in the months that follow. What could be the problem? In many cases, it could be a lack of change management, including adequate training, during rollout. Change management can guide the organization in effectively navigating the change created by the introduction of the new system of managing projects and programs. In this chapter we'll review the following aspects of portfolio rollout and change management:

1. Review the range of situations that provide the context for a portfolio rollout
2. Analyze why portfolio rollout efforts often fail
3. Discuss the politics surrounding portfolio rollout and change management
4. Discuss recommended best practices for portfolio rollout
5. Introduction to the mind map
6. Typical mind map structure for a portfolio office
7. Success factors for a portfolio mind map
8. Levels of portfolio maturity for this capability

THE WIDE SPECTRUM OF PORTFOLIO ROLLOUTS

It should be kept in mind that the term *portfolio rollout* can span a wide range of situations. In some organizations, there may be no portfolio management at all—therefore this rollout may constitute the first contact with a totally new concept. At other organizations, there may be some kind of portfolio management in place, and the present rollout may be an improvement or enhancement—possibly an attempt to go from Level 1 to Level 2 or even from Level 2 to Level 3. At other places, there may have been some kind of unsuccessful attempt in the past to implement portfolio management and this rollout is a *do-over*. Each of these situations comes with their own challenges and will have to be handled accordingly through effective change management. Although change management is an established discipline with specialized (and expensive) consultants, sometimes a back-to-the-basics approach can deliver the desired results.

WHY DO PORTFOLIO ROLLOUT EFFORTS OFTEN FAIL?

The following information includes some of the reasons why portfolio rollouts have faltered.

Reason #1: Inadequate Estimation of Impact

In the minds of portfolio managers, the changes they roll out seem simple, welcomed, and straight-forward. They may also seem to be a big improvement from the current suboptimal state of affairs. What they may not realize is that the organization may have adapted, however awkwardly, to the confusion or suboptimal situation. Any change now, even if for a better outcome, may create discomfort and uncertainty and is not likely to be warmly received. A prudent portfolio manager would do well to factor this potentially chilly reception while designing the rollout.

Reason #2: Incomplete Analysis of Affected Parties

It is important to methodically map out all of the current stakeholders and plan for how they would be affected by portfolio rollout. It is also important to consider the new stakeholders who would now come under the purview of portfolio management as a result of this rollout. Successful rollouts create a formal matrix of stakeholders, describe the expected impact for each stakeholder group, and also have a checkmark to show that each stakeholder group was helped in dealing with the rollout. This matrix is also useful to show the organization that the needs of all stakeholders were factored for the rollout and taken care of.

Reason #3: Inadequate Customization

Since the portfolio rollout affects different stakeholders to different degrees, it would be a mistake to provide the same level of training to everyone. Consider a project manager/coordinator who needs to be fully trained on the new templates, where to find them, where to submit them, etc. At the same time, a project team member at least needs minimal training—perhaps just an awareness that all projects are now managed as part of a portfolio. Providing the full extent of training to all is a waste of time and may even leave everyone feeling that *the new portfolio procedures are too complex*. There-fore, customization is required to provide the appropriate amount of training for the varied groups of stakeholders. Customized training, in turn, relies upon adequate impact estimation and stakeholder analysis as covered in Reasons #1 and #2.

Reason #4: Lack of Scenario-Based Training

Many portfolio rollout trainings miss the mark because they launch into a detailed explanation of the new portfolio policies and procedures that, while correct, are not really relevant to the day-to-day functioning of the stakeholders. It's much more useful for the training to focus on how the actions performed by the stakeholders today would change in the new process. For example, how does a stakeholder submit a project proposal for funding consideration? How does a project request more money? Etc. The section on mind maps later in this chapter addresses this need for delivering sce-nario-based help to the organization in detail.

Reason #5: Lack of Distinction from Earlier Failed Rollouts

In some organizations, prior rollouts of portfolio changes may not have been successful and may have created unfavorable opinions in the collective organization. In such situations, where an earlier rollout of portfolio management was attempted with mixed results, it becomes important to emphasize why this rollout is different. It may also help to frame this enhancement effort as a response to the short-comings of the previous attempt to roll out portfolio management.

Reason #6: Attempting Too Much Change

Every organization has a finite *change management capacity*—an ability to understand and process change. By trying to introduce too much change at once, the portfolio office runs the risk of failure. What are some examples of trying to do too much? For instance, trying to introduce a new enterprise portfolio management software at the same time as rolling out significant changes to the portfolio process that is currently in place. This would likely strain the organization and cause pushback and poor adoption of the whole setup. The recommendation would be to roll out the portfolio process first, let it mature for a bit, and then try to roll out the portfolio tool.

Reason #7: Failure to Account for Users' Lack of Retention

Sometimes an organization will launch an effective change management effort around a new portfolio process rollout. The change management and training could be well attended and well received; how-ever, inexplicably, the stakeholders may indicate dissatisfaction with the whole process a few months later. What could have gone wrong? The answer may lie in the availability of post-rollout resources.

It's a well-known fact that people have limited retention of training content that they may not ap-ply in practice immediately. For example, people may forget how to initiate a new project proposal unless they have done it a few times—and they may not get a chance to do it for some time after their training. It's very important to complement an effective training course with resources such as a train-ing website that people can refer to. It is also essential to make this training website an easy-to-use resource, as will be described later.

> KEY CONCEPT: Portfolio roll-out efforts often fail due to inadequate change management.

THE POLITICS OF PORTFOLIO CHANGE MANAGEMENT

As we covered in Chapter 16, everything about portfolio management can be political. This is due to the fact that a high-functioning portfolio forces accountability on all players. Stakeholders whose subpar performance was previously masked by the chaos now have to contend with high visibility and oversight from the portfolio office.

Stakeholders who are not supportive are often looking for the portfolio office to slip up and give them a chance to criticize the whole portfolio setup. A botched rollout would serve as the perfect opportunity for such a maneuver—a stakeholder could claim that the training was inadequate and hence call into question the entire competence of the portfolio office. By extension, they would also claim some lenience or a degree of exemption from following the portfolio procedures. How can this be dealt with? Some options are outlined here:

1. The recommended approach is to create a comprehensive stakeholder analysis to ensure that all stakeholders are accounted for. The best way to do this tactically is to prepare a matrix of stakeholders, accompanied by their official role, and list the impact to them caused by the roll out of portfolio management.

2. It helps to circulate this matrix to the whole organization (or as broadly as needed), asking to validate this matrix, and identify any additional stakeholders that may have been missed.
3. Further, during the actual training sessions, it's useful to capture which members from which team attended and then circulate this attendance record as part of the change management communications.

Collectively, the approach just described prevents sniping from certain teams that may try to claim that they *weren't trained*. The portfolio office can simply refer to the roster—one can either prove that many of the complaining team's members attended training or that many members did not attend, despite an invitation. In either case, this proves that the portfolio office is blameless.

> KEY CONCEPT: It is important to anticipate and navigate politics while planning portfolio change management.

RECOMMENDED BEST PRACTICES FOR PORTFOLIO ROLLOUT

Best Practice #1: Delivering Effective Training

Effective training is the product of careful design and well-crafted delivery. The portfolio office should make every effort to ensure that the training is relevant, concise, and designed to fit the users' needs. It would also help if the training itself were delivered by professional trainers. Too often, portfolio offices tend to rely on the in-team talent to deliver the training content, which may deliver underwhelming results in terms of audience engagement and retention. It is important that the portfolio office recognize the importance of the training/roll-out exercise and engage professionals to deliver the service.

Best Practice #2: A Network of Local Champions

Only a small percentage of people who attend a training session grasp everything that is imparted, record all relevant information, and remember to apply it correctly when the situation arises. This is all the more true for areas where the received training is not applied immediately. When the need does arise, most people would prefer consulting a person and being walked through the entire procedure, at least for the first time. A local champion is a person who fulfills exactly that need.

In this case, it would be a person—probably a project manager or project coordinator—who received intensive training and is able to function as an expert within their designated department. This person would be able to walk a project owner or any other stakeholder through any relevant portfolio procedure and give them the reassurance of working with a cohesive, functional system.

Best Practice #3: Website with Archived Training Materials

Imagine a successful portfolio rollout accompanied by effective training. Workshops are held and training materials are produced and distributed. What's the next logical step to make this a comprehensive effort? Archiving the training materials, including recordings of the training and posting them on an easy-to-navigate website, enables users to review them at a later date when they actually need to put the training concepts into practice. This arrangement also benefits new employees in the organization who joined after the comprehensive trainings were held.

Best Practice #4: Intuitive Navigation of the Portfolio Process and Materials

One of the most common complaints heard among the rank and file of an organization is, "I can't find what I need to get the job done." This is particularly true of portfolio management, where there are a lot of process materials, templates, and historical data that tend to pile up, creating a maze that is hard to navigate. This one factor could make all the difference between the organization adopting portfolio management processes or avoiding it and trying to work around it.

How do we balance these competing demands? On the one hand, we need to preserve and store all relevant data on the portfolio website, creating a huge pile to sort through. On the other hand, we need to get the right information to the right person as quickly as possible, enabling them to transact their portfolio work. One approach to accomplish this task is through the use of a mind map.

> KEY CONCEPT: The proven best practices listed above go a long way in ensuring successful change management.

WHAT IS A MIND MAP?

A mind map is a diagram used to visually organize information. A mind map is hierarchical and shows relationships among pieces of the whole. It is often created around a single concept, drawn as an image in the center of a blank page, to which associated representations of the central concept are added. Major ideas are connected directly to the central concept, and other ideas branch out from those. The utility of a mind map in representing information lies in its similarity to the human thought process, which involves starting with a broad outline and branching to the highly specific. The next section explains in detail how to use a mind map to ensure that the organization is able to navigate, locate, and use portfolio materials as part of the portfolio process.

HOW TO USE THE MIND MAP

Figure 21.1 shows a basic example of a mind map that helps partners of the portfolio office navigate through a mass of information. The big oval in the center stands for the *core idea* or *central topic* of portfolio management. Surrounding the central theme of *portfolio management* are the major topics that a typical stakeholder would be concerned with, including:

1. **New project initiation:** A stakeholder who wants to start a new project would start here and be guided on how to start a new project in accordance with portfolio policy. There would be resources on what the process is to start a new project, as well as how to use templates and other resources that would be relevant in enabling the stakeholder to submit a new project.
2. **Existing project maintenance:** A stakeholder who already has a current project in the portfolio would find this link as the logical starting point to transact with the portfolio. There would be resources on reporting the performance of the project back to the portfolio and staying in compliance with the other portfolio processes for an existing project.
3. **Historical data reference:** A person wanting to refer to historical portfolio data would find this link to be the ideal place to start looking for the particular data that they are interested in reviewing. Historical data could cover portfolio decisions, including funding and other approvals. It could also contain historical performance data.

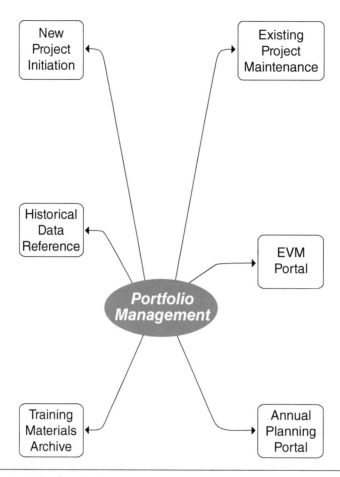

Figure 21.1   Basic example of a mind map

4. **EVM Portal:** EVM stands for earned value management. This is an advanced topic typically found in mature portfolios. It is included here for the sake of completeness. This portal would be the gateway for all matters related to EVM. This would include EVM artifacts for each project, such as the current year's month-by-month snapshots of EVM performance. All other EVM reports, such as aggregation, would also be found here.

5. **Annual planning portal:** This link would be the starting place for all topics related to the annual planning exercise. The process, the templates, and all of the artifacts related to annual planning would be accessed from this point.

6. **Training materials archive:** This link would be the gateway to all training materials, including archives of previously conducted training sessions. This is a valuable resource for people who could not attend training sessions or who need refreshers on the training content.

One version of a complete mind map for the whole portfolio is shown in Figure 21.2. Keep in mind that some subtopics can belong in more than one topic. That is perfectly alright because the ultimate aim is to let the user navigate to the desired content in one or more logical ways. The structure described above is the most typical and addresses all conceivable areas of a typical portfolio setup. Having said that, it is still possible that there may be slight differences in how each organization may want to structure their portfolio website content. Accordingly, there may be small differences in both the main topics as well as

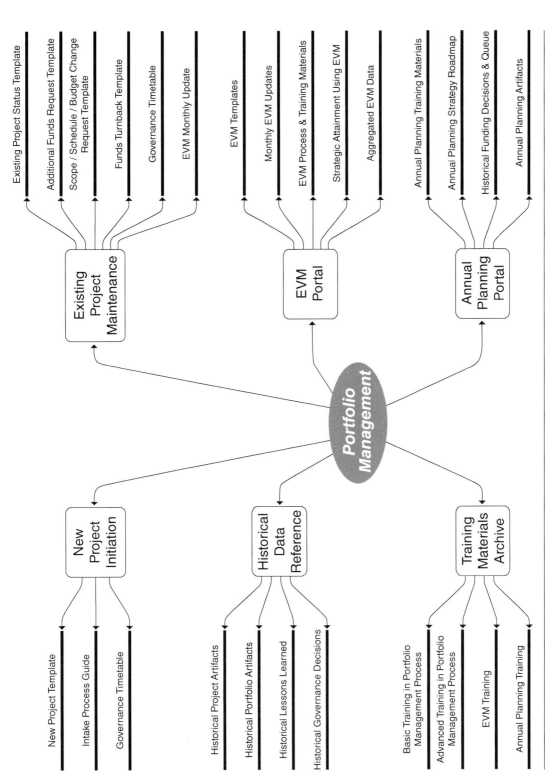

Figure 21.2 Complete mind map with full elaboration of all topics

the subtopics. However, the main rationale and use of the mind map still holds—it is one of the best tools to show and arrange information in a way that is easy for the users to navigate and understand.

POINTERS FOR SUCCESS IN USING A MIND MAP

A mind map is a powerful tool that allows a large mass of information to be effectively navigated and accessed by the partners of the portfolio office. Having a mind map cuts through the clutter of information and lets people get to what they actually want to do—it must always be kept in mind that most stakeholders are only interfacing with the portfolio as a means to an end.

When implemented and managed well, a mind map could prove to be a huge help to the mission of the portfolio office. This is because a mind map provides the user base with a familiar and unchanging interface, although the content behind it may be constantly growing. In this way, a functioning mind map creates a satisfied user base, which is a huge asset for the portfolio office and provides political capital for negotiating additional enhancements to the portfolio's capability. Here are some specific pointers that enable successful implementation and functioning of a mind map.

- **Pointer #1: Structure the mind map accurately:** For the mind map to serve its function, it needs to be designed in a way that both reflects the hierarchy of content as well as the thinking process of a typical user. The structure narrated in the previous section is a good starting point; however, organizations may have different needs and may have to change the mind map accordingly. The key design principle to keep in mind is that the main topics need to be broad, identifiable anchors and the subtopics need to be progressively more specific and detailed. It also helps to not have too many hierarchical levels in any branch of the mind map. Several iterations of the mind map may need to be performed before a stable version emerges that seems comprehensive and logical.
- **Pointer #2: Validate the mind map initially:** The mind map is meant to serve the needs of the typical user. Accordingly, it is appropriate that before launching the mind map, it should be validated with a group of users to ensure that it works the way it should. For example, the group of users could be given a list of resources that are most frequently searched for and asked to locate these resources using the mind map. User feedback should be carefully considered and changes made as appropriate in response to the feedback.
- **Pointer #3: Train users on how to use the mind map:** Although the mind map is supposed to be intuitively logical to use, it is still a good idea to hold a training session on how to use it. There are a couple of reasons why. For one, most people may not have seen a mind map and may not know how to use one. Second, training may serve to show all of the users that they simply need to start at the mind map in their search for information.
- **Pointer #4: Maintain the mind map regularly:** Although the mind map looks static, it needs to be remembered that it is only an overlay on top of dynamic content. The content changes all the time and the hyperlinks need to change accordingly. Failure to update the links results in broken links, which in turn leads to a loss of confidence on the users. Once users stop trusting/ using the mind map, it's very hard to bring them back and the whole artifact becomes obsolete. Therefore, regular updates of the mind map's links and frequent error checking to eliminate broken links are essential to the continued viability of the mind map. At the same time, only authorized personnel in the portfolio office should be tasked with updating the portfolio mind map. Quality control is essential to preserving the integrity and correctness of the mind map.
- **Pointer #5: Leverage the mind map frequently:** A frequently seen and used artifact stays in everyone's mind and continues to be utilized. A less visible artifact is slowly forgotten and ultimately falls into disuse. To ensure that the mind map stays in the limelight, it's a good practice

to prominently feature the mind map on the landing page of the portfolio website. It's also a good practice to frequently mention the mind map in portfolio communications, and to include a hyperlink to the mind map in communications emails.

- **Pointer #6: Employ mind map software:** Although the mind map described in the previous section was created in Microsoft Visio, mind maps can be built without any software. However, the use of a tool is recommended in some situations. The potential benefits of mind map software could be ease of use, ability to make changes and publish the output in a common file format such as a PDF, and so on. There are a wide variety of mind map tools available in the market. However, the one thing to keep in mind is that, ultimately, it's the end product (mind map) that matters. If the end product can be facilitated using mind map software, it may be a good idea that is worth pursuing.

KEY CONCEPT: Mind maps are a powerful change management tool.

LEVELS OF PORTFOLIO CAPABILITY MATURITY

Level 1

- The portfolio office and resources are likely to be rudimentary with modest capabilities, therefore many changes and rollouts of those changes are needed.
- When changes are introduced in the portfolio space, there may not be organized or planned roll-out efforts that accompany changes in the portfolio.
- There may not be an adequate estimation of the impact or complete analysis of who is affected by the rollout.
- Training may be *one-size-fits-all* and therefore lack customization.
- Training may also lack scenario-based focus and the recipients of training may find it hard to put the concepts learned into practice.
- The roll-out effort may not take into account the change management capacity of the organization and hence may attempt to change too much at once.
- Training may be imparted, but users may not have the facility to refer to archived training resources at a later time.
- No concept of a mind map exists—there may be a website with information that users find hard to navigate due to the mass of information.

Level 2

- The portfolio office and resources are likely to be moderately advanced, therefore some changes and rollouts of those changes are still needed.
- Some kind of planning and organization exists around roll-out efforts when changes are introduced in the portfolio space.
- Prior to roll-out efforts, estimation of the impact and analysis of affected parties may be performed, but this estimation/analysis may not be comprehensive.
- Some kind of customization and *tailoring to need* exists for training, but this may not cover all of the different kinds of stakeholders.
- Training may include scenario-based actions but all the scenarios may not have been accounted for—consequently, the recipients of training may find it hard to put some of the training concepts into practice.

- The roll-out effort takes into account the change management capacity of the organization and hence avoids trying to change too much at once.
- Training is delivered by in-house resources whose capabilities may not match that of professional trainers—consequently, training effectiveness may not be optimized.
- After the training is delivered, the users may not have the facility to refer to archived training resources, thus depriving them of a vital resource.

Level 3

- Although the portfolio office and resources are likely to be well advanced, the constantly improving portfolio office continues to introduce periodic changes and orchestrate the rollouts of those changes.
- Roll-out efforts are well planned and organized; sufficient coordination exists to ensure that the roll-out efforts do not clash with other organizational rollouts and/or changes.
- Prior to roll-out efforts, comprehensive estimation of impact and analysis of affected parties are performed to ensure that no stakeholder group is unaccounted for.
- The needs of the different kinds of stakeholders are taken into account to ensure that training is customized and *tailored to need* as much as possible.
- Training prominently features a comprehensive list of scenario-based actions—this ensures that the recipients of training are equipped to deploy the training content in the performance of their day-to-day actions.
- The roll-out effort factors in the change management capacity of the organization and hence avoids trying to change too much at once.
- Post-training, users have access to archived training resources, thus helping people who may need a refresher about the training content—this also helps users who may not have had a chance to attend training when it was offered.
- The concept of a mind map is well known to the organization and forms the gateway to accessing the resources of the portfolio website.
- The large and ever-growing portfolio website is navigated without any difficulty by the user base because of the familiar overlay of the mind map, which stays largely constant—and over the years, the addition of significant amounts of data to the website is still scalable and sustainable due to the existence of the mind map.

CHAPTER SUMMARY

This chapter explored a key area of portfolio management that is often overlooked—namely, the importance of managing the roll out of portfolio capabilities to the organization. Often, the lack of roll-out management contributes to poor stakeholder reception of what could otherwise be a well-implemented portfolio. The chapter began by reviewing a spectrum of situations that necessitate portfolio roll-out management. This was followed by an analysis of why portfolio roll-out efforts often fail, accompanied by a discussion of the politics surrounding portfolio rollout and change management. The next section in the chapter dealt with recommended best practices for portfolio rollout, which led to an introduction of a powerful technique to organize content—namely the mind map. A summary treatment of the typical mind map structure for a portfolio office was then provided, followed by a detailed listing of the success factors for a portfolio mind map. The chapter concluded with an analysis of the levels of maturity for this portfolio capability.

22

REAL-LIFE PORTFOLIO PROBLEMS AND SOLUTIONS

INTRODUCTION

There are many well-respected veterans of the field who have written fine texts on portfolio management that are very valuable when starting on the portfolio management journey. From personal experience, one question that the reader is often left with is: "How do I apply these concepts to the immediate problems I am facing as a portfolio manager today?" That question led to the thought that it would be useful to include a list of scenario-based solutions that a portfolio manager could deploy immediately in their organizations. I have also thought it would be useful to have a simple and direct checklist to walk through most portfolio topics to ensure that I have them covered in the real world.

Those thoughts, and the feedback from several accomplished colleagues, form the basis of this section of the book—namely, what happens when portfolio management meets the real world. Throughout this chapter you will find a listing of the most common obstacles one is likely to encounter as a portfolio manager and how to deal with them.

WHERE DO WE START?

Portfolio management can be overwhelming. The average portfolio has so much opportunity to improve that the most fundamental question facing portfolio managers is: "Where do I start improving my portfolio? Which problem do I solve first?" This is not a trivial question. Every organization is at a different point in its portfolio management journey. And every organization also has their peculiarities that may be unique to that place. Finally, some improvements are not easy to pull off and may not be the best investment of time and effort for the portfolio in its current state. Taken together, they constitute a custom problem to which there may not be a *one-size-fits-all* approach. So, the recommended solution is to simply start at the first problem scenario listed in the following section. If that scenario has already been handled in the organization, then simply move on to the next problem. It may still be a good idea to browse all the scenarios because there may be a perspective in the provided solution that the reader could still use to optimize their already-solved situation.

Situation #1: I Have Been Asked to Start a Portfolio Management Function from Scratch. How Do I Go About It?

It can be daunting to start a portfolio from scratch; however, it is also a great opportunity to build it right. Here's how one would go about it:

- First, build a list of projects that are currently being executed. This may require talking to the rank and file of the organization, removing some duplicate names, and some validation/iteration to create a good list.
- This then becomes the *official list of projects* or *the portfolio*. New projects cannot be added to this list without a formal entry procedure (explained in the following text).
- For the projects in this portfolio, collect the most basic and informative attributes such as:
    - Official name of the project
    - Brief project description
    - Name of the project manager
    - Who's the sponsor or customer (who are we doing this project for?)
    - Estimated start date and end date
- If your organization tracks project budget/money, the following become applicable:
    - Budget of the project (if known) (if not available, see Situation #2)
    - Current actuals (year to date) (if known)
    - How much more money each project will take to complete (if known)
- Also collect information from Finance about what the total budget allocated for the portfolio is—this is your portfolio budget.
- As mentioned before, once the project list is solidified, new projects cannot be added without the explicit involvement of the portfolio manager. This would involve filling out a basic intake form (refer to Chapter 4 for some pointers on what to include in the form). The form would then have to be reviewed and approved by portfolio governance, whose function is explained next.
- Share this list and the portfolio budget with *portfolio governance*—the decision makers of the portfolio—and explain that this is the preliminary portfolio. This should be a recurring meeting, preferably monthly. (What if there are no *decision makers* identified? Great—then you get to suggest who should be informed to make this a broad-based, participatory exercise).
- In addition to the previous information, the following data should be shared each month with portfolio governance:
    - New projects that were started (along with budget information, if applicable)
    - Projects that were completed (along with final actuals, if we are tracking money)

This is a very basic portfolio in flight. The journey has only begun.

Situation #2: No One Can Tell Me What the Budget Is for a Project

What happens when there isn't a formal budget for a project? This usually happens when projects are started without much oversight. When too many of these ad hoc projects are started, the expense begins to rack up and now the portfolio manager is tasked with bringing these under control. The challenge still remains to identify a budget for the project when no such formal budget was stated. Here are some pointers on how to proceed:

- If there is no budget for a project, the portfolio manager has to construct a simplified working budget. This could be done in a couple of ways:
    - The project manager needs to provide an estimate of how much it would take to complete the project—this is the standard estimate to complete. This, when added to the money already spent, forms the total budget of the project. (What if there are no actuals? See Situation #3.)

  ◻ The other alternative to creating a budget is to do a bottom-up estimvation. Although this is a little effort intensive, this forms a more solid number that can be used as a budget.
- Using the project plan, the portfolio manager needs to build (or guide the project manager to build) the list of major deliverables and their respective completion dates. Next to each deliverable is a dollar amount that is expected to be spent to reach that deliverable. Approximate numbers are fine!

Cautions in Situation #2

- Keep in mind that the project owner and the project manager own the budget number for the project and that the portfolio manager is only helping them build it.
- Too often, the project produces an inaccurate budget number—and then the portfolio manager is called out as the producer of the faulty estimate.
- To get around this, the portfolio manager can proceed in the following ways:
  ◻ The easiest way is to ask the project owner/manager to produce the estimate. This way the ownership is clearly established from the start.
  ◻ The next option is to explicitly obtain approval from the project owner/manager about the budget number created with the portfolio manager's help. This documented approval will be useful if the budget estimate is found to be faulty later.

Situation #3: No One Can Tell Me What the Actuals Are for a Project

In some organizations, actuals are not available for projects. Although this seems a little surprising, it may have to do with some decisions taken around implementation of the enterprise resource planning (ERP) system which hides the project costs among other buckets. However, it's quite clear that no portfolio can function well without being able to track actuals by project. Here are some pointers concerning how to start measuring actuals for a project:

- Finance should provide guidance on whether they use project codes (or can otherwise tie spend to a particular body of work). If they can, that's great—the solution may be as simple as a monthly report showing how much money was spent on this project code. However, this works only for purchase orders (POs) and external spend.
- We still need to account for the cost of internal labor spent on a project. If the organization uses time sheets, it should be a straightforward process to run a report that lists the total hours of labor spent against a project.
- Taken together, the POs and internal labor should account for most if not all the actuals of a project.
- What if we don't use time sheets? Things get tougher without the use of time sheets—we would need to get a fairly detailed breakdown of who worked on the project for how much percentage of their time, and turn those total number of hours into dollars using the standard labor rate. The result would be approximate and not an exact way to get the total cost of the project.

The aforementioned measures are enough to create a temporary solution to obtain (approximate) actuals for a project. In the long term, though, a systemic solution involving changes in the ERP system and the finance/accounting process of the organization is needed. A closer partnership with Finance is also needed in order to ensure that the previously mentioned concerns are taken into account when upgrading the ERP system or implementing fixes.

Situation #4: People Complain that Portfolio Management Is Too Cumbersome

A common situation encountered by most portfolio managers is the complaint from the organization stating that portfolio management is too cumbersome. The feedback is along the lines of: "You're adding too much process and we're not getting things done." The portfolio manager has to tread carefully here. Here are some pointers in navigating this situation:

- Acknowledge the feedback and promise to work with everyone to make the process more efficient. Why bother doing that? Simply because this is going to be a long, drawn-out exercise and the portfolio manager needs the support of the rank and file to complete the journey.
- Recognize where the feedback is coming from. The project owners and project managers are now having to deal with the changes introduced by the portfolio management process and procedures. They are no longer able to start projects at their discretion, run them without oversight, and close them out without an accounting of costs and benefits. The reduction in their *autonomy* creates the momentum to complain against the processes. Sometimes the feedback is just an indirect protest at the loss of power and autonomy that was previously available to the project owners and the project managers.
- Next, consider where changes can be made without diluting the intent or efficacy of the process:
    - Example 1: Simplify the project intake form.
    - Example 2: Be proactive in informing projects that it's their turn to present at the portfolio governance session that month.
    - The bottom line: Establish a sincere partnership with the stakeholders and demonstrate that this is a joint effort—that goes a long way toward achieving participation.
- All of the protests may not be uniform. Some stakeholders may have a genuine issue that can be remediated with some effort on the part of the portfolio office as outlined in the preceding examples. Other stakeholders may be chronic malcontents driven by the loss of their previous freedom. It is important to separate the two categories so that the malcontents are isolated as much as possible.
- Sometimes, people just don't want to play according to the new rules. In those situations, the portfolio manager has to channel the mandate given to them by executive management. Withholding approval for new projects, and/or approval of funding requests, may have to be done to drive home the point.
- A more subtle way of ensuring compliance is to let people fail in full public view. For example, have a stubborn project manager appear at the portfolio governance session and explain to the executives why their project is not meeting the agreed-upon portfolio standards.

Situation #5: Bad Projects Are Not Terminated

A common problem across organizations is that bad projects are simply not terminated. For some inexplicable reason, companies are determined to throw good money after bad projects that are highly unlikely to turn around or deliver. In many cases, it might be a political game. Everyone knows the project is a disaster but are simply unwilling to step up and make the much-needed decision to terminate. Historical precedence may play a huge role in the reluctance to terminate a project—*we've never terminated projects* is the mindset that needs to be remediated. Here are some pointers to address the situation:

- This is where strong governance is indispensable. One of the explicit mandates given to the portfolio governance team must be to terminate underperforming projects.
- The portfolio manager needs to provide to the portfolio governance members the data that helps to make up their mind.
- It also helps the governance members with the termination decisivon when they are provided with the enhanced monitoring list (EML). This offers an exit ramp and helps them see that some of the projects on the EML are doomed—and that the sooner they are terminated, the better.
- The portfolio manager can also use certain events to force the termination of projects:
  - During annual planning, data can be presented that shows why some existing bad projects should be *below the line.*
  - During portfolio rebalancing, underperformers can be served up as candidates for termination.
  - During approval of new project proposals, a case can be made that the new proposals can only be funded by terminating some underperforming projects and redirecting their spend to the new projects.
  - If portfolio governance is simply *unable to pull the trigger,* that is, terminate projects, the portfolio manager needs to approach the chief information officer (CIO) to make changes in the governance structure or composition.

Situation #6: We Don't Have a Portfolio Management Tool

Some organizations may embark on their portfolio management journey and feel the lack of a tool. While this may seem like a shortcoming, it may actually be a great opportunity. Many organizations have taken the plunge and adopted one of the popular portfolio management tools on the market (at a significant cost) and later regretted it (please refer to Situation #7). Having an inflexible and mismatched portfolio management tool is much worse than not having a tool in the first place. The latter situation can be molded to the portfolio's favor, but the former situation can be severely constricting and prevent the portfolio from developing to its potential. (This is exactly why using a simple adaptive platform like Smartsheet is a good idea.) Having said that, here's how to proceed in handling this situation:

- A portfolio management tool doesn't have to be costly, complex, and massive. Everything that a basic portfolio needs can be accomplished with Smartsheet at a really attractive price point.
- The key components of a portfolio management tool are the following:
  - An easy-to-use form to submit new project proposals
  - A list with configurable columns to capture key attributes of active projects
  - A simple workflow that can support the movement of items from one stakeholder to the next and keep track of the same
  - A simple repository to look up standard artifacts for each project
  - A repository to look up historical governance decisions for each project (audit trail)
- It's a straightforward, low-intensity effort to create the aforementioned functionality using Smartsheet.
- What if Smartsheet is simply not an option? In that case, the portfolio will have to make do with "low-tech" options—namely, throwing manpower and Microsoft Excel at the problem.
- The portfolio office may need to be staffed with a sufficient number of entry-level personnel who can carry out tasks such as composing various portfolio artifacts documents and ensuring that these are reviewed and approved by various stakeholders.

- At some point, as the organization grows, it becomes necessary to invest in a system like Smartsheet that can scale the portfolio without disproportionately increasing the size of the portfolio office. This is all that a portfolio tool needs to have.

Situation #7: We Have a Portfolio Management Tool and People Hate It

As described in Situation #6, organizations that have attempted portfolio management may have taken the plunge and paid for one of the well-known portfolio management tools on the market. This typically involves a significant expense as well as a huge effort in implementation. However, even at the end of this expensive exercise, it may also be quite likely that the people in the organization hate the tool and will do anything to avoid using it.

Why does this happen? Probably because the choice of portfolio tool was premature—the organization may not yet have traversed the difficult journey in setting up essential portfolio management capabilities (none of which have anything to do with a tool). When the choice of a tool is made prematurely, the organization gets *locked* into an inflexible software that restricts the rank and file from doing the things that make sense for the organization. What makes the whole situation worse from a portfolio manager's perspective is that the distaste for the tool often extends to the portfolio management process, too—people are resistant to following portfolio processes because these are implemented through the tool. Here are some pointers as to how to deal with this situation:

- Separate out the disliked portfolio software from day-to-day portfolio management. The enterprise portfolio tool can stay as the *official record*, but most of the day-to-day portfolio management tasks can run outside of the tool in a flexible platform like Smartsheet.
- This defuses the popular ire of the user base and lets them transact their business in a more user-friendly platform.
- When it becomes necessary to update the *official record*—also known as *the tool that no one likes to use*—the portfolio team can perform the update, which buffers the users from the undesirable experience.
- It does impose an extra load on the portfolio office to make this redundant entry in two systems, but it may be the most expedient thing to do for the present.
- Over the long term, the portfolio team would be well advised to retire the enterprise portfolio software entirely and move to Smartsheet.

Situation #8: Portfolio Manager Has No Power— "No One Listens to Me"

One of the maddening experiences for a portfolio manager is to realize that they may be quite low on the totem pole of the organization. In other words, they just don't wield enough power for people to listen to them and change the way projects are run. The irony is that the portfolio manager can enable projects to run better and deliver significant value to the organization, but sometimes no one wants to give their ideas a chance to work. Therefore, few things change and the status quo dominates. Here are some pointers on how to handle this most fundamental roadblock:

- Initially, the portfolio manager needs to be able to describe and sell a vision to upper management that shows the strategic value of a well-run portfolio. A successful portfolio manager needs to possess a fair amount of salesmanship in addition to technical skills.

- After securing executive buy-in, the portfolio manager needs to leverage that mandate to drive the first wave of desired change in behavior and processes.
- The portfolio manager then needs to demonstrate the benefits of the first wave of changes—perhaps a better intake, better visibility, and better management of project benefits? The aim is to establish a track record of continuous improvement for the portfolio journey. This reinforces the portfolio manager's credibility when they approach executive management for the mandate to drive additional change.
- If done successfully, the portfolio manager eventually becomes a credible, respected voice and is sought for input by the decision makers. The portfolio manager needs to then use that credibility to push for small incremental changes that cumulatively have a large effect in taking the portfolio where it needs to go.

Situation #9: We Don't Do Strategic Planning

Throughout this book, we've emphasized the portfolio as a vehicle to drive strategic change in accordance with the strategic roadmap. But here's a basic problem—what if the organization has no strategic plan? Or, as is much more common, what if there is no realistic or actionable strategic plan? Most organizations do have some kind of strategic plan, but it often has no bearing to action on the ground. In other words, there is no connective tissue between the lofty framework of strategic goals and the tactical actions of projects and programs. How can the portfolio manager bridge this divide?

- The portfolio manager can create a faux strategic plan as follows:
    - Define a few strategic imperatives—these can be generic, such as: growing revenue, increasing market share, increasing profitability/efficiency, or building strategic capabilities.
    - Decompose these strategic imperatives into smaller, more specific strategic priorities that are relevant to the organization.
    - Create a proposed alignment of the current projects and programs to the strategic priorities.
    - Present the previously mentioned version of the strategic landscape to the decision makers, including portfolio governance. This may spark some welcome dialogue that results in meaningful changes to the strategic roadmap.
    - The ultimate end product here is a strategic plan that is recognized as the official plan to be used as a compass for deciding what projects and programs to pursue.
- Sometimes, the aforementioned effort may meet with resistance, with some stakeholders questioning the mandate of the portfolio manager to create a strategic plan. In those situations, the portfolio manager should defer to the people who are wanting to create a strategic plan and focus instead on the end goal—to have a strategic plan and use it to decide what projects to execute. Another option would be to secure a mandate to define a draft plan with the understanding that key decision makers would then use the draft plan as a starting point to make changes and arrive at the final strategic plan.

Situation #10: Our Portfolio Process Has No Connection with Strategic Planning

As discussed in the previous situation, one of the common difficulties faced by a portfolio manager is to navigate a portfolio in the absence of a strategic plan. This situation covers a closely related problem—often, there is indeed a strategic plan in place, but one which has no connection with the portfolio. It may seem like the two activities—portfolio management and strategic planning—are run on two independent tracks with no possibility of intersection. How does the portfolio manager remedy the situation?

- This situation, while quite serious, is better than the previous one where there was no strategic plan to start with. Having a plan eliminates the need for the portfolio manager to create one. It also avoids all of the political wrangling about the mandate of a portfolio manager to play a role in strategy formulation.
- Starting with the official plan, the portfolio manager proceeds to decompose the high-level strategic imperatives into more tightly defined strategic priorities that are relevant to the organization.
- Then comes the exercise to map the current portfolio of projects and programs to the strategic priorities.
- The portfolio manager should expect to see some projects that do not align well to the strategic plan. In that case, a recommendation should be made about what to do with those projects. In most cases, we would want to complete those projects to avoid a complete write-off of the already spent funds for those projects. In a few situations, it may be worth considering a termination of the projects if the money spent is not significant and/or the project's objectives are nowhere near the strategic priorities.
- With the previous exercise, it should be expected that some dialogue may occur about the need to change the strategic plan. This is because the visibility created by the exercise now enables people to clearly see these two complementary entities—the portfolio and the strategic plan.
- Having done the previous exercise for the first time, the portfolio manager needs to ensure that the alignment continues going forward. Some of the ways to do that are:
  - Push for portfolio representation (ideally co-ownership) of the strategic planning activity.
  - Ensure that the portfolio annual planning process relies heavily on the strategic plan (see Chapter 15). Push for continuity of a strategic plan because a plan that changes every year is almost useless.
  - Ensure that portfolio intake considers strategic alignment (see Chapter 4). Every project that comes through project intake has to align to a strategic initiative or theme.
  - Ensure that portfolio tools such as earned value management (EVM) also report on the strategic attainment and progress made according to the strategic roadmap.
  - Provide these reports to portfolio governance and make recommendations.

Situation #11: People Want to Tie Their Projects to High-Priority Strategic Programs to Achieve Funding

Once the basic discipline of portfolio intake management takes hold, other kinds of problems begin to emerge. Now that people are prevented from starting projects willy-nilly, they try to align themselves with established, strategic programs in order to get past the hurdle of intake management. How can this be addressed?

- The program manager of the high-priority program needs to agree that this particular project belongs to their program and is included in the program budget.
- The portfolio office needs to enable this signoff from the program manager in one of the following ways:
  - As a low-tech solution, the program manager sends an email approving the inclusion of the new request in their approved program. This email can be added to the supporting documentation for the new request.

> ❏ As a more high-tech solution, a workflow in the Smartsheet intake list routes requests to the correct program manager when the corresponding program is chosen in the drop-down. The program manager needs to approve in Smartsheet and then the workflow reverts to the portfolio office.
>
> ❏ The systemic, high-tech approach is always preferable because it takes all unnecessary interaction out of the loop, with less chance for errors, too.

Note that there is a possibility that the program manager may not keep track of how the incoming projects add up to a sum that may exceed the program budget. It is prudent for the portfolio office to keep a running total and raise the flag when the incoming requests cumulatively begin to approach the program budget.

Situation #12: People Start New Projects Without Informing the Portfolio Manager

In organizations that are yet to implement a portfolio, it's common to see projects being started without prior communication or approval. Due to organizational inertia, this practice may continue even after portfolio rollout. What options does a portfolio manager have to curtail such behavior and regain control over project initiation?

- The portfolio manager needs to partner with Finance (see Chapter 20 on how to partner with Finance) and request their help in making sure only POs against authorized projects are approved. This would mean POs that are charged against unauthorized projects will *not* be approved. It's better to make this a systemic implementation such that the financial ERP system would automatically reject such POs.
- The portfolio manager should not make exceptions to these projects that were started on the sly. For example, these projects cannot be presented at the governance meetings until they go through intake.
- Additionally, the portfolio manager should approach the project owners and ascertain why the project was started without notifying the portfolio team.
- Finally, the portfolio manager should recommend that there should be some kind of official disapproval made known from the CIO's office toward stakeholders who persist in starting projects without due authorization.

Situation #13: People Want to Misrepresent the True Status of Projects

One of the most persistent problems faced by portfolio managers has to do with project owners trying to misrepresent the true status of projects. This is typically done to buy time for troubled projects in the hopes that the project manager can turn things around. The project owners may also believe that the problems in the project may work themselves out. Sometimes the project owners are quite unaware of the true status and pass along their incomplete or false understanding of the status to the portfolio. What can be done in such a situation? Here are some pointers:

- The portfolio manager needs to understand that the traditional methods of reporting status—for example: red, yellow, and green (R/Y/G)—are simply too subjective to provide a precise readout of project status. Subjective R/Y/G is a system where the project manager decides whether the project is red, yellow, or green based on their judgment.
- The portfolio manager must push the projects to start using objective R/Y/G—a system which uses definite criteria to decide if a project is red, yellow, or green.

- If the organization is advanced enough (or there is enough appetite), the portfolio can consider using advanced techniques like EVM.

Situation #14: People Want to Evade Measurement of Project Benefits

Project owners promise the moon when seeking funding, but sometimes become hard to find when it's time to measure the actual benefits delivered by the projects. One common tactic is to claim that the benefits will only be delivered at the end of the project, at which point the project's money is already spent and there is little recourse. How can the portfolio manager make projects accountable for their promised benefits?

- The portfolio manager needs to start nudging the organization toward following a benefits realization process. The building blocks are outlined here:
  - The first step in measuring benefits is to create a standard taxonomy in describing benefits. All projects need to use the standard taxonomy in describing their benefits. Projects that refuse to do this need to be sent back at the governance review with a direction to come back with the benefits in the standard format.
  - The next step is to make it mandatory for projects to declare the earliest time that benefits can be produced by the project. Projects that declare that benefits can only be delivered at the end of the project should be treated as high-risk investments where nothing can be done if the project does not produce benefits as promised. Instead, projects that can start delivering benefits earlier should be emphasized for funding consideration.
  - The next step is to constitute a benefits review council that meets regularly and reviews the benefits of all projects. A key component of this review is to compare the current benefits with the promised benefits and take action if there is significant variance between the two.

Situation #15: People Don't Want to Follow Process

Once the building blocks of the portfolio management process are implemented, the next major problem for a portfolio manager is to contend with people who want to be granted exceptions to the process. For example, some project owners may want to bring a PowerPoint in lieu of filling out the intake form. Others may want to use their own status reporting system—such as the notoriously ineffective R/Y/G system. How should the portfolio manager deal with this situation?

- In the beginning of the portfolio journey, it may be a good idea for the portfolio office to relax the rules and allow people some latitude in following process and using the official templates.
- However, as time passes, the portfolio office needs to slowly increase the rigor associated with the process. When it comes to people who will not follow the process, a couple of options are available—one is to *not transact*, that is, the portfolio will simply not entertain requests that do not follow process. In other words, a project owner who will not fill out the project intake form will not have their project considered at the intake meeting. The other option is to let the project *fail in full public view*—for example, letting the project owner explain to the governance committee why they are not able to produce performance data for their project in the format that the governance committee has come to expect from all projects.
- In summary, the portfolio office is able to drive compliance by controlling the portfolio resources, primarily funding. If a project's stakeholders refuse to follow process, they may find themselves locked out of funding and other portfolio resources. The portfolio office needs to have (and confirm) backing from executive management before refusing to engage with truant stakeholders.

Situation #16: People Complain that the Portfolio Website Is Too Hard to Navigate

As the portfolio grows and the portfolio office deploys more process and artifacts, one predictable effect is the growth of records and documents and the need to keep everything organized. This usually takes the form of a portfolio website, where all the materials and historical records related to the portfolio are stored for reference by the organization. The unintended side effect of a large and growing website is that people find it hard to locate what they're looking for. This frustration may have serious effects if people are unable to follow portfolio process or if their dissatisfaction with the website turns into dissatisfaction with the functioning of the portfolio office. How should the portfolio office handle this situation?

- The primary factor to consider when designing a portfolio website is that most stakeholders have only a basic need or transaction that they need to carry out on the website. In other words, a successful portfolio website is one that enables the vast majority of its users to perform their actions quickly and efficiently. Although this sounds simple, this can be problematic because everyone may have a slightly different simple transaction to execute and it could be hard to optimize the website to accommodate everyone's perspective.
- One tool that can help overcome this situation is the mind map. The fundamental premise of the mind map is that everyone starts from a common place and are able to quickly navigate to the specific task that they need transacted.

KEY CONCEPT: A variety of standard situations are listed above for the portfolio manager to anticipate and accordingly mitigate to ensure smooth portfolio functioning.

CHAPTER SUMMARY

In this chapter we explored all of the common problems faced by portfolio managers as they attempt to implement portfolio management best practices. The solutions explored in response to each of these problems consist of a focused approach in drawing content from the other chapters in this book. Portfolio managers are encouraged to go through all of the problems and solutions listed here, as there may be insight that could prove useful at some point in their implementation journey.

INDEX